Crime Scene Investigation

Second edition

Crime Scene Investigation

Methods and Procedures

Second Edition

Ian K. Pepper

 McGraw Hill

Open University Press

Open University Press
McGraw-Hill Education
McGraw-Hill House
Shoppenhangers Road
Maidenhead
Berkshire
England
SL6 2QL

email: enquiries@openup.co.uk
world wide web: www.openup.co.uk

and Two Penn Plaza, New York, NY 10121-2289, USA

First published 2005

A catalogue record of this book is available from the British Library

ISBN-13: 978-0-33-523441-7 (pb)
ISBN-10: 0335214916 (hb)

Library of Congress Cataloging-in-Publication Data
CIP data applied for

Typeset by RefineCatch Limited, Bungay, Suffolk
Printed in the UK by Bell & Bain Ltd., Glasgow

Fictitious names of companies, products, people, characters and/or data that may
be used herein (in case studies or in examples) are not intended to represent any
real individual, company, product or event.

Mixed Sources
Product group from well-managed
forests and other controlled sources
www.fsc.org Cert no. TT-COC-002769
© 1996 Forest Stewardship Council
FSC

The **McGraw·Hill** Companies

To my grandparents Albert and Christiana Depledge, Colin and Daisy Pepper.

Contents

Table of Statutes   ix

Abbreviations   xi

Introduction   1

1 The history and contemporary structure of the police, scientific
services and crime scene investigation in the United Kingdom   3

2 Approaching the crime scene, packaging the evidence and the
documentation required   17

3 The basics of crime scene photography   30

4 Trace evidence: fibres, glass, hairs, paint and soil   45

5 Impressions: footwear marks, instrument marks, glove marks
and tyres   55

6 Deoxyribonucleic acid (DNA) and body fluids   65

7 Fingerprints   78

8 The investigation of a fire scene   104

9 Firearms   111

10 Terrorism, mass murder and disaster (major incidents)   122

11 The leadership and management of the forensic examination of a
major crime scene   132

12 Other sources of evidence for the crime scene investigator   147

13 Health and safety at a crime scene   165

14 The Criminal Law Courts in the United Kingdom   174

15 Organizations related to crime scene investigation   184

Answers to questions   192
References   198
Index   206

Table of Statutes

Air Force Act (1955)
Armed Forces Act (2006)
Army Act (1955)
Crime and Disorder Act (1998)
Criminal Justice Act (1967)
Criminal Justice Act (2003)
Criminal Justice and Police Act (2001)
Criminal Procedures and Investigation Act (1996)
Firearms Act (1968)
Fire and Rescue Services Act (2004)
Health and Safety at Work Act (1974)
Judicature (Northern Ireland) Act (1978)
Judiciary and Courts (Scotland) Act (2008)
Justice of the Peace Act (1361)
Metropolitan Police Act (1829)
Misuse of Drugs Act (1971)
Municipal Corporation Act (1835)
Naval Discipline Act (1957)
Police Act (1919)
Police Act (1964)
Police and Criminal Evidence Act (1984)
Police Reform Act (2002)
Serious Organised Crime and Police Act (2005)
Special Constables Act (1831)
Terrorism Act (2000)
Violent Crime Reduction Act (2006)

Abbreviations

Like any large organization, the police service has developed its own 'language' that may be confusing to an aspiring or new forensic practitioner. Listed here are some common abbreviations and what they stand for.

AAFS   American Academy of Forensic Sciences
ACE-V   analysed, compared, evaluated and verified
ACPO   Association of Chief Police Officers
AIB   Accident Investigation Branch
ASA   American Standards Association
ASCLD   American Society of Crime Laboratory Directors
CAP   Common approach path
CBRN   chemical, biological, radiological and nuclear
CID   Criminal Investigation Department
CJA   Criminal Justice Act 1967
CJPO   Criminal Justice and Public Order Act 1995
CODIS   Combined DNA Index System
COSHH   Control of Substances Hazardous to Health
CPA   Crime pattern analyst
CPS   Crown Prosecution Service
CRFP   Council for the Registration of Forensic Practitioners
CRO   Criminal Records Office
CSE   crime scene examiner
CSI   crime scene investigator
CSM   crime scene manager
DFO   Diazafluoren-9-One
DMORT   Disaster Mortuary Operational Response Team
DNA   Deoxyribonucleic acid
DPP   Director of Public Prosecutions
DVI   Disaster victim identification
EOD   Explosives Ordnance Disposal
ESDA   Electrostatic detection apparatus
ESLA   Electrostatic lifting apparatus
FAIR   Forensic after incident review
FBI   Federal Bureau of Investigation
FDL   Fingerprint Development Laboratory
FDR   firearms discharge residue

FIO	Force intelligence officer
FIT	Fire Investigation Team
FLINTS	Force Linked Intelligence System
FLO	Family liaison officer
FME	Forensic medical examiner
FSAG	Forensic Science Advisory Group
FSS	Forensic Science Service
GF111	Form used to forward crime scene stains for a speculative search against the DNA database
GPS	Global positioning system
GRIM	Glass refractive index measurement
GSR	Gunshot residue
HE	High explosives
HMCS	Her Majesty's Court Service
HOLMES	Home Office Large Major Enquiry System
HOSDB	Home Office Scientific Development Branch
HSE	Health and Safety Executive
IAFIS	Integrated Automatic Fingerprint Identification System
IAI	International Association for Identification
IBIS	Integrated Ballistic Identification System
Ident1	National finger and palm print identification database
IED	Improvised explosive device
Interpol	International Criminal Police Organization
ISO	International Standards Organization
JP	Justice of the Peace
KM	Kastle mayer
Lantern	Hand-held fingerprint scanner
LCN	Low copy number DNA
LIO	Local intelligence officer
Livescan	System allowing the electronic scanning of fingerprints
LMG	Leucomalachite green
LSD	Lysergic acid diethylamide
MDAT	Major Disaster Advisory Team
MG11	Statement of witness form
MG/FSP	Form used to submit samples recovered from the crime scene for comparison with samples recovered from a suspect
MIDaS	Mobile Identification at Scene
MLP	multilocus probe
NaBIS	National Ballistics Intelligence Service
NAFIS	National Automated Fingerprint Identification System
NCIS	National Criminal Intelligence Service
NCOF	National Crime and Operations Faculty
NCS	National Crime Squad

NDNAD	National DNA Database
NHTCU	National Hi-Tec Crime Unit
NIM	National Intelligence Model
NOS	National Occupational Standards
NPIA	National Police Improvement Agency
NSLEC	National Specialist Law Enforcement Centre
NTCSSCI	National Training Centre for Scientific Support to Crime Investigation
PACE	Police and Criminal Evidence Act 1984
PCR	Polymerase chain reaction
PCSO	police community support officer
PITO	Police Information and Technology Organization
PM	Post-mortem examination
PNC	Police National Computer
POLSA	Police search adviser
PPE	Personal protective equipment
PSDB	Police Scientific Development Branch
R v	Regina versus
RVP	Rendezvous point
SARC	Sexual Assault Referral Centre
SERM	Scene Evidence Recovery Manager
SGM	Second generation multiplex
SICAR	Shoeprint image capture and retrieval
SIO	Senior Investigating Police Officer
SLP	Single locus probe
SLR	Single lens reflex
SOCA	Serious and Organised Crime Agency
SOCO	Scenes of crime officer
SSC	Scientific support coordinator
SSM	Scientific support manager
STR	Short tandem repeat
SUDI	Sudden unexplained death of an infant
TGM	Third generation multiplex
TSU	Technical Support Unit
TTL	Through the lens
UV	Ultraviolet
VCSI	Volume crime scene investigator
VIPER	Video Identification Parade Electronic Recording
WORM	Write once, read many

Introduction

The investigation of a crime is like putting together a jigsaw. No one person has all the pieces but some of the key shapes can be found at the crime scene. There is only one opportunity for the crime scene investigator (CSI) to recover forensic evidence from the scene of the crime. The evidence may be of a scientific nature such as DNA or unique marks on bullets; it may be minute such as fibres, hairs or paint flakes, or even obscure such as knots or diatoms. Whatever the type of evidence, the CSIs are at the forefront of the investigation and if they don't recover the evidence, then a forensic specialist cannot identify from where and whom it came.

The nature of both policing and forensic investigation continues to lead to new ideas and their associated technological advances such as a National Ballistics Intelligence Service, mobile fingerprint scanners and the wider use of digital photography. New Home Office appointments, such as that of the Forensic Science Regulator, ensure that quality processes are adhered to across the wide range of forensic science services. Developments in the forensic investigation of crime scenes continue to be dynamic.

Whatever the developments, the three elements of the investigation of a crime continue to be the same: the history leading to the offence taking place, the crime scene itself, and the up-to-date knowledge and skills of those investigating the event. With the importance of forensic evidence in the detection and prosecution of offenders, the knowledge, skills and abilities of those who examine the scenes of crimes, the CSIs, must be both maintained and continually enhanced. Crime scene investigators continue to attend numerous crime scenes every day recovering essential evidence, for example, during the police reporting year of 2004/2005, crime scene investigators across England and Wales examined over 900,000 crime scenes (Newburn et al. 2007). The evidence collected is of paramount importance to investigations, for example, during the crime recording year of 2008/2009 some 832 murders, manslaughters and rapes were matched using evidence placed on the DNA database (Johnson 2009).

As an operational CSI within an urban police force in the United Kingdom over a number of years I attended in the region of 9000 crime scenes ranging from multiple murders and robberies to burglaries and stolen vehicles. I have also been privileged to work as a fingerprint examiner in a large Fingerprint Bureau, making a number of fingerprint identifications from finger marks recovered from crime scenes by CSIs. As a lecturer and team leader at the

National Training Centre for Scientific Support to Crime Investigation, I have delivered training in the investigation of crime scenes across the UK, the Far East, the Middle East and Africa. Now as a university lecturer I work as a member of a team educating the CSIs and police officers of the future.

This text guides an aspiring or newly appointed CSI through the methods and procedures for the accurate recording and recovery of evidence from the scene of a crime, while providing a broad understanding of the development and context within which a modern CSI must operate effectively as an integral member of investigative teams.

1 The history and contemporary structure of the police, scientific services and crime scene investigation in the United Kingdom

1.1 The early years

Critchley (1967) suggests that the birthplace of the police system in England and Wales can be found in the ancient customs of the Anglo-Saxons. The tythingman was responsible for justice over a loose group of families. Such families were brought together for their common good. Any wrongdoing by an individual meant that they had to be brought by the tythingman to justice. The tythings were grouped under a royal reeve who exercised judicial powers. The royal reeve was answerable to the local shire reeve (or sheriff) who in turn was answerable to the king.

The Norman Conquest of England in 1066 brought a culture that attempted to dominate its new subjects, which sometimes led to barbaric outcomes. In 1124, a court found 44 men guilty of theft and publicly hanged them and blinded several others (Critchley 1967). The Normans did, however, establish the unpaid role of constable. The constable was appointed annually from a rota of local eligible males who lived in the area. His role was to report to the manor any incidents that occurred within the vicinity.

In 1285, the Statute of Winchester established the need for fortified towns to have a number of watchmen who would patrol the gates between sunset and sunrise apprehending strangers. Reporting to the constable, the watchmen could call on the whole town using a 'hue and cry' to summon all males between the ages of 15 and 60 to assist in the apprehension of a stranger.

In 1361, the Justice of the Peace Act enabled the Crown to appoint individuals as Justices of the Peace (JPs) to have responsibility for law and order and as such have responsibility over any police.

The eighteenth century witnessed a population explosion and growth of large industrial areas. London became the largest city with over a million inhabitants. London, being a centre of trade and the capital, became a haven of crime and criminals. Since 1663, the capital had employed watchmen called Charlies, named after King Charles II who was instrumental in the scheme

(Critchley 1967). They patrolled London's streets calling out the time, but they were poorly paid, relatively ineffective and would often turn away from trouble or ignore it for a bribe.

In the mid-eighteenth century two brothers who were both magistrates, Henry and John Fielding, published articles on cases over which they had presided in an effort to illustrate the level to which public order and crime had sunk in eighteenth-century England. In 1750, Henry Fielding created a small band of paid constables into a team of 'thief takers' led by him and based at his Bow Street offices. Their aim was to tackle the robbery gangs which were plaguing London. They had initial successes capturing some dangerous criminals and, although disbanded after a year, they were reformed in 1753 to tackle the rising number of murders which were occurring in the capital. Within a few weeks they had successfully broken up the gangs of murderers. On Henry Fielding's death, his brother John Fielding continued his work, gaining financial support for the continued establishment of the so-called 'Bow Street Runners'. John established horseborne patrols on the roads leading into London to chase and capture highwaymen. He also saw the importance of intelligence using his Bow Street offices as a centre through which descriptions of suspects could be gathered and disseminated around London.

For a week in June 1780 London came under mob rule (Emsley 1991). Over three hundred people were killed or injured; 72 houses and four gaols were destroyed. The army was finally used to viciously quell the 'Gordon riots' and eventually 25 individuals were found guilty and executed for their part in the mayhem (Radzinowicz 1956b). Unease spread across London at the way in which the riots had risen and been quelled. No longer could a few constables, assisted by the public, be relied upon to police the growing metropolis of London.

A champion of the need for the establishment of a full-time police force was the magistrate Patrick Colquhoun. Research he conducted demonstrated that in the year ending in January 1798 goods stolen and lost from the port area of London equated to over half a million pounds, with nearly half of these goods being taken from the West India merchants (Radzinowicz 1956a). So, in June 1798, funded mainly by the shipping merchants, a force of 60 full-time paid officers was established (Critchley 1967). The officers were given reasonable pay and rules of conduct establishing what was and was not expected of them. The project was immensely successful and in 1800 an Act of Parliament turned the private venture into a public body.

In April 1829, the then Home Secretary, Sir Robert Peel, introduced the Metropolitan Police Act. This established the metropolitan police district as an area extending 7 miles from the centre of London. A force of suitable men was to be recruited and sworn in as constables. They were to have the powers and privileges of a constable at common law. The force was to have its own budget and was to be run by two commissioners: a military man, ex-Colonel Charles

Rowan, and an Irish barrister Richard Mayne. They were to report directly to the Home Secretary. Richard Mayne suggested that, 'The primary object of an efficient police is the prevention of crime: the protection of life and property, the preservation of public tranquillity, and the absence of crime, will alone prove whether those efforts have been successful' (Metropolitan Police 2002). Offices were established for the two new commissioners at 4 Whitehall Place, which backed onto a narrow, little-known lane called 'Scotland Yard'. The Metropolitan Police district was split into 17 divisions, each of which was to be run by a Superintendent supported by an establishment of 56 men consisting of constables, sergeants and inspectors.

The constables were paid one guinea a week and wore a non-military uniform consisting of a blue tailed coat, blue trousers and black top hat with a strengthened crown. They carried a rattle and truncheon concealed beneath their coat. Recruits had to be under 35, of good physique, at least five foot seven inches tall, literate and of good character (Critchley 1967). By 1830, the Metropolitan Police Force had grown in numbers exceeding over 3000 men and the constables had been nicknamed 'peelers' or 'bobbies' after their founder. In 1831, the Special Constables Act empowered local magistrates to conscript men during time of riot and in 1835 the Municipal Corporation Act required the establishment of regular police forces throughout England and Wales. The first detective department was founded in the Metropolitan Police during the early 1840s. Women were not recruited into the police service until the start of the First World War in 1914 when the Women Police Service was established (Fido and Skinner 1999).

Similar developments were occurring elsewhere in the world. In the USA immigrants took with them the traditions of sheriffs. Perhaps the earliest recorded appointment of a county sheriff in the USA was in Virginia during 1634 (Haberfeld 2002). In 1789, George Washington appointed US Marshals to enforce the law across the state boundaries in the USA, but only Texas had a police force that operated across a whole state (Haberfeld 2002). In 1834, the first full-time constable was appointed to police parts of Toronto in Canada. Then, in 1844, the New York City Police was formed to police the rapidly expanding large urban areas of New York. In 1862, the New South Wales Police was established to police a large portion of Australia. As part of their new uniforms the New York City Police adopted an eight-point copper star as its badge of office. Soon these police became known as 'coppers or cops' (Bresler 1992). These nicknames stuck and are now in general use as slang for the police across the world.

1.2 The identification of criminals before the use of fingerprints

Prior to the 1840s the methods of identification of criminals were very limited, such as an artist's impression with a rough description or the branding of repeat offenders (recidivists) with hot irons. The addition of photography in the 1840s aided this identification process. Bresler (1992) suggests that in Brussels during 1843 the police took the first ever photograph of a criminal.

In France in early 1879, a young man, Alphonse Bertillon, was employed by the police in Paris to file these many descriptions and photographs. Having had a scientific education Bertillon became frustrated with an identification process that was undoubtedly flawed, leading to many miscarriages of justice. After only a few months Bertillon wrote a paper that demonstrated that by using a number of measurements of different parts of the body he could show that no two individuals were exactly alike. His system of identification used 11 measurements of varying parts of the body ranging from the length and breadth of the head to distance between elbow joint and fingertip. Called anthropometry, the system relied upon accurate measurements to identify the repeat offenders. Such a system did have some recorded success with 26 recidivists being identified in the last three months of 1883 (Rhodes 1956). The news of such success drew attention to his work from across Europe and the USA. Bertillon built on this success, implementing the use of a metric scale when he took photographs of evidence, such as tool marks and footprints, at crime scenes to which he could then apply his basic method of identification in his workshop (Rhodes 1956). In contemporary terms he was the first real crime scene investigator and established one of the first crime laboratories.

Edward Henry (see Chapter 7) introduced the anthropometric system of identification into colonial India in 1892. Then, in 1894, anthropometry was accepted as a means of identification in England, but the number of Bertillon's measurements was reduced to five and was to be accompanied by a set of ten fingerprints that were to be taken from every offender (Thorwald 1965). The anthropometric system of identification did, however, rely on the accuracy of the measurements of the suspects taken by different police officers, with vary-ing equipment at different times. Bertillon later added the use of fingerprints to his French system but only as a supportive means of identification. The use of anthropometry was later discarded as a means of accurate identification (in England in 1900). Despite this, Bertillon is generally regarded as putting the identification of individuals on a scientific basis and raising the profile of the use of science in the investigation of crime.

A pupil and close friend of Bertillon was Dr Edmond Locard who, in 1910, established the first real police forensic laboratory to compare evidence recovered from the crime scene with that from suspect. Locard was particularly interested in poroscopy – the distribution of the sweat pores on fingerprints. But he is best remembered for his principle of exchange of evidence. In 1910, Locard successfully recovered evidence from under the fingernails of a murder victim. Then in 1920 he first published his principle suggesting that when one object comes into contact with another something is exchanged between and taken away by both objects. Locard's principle is the basis of the transfer and recovery of all forensic evidence.

To understand the principle, imagine:
'A' = Angora sweater
'B' = Blazer
How will fibres be exchanged between them if they touch each other?

Figure 1.1   Locard's principle

1.3 The structure of the contemporary police

At the time of the Police Act (1919) there were over 100 police forces across England and Wales. The act formalized national police pay and conditions and forbade policemen the right to strike. Another Police Act (1964) set the basis for the police service that we have today. It set out the role of the individuals and agencies involved in running the police service. The Home Secretary became responsible for ensuring that the police service was run efficiently. A police authority (consisting of councillors and magistrates) was established in each force area, ensuring that adequate policing was delivered to the area with suitable and sufficient equipment; they would also hire the Chief Constable. A Chief Constable would be responsible for the control of the force including appointments. Such a tripartite system of power sharing meant that no one individual had overall control of the police and its actions. The Act also extended the powers of a police constable from his own force to all forces across England and Wales. This Act gave the impetus for the eventual amalgamation of over 100 police forces to the largely autonomous 43 Home Office Police Forces we have today.

The push for financial prudence by the government in the 1980s led to the large-scale civilianization of a number of policing duties. A circular from the Home Office (1988) to all police authorities and Chief Constables highlighted 25 different duties that could efficiently be conducted by civilian staff. These roles ranged from clerical and administrative work to scenes of crime and forensic examinations. Hence no longer did one have to be a police constable to work within the police service. The largest police force remains the Metropolitan Police Service with over 32,000 police officers, 14,000 civilian support staff, a number of special constables (volunteer part-time police officers) and a multi-billion pound annual budget. In comparison the Dumfries and Galloway Constabulary have just over 470 officers and 260 civilian staff and a budget of several million pounds. In total the contemporary police service across the United Kingdom employs some 260,000 individuals in a range of police and civilian roles.

The 43 Home Office Police Forces of England and Wales, the eight Scottish Police Forces, the Police Service of Northern Ireland and a number of other specialist law enforcement agencies such as the British Transport Police, the Civil Nuclear Constabulary and the Ministry of Defence Police have the support of a number of new roles within law enforcement and a number of national organizations. For example, the Police Reform Act (2002) established the uniformed role of police community support officer (PCSO) with a target recruitment of 25,000. PCSOs nationally work within the community to reassure the public and deal with minor incidents such as criminal damage. The Serious and Organised Crime and Police Act (2005) established the Serious and Organised Crime Agency (SOCA) which became operational in 2006. SOCA amalgamated the roles of the National Criminal Intelligence Service (NCIS), the National Crime Squad (NCS) and the investigative wings of HM Revenue and Customs along with those of the UK Immigration Service. The role of SOCA is to gather, store and analyse information on serious organized criminal activities, which can then be investigated and disrupted. The National Police Improvement Agency (NPIA) was established in April 2007 through the amalgamation of a number of existing police agencies such as the Central Police Training and Development Authority (Centrex) and the Police Information and Technology Organisation (PITO), and aims to deliver effective, efficient and up-to-date training and educational programmes to the police across England and Wales while developing leading-edge information and communication technology solutions for contemporary policing. The Police Scientific Development Branch (PSDB) is a Home Office Unit of scientists, technologists and researchers providing technical advice and guidance to ensure the effectiveness and efficiency of the police service. Their developments range from the high-visibility paint schemes for police helicopters, the best chemicals to develop fingerprints and the best brushes to apply certain fingerprint powders.

The future of the police service appears to fall into two distinct categories, a focus on neighbourhood policing to meet the needs of local communities while developing more centralized services such as those already evolving within the arenas of investigation, intelligence, counter-terrorism and information technology. The smaller police forces are going to have to work with their colleagues on a regional basis. Such regionalization will reduce the duplication and expense of services such as air support units, underwater search units and counter-terrorism. This regionalization will ease the movement of personnel and the sharing of information across police force boundaries and provide a more cost-effective and efficient police service – after all, the criminal does not stop at county boundaries.

1.4 Structure of the contemporary scientific support department

Each of the 43 Home Office police forces in England and Wales, the eight police forces in Scotland and the Police Service of Northern Ireland has a scientific support manager (SSM) who heads each individual scientific support department, as do a number of the other law enforcement agencies such as the Ministry of Defence Police, the Royal Air Force and Royal Military Police and States of Jersey Police. An SSM may be a police officer or civilian crime scene investigation/forensic specialist, with the prime requirement being that they should have strong management skills (Touche Ross 1987). The SSM controls the day-to-day management, including personnel, finance and organization, of the police photography, scenes of crime and fingerprint departments and may occasionally also have responsibility for other specialist departments such as Technical Support Units.

Each specialist department has a departmental head, usually a specialist from within the appropriate discipline. In a typical force structure the fingerprint bureau and the photographic department are based centrally, often in the police force headquarters; whereas in the crime scene investigation department, the Head of Crime Scene Investigation is based at a central location, and the crime scene investigators (CSI) are deployed in sections. These sections are either based geographically, covering large areas, or divisionally, working solely as a resource within that particular police divisional area. Each section has at least one crime scene manager/supervisor who has line management responsibility for those particular CSIs.

The number of CSIs employed within a police force varies enormously in relation to the size of the force, from 10 to well over 150. The same can be said for all of the specialist departments.

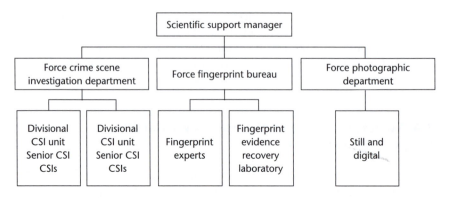

Figure 1.2   A typical UK scientific support unit

1.5 The training of the modern crime scene investigator

The Touche Ross Report (1987) highlighted an enormous difference between the training, expected roles and success of crime scene investigators (then called scenes of crime officers) from force to force. The 1987 report recommended that a formal, standardized training package should be delivered to all CSIs covering the core elements of fingerprint and forensic evidence recovery and basic photography. It went on to suggest that CSIs should receive regular updates as technology advances. At the time the report was written, three police centres, one in Durham, one in Wakefield and the other at Hendon, offered formal national training courses in scenes of crime examination.

As a result of the Touche Ross Report, Durham Constabulary took a brave move to establish the National Training Centre for Scientific Support to Crime Investigation (NTCSSCI). The NTCSSCI runs scenes of crime courses for the majority of police forces in the United Kingdom and has had success delivering similar training programmes overseas. The Scientific Support College based at Hendon runs courses for the Metropolitan Police Service and several forces have opted to continue to train their own personnel in-house to the national standard or opted to recruit graduates with specific crime scene investigation knowledge and skills who have then been inducted into specific force procedures. The initial scenes of crime courses all follow broadly the recommendations of the core elements identified in the Touche Ross Report; the courses vary in duration between eight and twelve weeks and can now be completed as separate modules. Refresher and specialist courses, such as crime scene management, blood spatter interpretation or fire investigation, are on offer to CSIs from a number of differing sources ranging from the NTCSSCI and the Forensic Science Service to specialist companies.

The introduction of the roles of the volume crime scene investigator (VCSI) and forensic vehicle examiner within police forces has greatly increased the number of operational scenes of crime personnel. Trained in a much shorter time, three to four weeks as opposed to eight to twelve weeks, they are specialists trained to deal with volume crime scenes involving stolen vehicles, thefts and burglaries from premises such as garages. It is not uncommon for trained and experienced VCSIs to complete a short conversion course of several weeks to enable them to be employed as a fully skilled CSI.

The introduction of Skills for Justice during 2004 as the national training organization for the police service (see Chapter 15) developed a portfolio of national occupational standards which new and experienced CSIs/VCSIs should achieve and demonstrate competence in. There are a range of National Occupational Standards (NOS) which are specific education and training units. These units are further sub-divided into a number of elements, each of which has a number of performance criteria, a range of situations, along with knowledge and understanding, all of which should be achieved to be awarded the NOS. There are a number of specific Crime Scene Investigator NOS units such as 'Starting the Crime Scene Investigation Process' and 'Evaluating the Crime Scene Investigation' along with more generic units which apply to all law enforcement occupations such as 'Communicate effectively with people' and 'Ensure your own actions reduce risks to health and safety', these are then linked together to form a complete role profile (Skills for Justice 2009).

1.6 The role of the modern crime scene investigator

The general perception of the role of the modern crime scene investigator is often influenced by the strong images portrayed in the popular media of detectives who conduct the crime scene investigation in large teams wearing smart suits, but very little protective clothing, who recover evidence to compare within their own forensic laboratory. This fictional portrayal, based on fact but skewed to make good television, does not reflect what occurs in reality. CSIs (also known by other names such as crime scene examiner and forensic investigator) often work on their own, are very aware of the need to wear protective clothing ranging from gloves to oversuits, and recover the evidence for a forensic scientist to examine within a specialist forensic laboratory. A joint project by the Association of Chief Police Officers and Forensic Science Service (ACPO/FSS 1996) built on the work of others such as the Touche Ross Report and identified a number of roles required of a CSI. These are:

- photography or video photography at scenes of crime, victims and property;
- search for and recovery of physical evidence;
- detection and recovery of fingerprints and palm prints at scenes of crime;

- packaging and storage of physical evidence preventing contamination;
- maintenance of intelligence indices on *modus operandi*, footwear marks, etc.;
- provision of advice on scientific matters;
- preparation of statements and giving evidence in court.

Broadly, the roles and responsibilities of a CSI remain the same today. There is little difference in the roles and responsibilities of CSIs in the UK and the USA, with most other countries following one of these two models (see typical job descriptions of a CSI in the UK and in the USA in Appendices 1.1 and 1.2).

There are approximately 3000 operational CSIs in the United Kingdom. On a daily basis these multi-skilled CSIs individually manage the examination and recovery of photographic, forensic and fingerprint evidence at volume crime scenes such as burglaries and thefts from motor vehicles. Research from data supplied by several police forces for the years 2000/2001, which was conducted by Williams (2004) into the workloads of CSIs, suggests that overall crime scene examinations per year per CSI range between 572 and 348 in the data examined with the percentage of burglaries and vehicle crime examinations ranging between 48–61 per cent of the total examinations completed.

Today the role of the CSI places an even greater emphasis on ensuring that contamination of the evidence cannot take place and the most up-to-date techniques are used to optimum effect. The continuity of the evidence, i.e. ensuring that the location of the evidence can be accounted for all of the way from the crime scene to the court, should be initiated by the CSI during the initial stages of the enquiry. The CSI must always make sure that the documentation relating to the recording, recovery and storage of the sample is accurate and complete.

The modern CSI must constantly think 'outside of the box', identifying and making decisions as to how evidence could be contaminated or destroyed before it happens. Contamination of evidence at the crime scene, during storage and transportation, and in the laboratory can take place due to the incorrect or poor packaging of samples, inappropriate practices or secondary transfer. Incorrect or poor packaging could, for example, be the removal of samples from a crime scene without sealing the packaging; the mere suggestion that this had occurred during a murder enquiry can lead to questions being asked in court. Inappropriate practices could be the CSI not wearing the correct protective clothing or coughing and sneezing over samples recovered for DNA analysis. Secondary transfer could be due to both a victim of an assault and the suspect being transported to the police station at different times but in the same police car. The car could be the means of transferring, for example, fibres between the victim and suspect without their ever coming into contact with each other. Good working practices, the availability of protective clothing and forward thinking can assist in negating such opportunities for contamination to take place. For example, a member of the ambulance service attended the scene of a murder where unfortunately, while checking for the vital signs of life, he stood and knelt in the victim's blood. His boots and clothes were almost immediately seized and securely packaged by the police, removing the opportunity for these items to become a source of secondary transfer of forensic evidence. As a result of this event he now carries paper suits and overshoes to wear at such scenes in order to prevent the likelihood of contamination taking place.

Career progression within the crime scene investigation field is somewhat limited by the number of vacancies, however, with time and experience (and in some police forces the requirement to have attended specific training courses and hold a Diploma in Crime Scene Examination or similar), it is possible for a CSI to become a senior CSI/supervisor managing a particular divisional unit of around ten CSIs/VCSIs. Each force has a head of crime scene investigation, who in turn can progress to become the scientific support manager. Usually working at the force headquarters is the crime scene investigation/forensic trainer; an experienced CSI (in some police forces the requirement is also to hold a Diploma in Crime Scene Examination or similar and a teaching qualification), the trainer has responsibility to keep CSI staff up to date with developments and to provide scene awareness training for police officers.

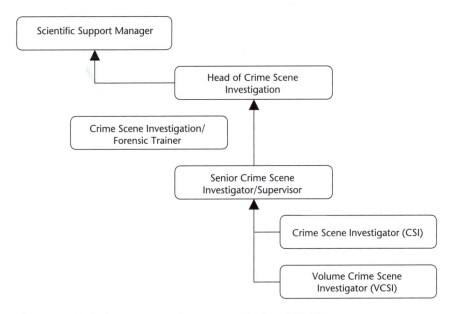

Figure 1.3   Typical career progression opportunities for a CSI/VCSI

The future for the CSI appears extremely exciting. With the demise of the Council for the Registration of Forensic Practitioners and the rise of National Occupational Standards as a means of demonstrating forensic competence, working alongside the national oversight provided by the forensic regulator can only enhance the status of the CSI and ensure common standards. The employment of graduates with underpinning knowledge and skills from the educational disciplines of crime scene and forensic investigation, either directly into operational roles within police forces or indirectly achieving graduate status (such as Foundation Degrees) through work-based training, must enhance the professional standing of the CSI. Opportunities exist for CSIs to work nationally with agencies such as SOCA or the UK Border Agency and internationally with the Foreign and Commonwealth Office, perhaps dealing with investigations into organized crime and disasters overseas, such as those involved in the investigations of the mass graves in the former Yugoslavia during the late 1990s. The involvement of the CSI in the investigative process will grow with the inclusion of intelligence gathered by the CSI from crime scenes in both local and national intelligence systems. Examination and the consequent recovery of evidence will become more automated. For example, the 'online' transfer of latent fingerprints from the crime scene for comparison against the fingerprint database or transfer of a footwear mark to the footwear specialist via a digital camera, laptop computer and mobile telephone will allow speedier analysis and hence earlier arrest of the offender. But, as with the past 150 years, the CSI of the future must continue to have an enquiring mind and an eye for detail, linked to the contemporary knowledge and skills to recover photographic, forensic and fingerprint evidence from the scene of any crime.

Appendix 1.1

Typical job description for a crime scene investigator in the UK

Main responsibilities:

- The examination of crime scenes and associated property for forensic and fingerprint evidence
- The taking of photographs/digital images of crime scenes and other incidents
- Attending, taking photographs and involvement in the recovery of evidence at post-mortems
- Documentation, storage and processing of evidence in a thorough and correct manner
- Attending court and providing evidence as required
- Provision of advice and guidance on forensic matters

- Liaising with other police departments and outside agencies as required

The knowledge, skills and abilities the applicant must possess include:

- Excellent observational skills
- Good interpersonal skills with the ability to deal with victims of crime
- The ability to handle stressful situations and deal with uncomfortable issues
- The ability to maintain records accurately and completely
- IT literate and the ability to utilize computer applications
- The willingness to accept responsibility for his or her own work
- An appropriate level of fitness as the lifting of equipment will be necessary
- A current driving licence
- A flexible approach to working hours
- A demonstrable interest in the use of science to detect crime
- A proactive approach to self-development
- A willingness to attend internal and external training courses

Appendix 1.2

Typical job description for a crime scene investigator in the USA

Main responsibilities:

- Responding to major crime scenes
- Photographing crime scenes
- Searching for evidence relating to the crime
- Searching and processing latent fingerprint evidence
- Preparation of cases
- Providing testimony in court as required
- Fingerprinting individuals

The knowledge, skills and abilities the applicant must possess include:

- The ability to deal effectively and courteously with others
- The ability to express him or herself clearly both orally and in writing
- The ability to observe scenes analytically and objectively
- The ability to record scenes clearly and completely
- The ability to work with adverse conditions, such as fingerprinting corpses

- The ability to lift heavy weights
- Able to work with chemicals used in crime scene investigation
- Able to work both inside and outside in all weather conditions
- Able to work unsociable hours on various shifts or callout

Self-assessment questions

Answer the following questions without reference to the chapter:

1 Who developed the anthropometric system of identification?

2 What does Locard's principle state?

3 Which Act established the uniformed role of the police community support officer?

4 What do the initials PSDB stand for?

5 Who 'aims to deliver effective, efficient and up-to-date training'?

6 What do the initials SOCA stand for?

7 How many police employees are there across the United Kingdom?

8 Who controls the day-to-day management of the Scientific Support Department?

9 What do the initials VCSI stand for?

10 What are the core roles of a crime scene investigator?

---

2 Approaching the crime scene, packaging the evidence and the documentation required

The thorough and conscientious examination and recording of the crime scene are of paramount importance – after all, the crime scene investigator only has one opportunity to recover the evidence that may detect and prove the case. As an operational CSI I can vividly remember finding some blood at the scene of a double child murder that was to become the only evidence that linked the offender to the crime. If this had not been recorded and recovered correctly, then this murder may never have been solved and the individual never convicted.

2.1 Approaching the scene of the crime

CSIs attend a host of different types of crime scenes, at different times of day and night in all weathers. Such scenes can range from murders and robberies to burglaries and thefts and the scenes can be in a range of different locations from those with high density population in deprived areas to crime scenes in less deprived areas. Research conducted by Adderley and Bond (2008) using data from three years relating to burglaries and vehicle crime in the Northamptonshire Police area, suggest that the time CSIs spend examining scenes for forensic evidence is not affected by the location of the crime, but the evidence types recovered can be affected. Before leaving the police station or office to attend any type of crime scene CSIs must check what type of crime scene they are attending, and that they have suitable, sufficient and full working equipment to carry out the examination. A list of equipment that a CSI must have available can be found in the appendix.

When a CSI first arrives at the scene of a burglary or theft, he or she must identify him/herself to the injured party and show a police identification card. The CSI must explain his/her role to the injured party, which is to examine the scene for any evidence that may assist the enquiry. If the CSI is attending a major incident, such as a suspicious death, then he or she must initially locate the rendezvous point (RVP). The RVP will be staffed by a police officer who will record the details of all individuals who enter and leave the crime scene (see Chapter 11).

The CSI shouldn't be afraid to talk to the injured parties and gather information from them; they may even tell the CSI who they believe burgled their premises or stole their laptop. Of course the injured party may be mistaken, but any information the CSI gathers may eventually be of use to the investigation. The type of questions the CSI should ask at the scene of a burglary are:

- Where and how did the intruder get into the premises?
- Where and how did the intruder get out?
- Where has the intruder been?
- What has the intruder taken?
- When did it happen?
- When did they find the burglary or theft?
- Did anyone see the intruder? If so, have they spoken to the police?
- When were the windows and doors last cleaned? This question will assist in providing a time frame during which the evidence such as blood or fingerprints could have been deposited.

All the information gathered must be comprehensively noted on a new crime scene investigation report form. These notes then become the original notes made by the CSI at the time of the examination and must be retained to assist with the investigation, to refresh the memory of the CSI of his/her actions at the crime scene and for court purposes.

Having collated as much information as possible, the CSI must ensure that he or she locates and recovers all of the evidence at the scene of the crime, therefore time spent thinking about the process is well spent. The best way to ensure that the whole scene is examined is mentally to break down the scene into zones; perhaps the point of entry could be one zone, the rest of the room that was broken into a second zone, and the garden a third. The CSI should ensure that each zone is searched and examined for sources of evidence before the next zone is moved onto. At large major crime scenes, such as a scene of an explosion, the scene is physically broken down using police barrier tape into separate zones for searching by specially trained police search teams and the examination by the CSI and possibly other specialists such as a forensic chemist.

Once zoned, the CSI needs to consider the potential effects of the weather on sources of evidence. Consideration should be given to covering footwear marks with buckets to protect them or recovering items that may have been in contact with body fluids or fingerprints to protect them against the elements, as the rain may wash them away or the sun may dry them out. After completing photographs recording the scene of the incident, the CSI examines the exterior of the premises for forensic and fingerprint evidence before starting the examination of the inside. This ensures that evidence is not blown away in the wind, for example. Before starting the fingerprint examination the CSI must gain the permission of the injured party or parties to ensure that they agree to the use of powders, as they can make a mess, but the CSI must also advise them that he or she will clean up afterwards.

The Police Reform Act (2002) allows Chief Constables to designate suitable, capable and adequately trained civilian specialists as investigators. Prior to the 2002 Act, civilian CSIs relied on implied consent to recover evidence found, such as an apparently bloodstained ornament, from the scene of the crime. The 2002 Police Reform Act now allows a designated civilian CSI to seize such evidence without the consent of the owner in order to prevent it being lost or destroyed (Home Office 2002). The evidence seized for the purposes of investigating a crime 'may be retained . . . for use as evidence at a trial for an offence or for forensic examination' (English and Card 2003). It would be prudent for the CSI to provide an injured party with a receipt for property taken away.

Once the CSI has completed the examination, any rubbish, such as ends of sellotape or seals from tamper-evident bags, should be collected and all of the surfaces that have been powdered should be cleaned. The CSI finally decides if elimination DNA samples, fingerprints or footwear marks should be taken from the injured party and from anyone else who has legitimate access: these can only be taken with the consent of the donor. Any elimination fingerprints or footwear marks are compared by specialist staff on a one-to-one basis with those recovered from the crime scene, whereas elimination DNA can either be profiled and compared solely with the suspect DNA profiles from that particular crime or, with the specific consent of the donor, the profile can be loaded on to the national DNA database.

Before leaving the scene the CSI may also give the injured party basic crime prevention advice. Although referrals should always be made to the local crime prevention/reduction officer, basic advice that could be provided include the use of an alarm or security lighting, solid exterior doors with good locks and locks on the windows. The injured party may well have been affected by becoming a victim of crime and as such should be told about the Victim Support Scheme. This is a national charity that provides support and assistance to victims of crime, their dependants and witnesses. It aims to raise the awareness of the public of the effects on individuals of crime. Victim Support also operates a volunteer Court Witness Service providing support for those who have to give evidence in a court.

2.2 The principles of packaging

There are a number of different types of packaging materials with which a CSI must become familiar. Polythene bags are used in large quantities; some are clear and others have labels printed on them ready to be filled out with information about the type of evidence that is in the bags, where it was recovered from, when it was recovered and who recovered it. Tamper-evident bags are polythene bags with an adhesive seal, once sealed they display a 'void' message along the seal if tampered with. Polythene bags would be used for packaging items such as fibre tapings mounted on plastic sheets or paint samples that had been placed in a paper wrap. Brown paper sacks are used to package soil samples or items of clothing, as the sample would rot and decay if placed in polythene bags. Boxes are used for sharp objects such as glass, which should be sellotaped to the bottom of the box, or firearms that must be secured with string within the box. Circular plastic tubes, termed knife tubes, are used for safely packaging sharp instruments such as knives or screwdrivers. Nylon bags are used for fire debris or items which have been in contact with explosives. The nylon bags must be secured at the top with a plastic tie, sellotape or string, ensuring an airtight seal.

Whichever type of packaging is used, it must always be securely sealed, with any potential opening in the packaging sealed, so that minute traces of evidence cannot drop from the packaging or enter into the packaging. Polythene bags and paper sacks must always be folded over twice at the top before sealing to ensure evidence cannot fall out. The packaging must be labelled by the CSI with the four minimum details of the name of the person recovering the sample, the date it was recovered, the location from which it was recovered and an identifying mark (see section 'The CJA label') written on it. A CJA label should then be added if it is not pre-printed on the packaging.

The preferred method of working is to recover each individual sample, package the sample, seal the packaging, then label the packaging before moving on to the recovery of another sample. The required packaging should be taken to the sample rather than the sample to the packaging. In this way evidence is not being transported around the scene by the CSI.

Incorrect or poor packaging linked to inappropriate practices may give rise to the possibility of contamination of the evidence.

Figure 2.1   Folding the top of a paper sack over twice before sealing ensures evidence will not be lost

2.3 Documentation

Accurate note taking of the examination of the scene of the crime, completion of Criminal Justice Act (CJA) labels and the later completion of statements cannot be emphasized enough. The 1996 Criminal Procedures and Investigation Act created the requirement for both the prosecution and defence to disclose any material that may undermine the case in order to ensure the fairness of any subsequent court case. The defence may also apply for a court order to gain access to information that the prosecution may possess that could assist in the case for the defence. Therefore, all of the evidence, including the paperwork that the CSI completes, can be required to be produced before a court of law.

Crime scene investigation report form

All the police forces across the United Kingdom use different formats for crime scene investigation report forms, either in a hard paper copy (usually in the form of a booklet) or electronically using information technology (IT). Whichever form is used, there are some basic principles to be followed. The notes should always contain the name of the CSI, a unique reference number, the date the notes are written, along with the start time and completion time of the examination. A description of the premises or location is worthwhile to 'set the scene' of the crime such as 'a three bedroomed bungalow with a front garden facing on to the main road and fields to the rear', and the weather conditions at the time of the examination may later have significance on why evidence was or wasn't found. It is important that the *modus operandi* (how the crime has been committed) section of the report form is completed as this may provide information of use to the investigation. English and English (2003b) suggest that when a law enforcement employee considers the *modus operandi*, he or she should record the following as a minimum:

- the type of person or property attacked;
- a description of the point of entry;
- a description of how entry was gained;
- the objective of the crime;
- the time of the crime;
- the minimum number of people who may have been involved in the commission of the crime;
- whether a vehicle was used;
- any trademarks of the crime (such as always stealing particular items);
- if the offence involves deception (such as a bogus official), the style of the approach to gain entry and the details of any tale given by the offender.

The CSI must always complete the report at the time of the examination. The notes must be comprehensive and factual, identifying what was done in a logical sequence. The exact locations of every piece of evidence recovered should be detailed on the form. This should include details such as the evidence being on a windowsill inside of the window in the lounge. It is also good practice to draw diagrams of the crime scene on the report form, which must include measurements such as the size of windows climbed through, and the height at which samples, such as blood spatter, were found above the ground. A title showing whether the diagram is from the outside or inside also needs to be included. The patterns of any visible footwear marks at the crime scene should also be added to the report form as an initial means of intelligence gathering. Any alterations by the CSI completing the form should be crossed out, not obliterated, but initialled and dated.

The crime scene investigation report form will later allow the CSI to write an accurate and meaningful statement. If the notes were completed at the time of the examination, it is likely that the CSI will be allowed to use them to refer to while giving evidence in a court of law. It is also likely that the crime scene investigation report form will be used by the police-investigating officer as a primary source of intelligence when attempting to link crime scenes and by the fingerprint or forensic examiner when trying to judge the value of certain evidence.

CRIME SCENE INVESTIGATION REPORT FORM

Offence Type:	Crime Scene Investigator:
Division:	Investigating Officer:
Date examined: Time: Start:	Crime Ref. No. Finish:
Location of offence:	Weather:

Name of Injured Party (if known):

MO:

Details of Examination	Photographs Y/N Number taken:
	Footwear marks found Y/N
	Tool mark Y/N Type:
	DNA found Y/N
	Finger/Palm marks found Y/N Number:
	Glove marks Y/N Type:
	Eliminations Fingerprints Y/N Number of sets:
	DNA Y/N Number of samples:

Signed	Date

Figure 2.2   Crime scene investigation report form

The CJA label

Criminal Justice Act (1967) labels, or their equivalent that may be pre-printed onto bags, need to be attached to the packaging of every piece of forensic evidence recovered at a crime scene. The label provides an accurate record for the court, detailing what is in the sample, where it was recovered from, when it

Continuity

Name: _____
Signature: _____
Date/time: _____

Name: _____
Signature: _____
Date/time: _____

Name: _____
Signature: _____
Date/time: _____

Name: _____
Signature: _____
Date/time: _____

Major incident No.: _____

R. v. _____

Court use only
Court Exhibit No.
Court   Date

Police use only
Crime Ref. No:
Officer in case:
Police Force:
Description of item: _____
_____

Where seized/produced: _____
_____

Time/date seized/produced: _____

Seized/produced by: _____
Signed: _____
Identifying mark: _____

Lab use only:

Figure 2.3 A CJA label

was recovered and by whom. It is on this label that the unique identifying mark given to a particular sample at a particular scene will first appear. The unique identifying mark is usually the initials of the person who recovered the sample and the number of the sample in sequence of recovery and is sometimes pre-fixed by a CSI job number. As such, a unique mark could be 12345 IKP 5, where 12345 is the job number, IKP are my initials and 5 is the fifth sample recovered. The label also shows the signature of everyone who has handled the sample since its recovery, including that of the CSI. This is known as the chain of continuity of the evidence.

Statements

A statement is the written record of the activities of the CSI at the scene of the crime that, under the 1967 Criminal Justice Act, may later be presented to a court. Such a statement (completed on an MG11 statement from witness form) must contain a signed declaration that its contents are to the best of one's knowledge true and any evidence provided that is known or believed to be untrue may lead to prosecution. Statements are usually written or, using a computer, word processed by CSIs at the request of the Crown Prosecution Service (CPS); they should be structured, clear and comprehensive, always observing the rules of disclosure under the Criminal Procedures and Investigation Act (1996). The statement details the facts of what was done at the scene and what happened to the evidence recovered, including the security and continuity of the samples. Hearsay evidence (what someone else has said has happened) should not routinely be included in the statement, although there may be occasions when this is relevant to the case so the CSI may be directed by the CPS to include it.

Generally, when writing a statement, the CSI must begin by identifying his/her role as a CSI and list any relevant qualifications, such as a BSc (Hons) in Crime Scene Science or a Foundation Degree in Crime Scene Investigation. The statement should then detail who the CSI is employed by and the date and time he or she attended a particular address or location. This will allow anyone reading the statement to judge the professional standing of the CSI and identify how he or she was involved in a particular enquiry. Usually the statement would briefly describe the location that the CSI attended and then detail the photographs that were taken, the samples that were recovered and the fingerprint examination the CSI conducted. He or she must add to the statement when the examination of the crime scene was concluded and then what the CSI did with the photographs, forensic samples and fingerprints recovered from the scene, such as placing them into secure storage or handing them to an individual for processing or analysis. The CSI must finish the statement by signing the bottom of every page. To ensure that no one can add anything to the statement the CSI will ensure that no blank lines are left between paragraphs and, whether hand-written or word processed, they should sign the statement immediately after the very last word.

All CSIs write their own statement directly from the notes they made at the crime scene, which it should match in every detail. In my experience the more detailed and comprehensive the statement, the less likely the CSI is to be called to give evidence in court.

Forensic submissions

Two types of form are routinely completed by CSIs to submit samples for forensic examination. The GF111 form is used to forward crime scene stains (such as a swab of blood recovered by the CSI from the interior of a window frame, the suspected point of entry) that may contain DNA for a speculative search against known DNA samples of the National DNA Database (NDNAD) and also, if unidentified, inclusion on the NDNAD. MG/FSP forms are used to submit samples recovered from the crime scene for comparison with samples recovered from a suspect. It is often challenging to decide which samples would be the most appropriate to submit for forensic examination on an MG/FSP form. As a general principle, the samples should be selected which provide the best evidence to prove or disprove an individual's involvement in the incident. It is important to remember that as both of these processes occur outside a police force, there are charges levied, so the forms, along with the submissions, must be checked and authorized by the appropriate budget holder.

2.4 Evidence management systems

One of the first systems used to manage the immense amounts of information, including that of a forensic nature, gathered during a major enquiry was the Home Office Large Major Enquiry System (HOLMES). However, the use of information technology (IT) to manage the day-to-day collection and movement of samples within police scientific services has been slow to develop and take over from paper-based property logs. Police strategy is now determined to integrate the use of IT across the whole service (Home Office Science Policy Unit 2003), so the capabilities for the management of information within the scientific arena must be enhanced. The HOLMES IT system has now migrated to the HOLMES II computerized system used by all 43 police forces across England and Wales (Adderley and Musgrove 2001). The system is used to record, analyse and link data from descriptions, documents, forensic samples and information collected as part of a major investigation.

However, there are predominantly three main systems, SOCRATES, Locard and FLINTS, in daily use in CSI departments across the police and law enforcement agencies in the United Kingdom.

The SOCRATES integrated evidence management system has been developed in consultation with forensic practitioners on a modular basis to allow police forces to customize their choice of computer systems. SOCRATES contains modules for use by CSIs (named SOCKET) which provides information on who attended a particular crime scene, when they attended and which samples were recovered. Also included in the system is the ability for information to be input directly onto SOCKET from the crime scene using a laptop computer. Other modules available in the suite include SOCIMS, which tracks forensic submissions, and GENIE, which tracks DNA samples. The photographic departments may use PRISM and fingerprint bureaux the FLARE system to manage both photographic and fingerprint submissions. SOCRATES is compatible with bar code readers allowing the unique identification of evidence throughout the chain of continuity.

The Locard integrated and automated evidence tracking system also provides the scientific support department with a suite of modules that can be tailored to suit the requirements of each user. The modules available deal with incident logging, exhibit continuity, chemical processing, photography and video, DNA, fingerprints, suspect intelligence, monitoring and audit trails. Locard will allow the user to input information into the system directly from the crime scene using a laptop computer.

Both systems will automatically create hard copies of the forms necessary to forward samples for further analysis, such as those required by forensic science providers or fingerprint bureaux.

The Force Linked Intelligence System (FLINTS) was developed jointly by West Midlands Police and the Forensic Science Service. This computerized system collates and searches all the information routinely collected by a law enforcement agency such as command and control logs, crime reports and firearms registers. Forensic evidence such as DNA, footwear and toolmarks, along with fingerprint evidence, is also input into FLINTS. Using all of this information the system can identify links between individuals and crime scenes and identify criminal networks and crime hotspots. The system is in use by several police forces.

Appendix 2.1

List of equipment available to a Crime Scene Investigator

Personal equipment

Crime scene case containing:

- Selection of sizes of tamper-evident/polythene bags
- Selection of sizes of brown paper sacks
- Selection of plastic tubes and pots
- Disposable scalpels
- Sterile swabs

- Sterile water
- A4 paper
- Small labels for identifying evidence in photographs
- Sellotape
- CJA labels
- Scissors
- Disposable tweezers
- Magnifying glass
- Selection of fingerprinting powders
- Selection of types of fingerprint powder brushes
- Low tack adhesive fingerprint lifting tape
- Low tack adhesive footwear size lifting tape
- Fingerprint size clear plastic
- Footwear size clear plastic
- Indelible pen to write on clear plastic
- Crime scene investigation report forms
- Clipboard
- Tape measure
- Personal health and safety equipment such as latex/nitrile gloves, facemask/respirator, one-piece disposable suit, etc. (see Chapter 13)

Shared equipment (often kept in a vehicle)

- Camera kit with a selection of lenses, flashgun, tripod and film
- DNA elimination swabbing kits
- Elimination fingerprint forms
- Pre-inked elimination fingerprint strips
- Electrostatic lifting apparatus (ESLA)
- Thermometer
- Selection of boxes (usually flat pack)
- Casting mediums for footwear and instrument marks
- String
- Body bag
- Shovel
- Screwdriver
- Door wedge
- Torch
- Police 'Crime scene/do not cross' barrier tape
- 'Rendezvous Point' sign
- Large plastic numbers to identify evidence in photographs
- Mobile telephone and/or police radio
- First aid kit
- Biological hazard bags and sharps bin

Equipment taken to specific scenes

- Video camera
- Digital camera
- Nylon bags and plastic bag ties (to package evidence at a scene of a suspicious fire)
- Firearms discharge residue swabbing kit (to recover evidence from a suspect and victim in a firearms case)
- Forensic medical examination kit (to recover evidence from victims or suspects in sexual offence cases)
- Stepping plates (used to enter a scene without damaging evidence on the floor)
- Crime scene tent (used to protect a scene from the weather and prying eyes)
- Floodlights
- Hand-held global positioning system (GPS) to uniquely locate evidence in remote areas

---

Self-assessment questions

Answer the following questions without reference to the chapter:

1   What is the first thing a CSI should do on arrival at the scene of a crime?

2   Where should the CSI record all the information gathered from an injured party?

3   Which Act allows Chief Constables to designate investigators?

4   Which national charitable organization provides support and assistance to victims of crime?

5   When should a scene of crime report form be completed?

6   What should be attached to every piece of forensic evidence recovered from a crime scene?

7   When writing a statement, what should be at the bottom of every page?

8   What is hearsay evidence?

9   What must both the prosecution and defence disclose?

10   Name the main computerized management system used to record, analyse and link data in a major investigation.

3 The basics of crime scene photography

Almost every day crime scene investigators utilize their photographic skills to record evidence at the scene of a crime. Whether the evidence is located inside or outside, during the day or the night and whatever the weather, the photographs that they take are not a piece of creative work but an actual, accurate permanent record of the evidence as it was found. Warlen (1995) adds that photographs can also be used to help witnesses recall events and assist in clarifying the statements of witnesses in a court.

Like most CSIs, when operational, I took thousands of photographs recording victims of murder, both at the scene and the mortuary, victims of assault, burnt-out houses, footwear marks in soil, car engine numbers, even aerial photographs from helicopters. The variety of photographic challenges presented to a CSI means that a good understanding of basic photographic theory is essential. Equally important, though, is the practical experience of taking photographs for which there is no substitute.

3.1 The basics of crime scene photography

Photography is the recording of an image onto light-sensitive film or electronic sensor. The requirement for light, or the lack of light causing shadow, is an essential element in photography. Light itself travels in straight lines and at the immense speed of 299,790 kilometres (186,000 miles) per second. As the light reflected from an object passes through the lens of a camera it slows and bends (converges) to form an image. Traditionally the image is formed on film that has been covered with silver halide, which is sensitive to light, and placed at the rear of the camera. When chemically processed, the minute crystals of silver halide that have been exposed to light react differently to those that have not and the image is produced in the form of a negative. In order for a final print to be made, light must once again be shone through the negative onto light-sensitive photographic paper; this too must be chemically treated to develop the image. Since the 1980s developments in digital technology have allowed the development of cameras capable of capturing the photographic image on a light-sensitive electronic array.

The majority of the police crime scene investigation departments in the United Kingdom use either a digital or 35mm traditional 'wet film' SLR (single lens reflex) camera; many are of the Nikon type such as digital D70 or D2X or alternatively the 35mm film FM 2. However, no type of camera is prescribed by the Home Office for use by police crime scene investigation units. The 35mm in film terminology refers to the size of the negative produced on the film, which in reality is 24 × 36mm in size (Stroebel and Zakia 1993), whereas with digital cameras the image is recorded on sensors rather than film with the physical dimensions of the group of sensors being smaller than a 35mm film negative. The abbreviation SLR refers to using the same lens for both viewing and photographing an image. A mirror mechanically held at 45 degrees to the lens reflects the light up to a viewfinder, allowing the photographer to see the image that will appear on the film or digital sensors. Immediately before the shutter is opened and the photograph is taken, the mirror flips up, closing off the viewfinder from light. The added bonus of a digital camera is that the image taken and recorded on the sensors is usually displayed on the LCD screen on the rear of the camera.

In order to operate effectively, an SLR camera will have a lens on which the photographer can alter the point of focus; the focusing ring alters the point that the photographer wishes to be in sharp focus. Aperture settings on the lens allow the photographer to alter the size of the hole within the lens through which light can pass. Based on the 'f system' of ratio measurement developed by the Royal Photographic Society in nineteenth-century Britain (Miller 2006), small apertures (or a small opening in the lens) such as f16 or f22 mean that less light will enter the lens in a set time than larger apertures such as f2.8 or f4. The aperature range displayed either on the camera lens or digitally within the camera usually follows the sequence of f2, f2.8, f4, f5.6, f8, f11, f16, f22, each step up the numbers decreasing the light allowed into the lens. The lenses themselves come in different sizes from 28mm wide-angle lenses to 120mm telephoto lenses. A standard lens for a 35mm film camera is a 50mm lens. This 50mm lens reproduces on the film an image roughly equating to what can be seen if the eye is held still, so may be used to photograph evidence as the CSI sees it. In the case of digital SLRs, as the group of sensors varies in size, the equivalent of a standard lens alters from camera to camera; with a few exceptions, the standard is unlikely to be 50mm lens, so the recommendation would be to check with the instruction manual. A wide-angle lens provides a wide angle of view and would perhaps be used to photograph a room, while a telephoto (or zoom) lens provides a narrow angle of view but can be used to photograph images at a greater distance.

A by-product of altering the apertures is depth of field. Using a smaller aperture such as f22 (a big number), the distance between the closest and farthest points that will appear to be in focus in a final print will be greater than at larger aperture settings such as f4.5 (a small number). This may be of use when photographing, for example, the victim of an assault in his or her own home: although the CSI may wish to see the injuries on the face of the assault victim in focus, the background, such as a large pattern wallpaper, may be better out of focus so as not to distract the jury looking at the photograph from the victim's injury. Consequently an aperture setting of f5.6 will allow this, as if the injury is focused upon, the background will be out of focus. Alternatively at an outdoor murder scene with evidence strewn along a road, an aperture setting of f22 will allow all the evidence to be seen in focus along the whole road in the final photographic print.

The camera body will have some means of controlling the shutter speed and a shutter release button. Operated by pressing the shutter release button on top of the camera body, the shutter speed is the speed at which a mechanical device within either the lens or the body of a camera opens and closes across the film, exposing it to light. Changed by a dial located on top of the camera, shutter speeds vary from as slow as one second to faster than 1/1000th of a second. If, for example, you were photographing a police helicopter with its rotors turning, then using a fast shutter speed, such as 1/500th of a second, will freeze movement allowing individual rotor blades to be seen in the final photograph, while a slower shutter speed, such as 1/8th of a second, will create the effect of movement allowing a disc to be seen on top of the helicopter rather than individual rotor blades. If a long shutter speed is required, usually 1/250th of a second or slower, then a cable release and tripod should be used. A cable release, attached to the camera, will allow the shutter to be fired without the CSI touching the shutter release button. Therefore the possibility of the camera moving during the long exposure, causing 'camera shake' on the final photographic print, will be reduced. Some cameras also have the letter 'B' on the shutter speed dial meaning 'brief'. Setting the letter 'B' will allow the shutter to be opened and left open, sometimes exposing the film for several minutes, until the photographer closes the shutter. This would be used when photographing a scene at night when the film will need light to be introduced from a flashgun.

In order to measure the exposure required to record the crime scene, the photographer will use either the camera TTL (through the lens) metering system or a hand-held light meter. The TTL metering system is good for obtaining a general reading of the light reflected from all of the surfaces in the photograph (termed reflected light reading), while a hand-held meter has the added benefit of being able to be used to take a meter reading of the light falling onto the subject in the photograph (termed incident light reading). Once the light has been measured, the photographer will balance the size of the aperture

Figure 3.1a Depth of field at f4.5

Figure 3.1b Depth of field at f22: note that the fence post behind the pliers is in focus at f22

required for the photograph with the best shutter speed or vice versa in order to determine the preferred exposure.

If a flashgun is to be used linked to the camera with a synchronization lead, then the camera flash synchronization speed should be set on the shutter speed dial. This synchronization speed is the minimum to allow light to be emitted from a flashgun, reflected from the surface and returned to the film before the shutter closes. Flashguns are used when either insufficient light is being reflected from the object in the photograph, such as inside a house or a car, or shadows need to be eliminated because of strong daylight, such as seeing a knife under a car in strong sunlight. Flashguns come in numerous shapes, sizes and powers. As a general rule, large powerful flashguns are good for general scene work while smaller, less powerful flashguns should be used for photographing evidence close up, such as fingerprints or instrument marks. Specially designed flashguns called 'ring flashes' can be screwed to the front of a lens and used to provide even lighting from all sides across the subject being photographed. Routinely the flashgun should have its aperture settings the same as that on the camera. However, on occasions it may be necessary to alter the settings so that the flash doesn't give out as much light, for example, to eliminate the shadows, or give out more light, for example, to photograph the very black inside of a fire-damaged room.

The choices of photographic film range from black and white to colour. The choice of black and white or colour film is dictated in the main by the requirements of the end user of your photographs. For example, the scene of a murder would be better recorded on colour film to show everything in detail, while fingerprints would be better photographed with black and white

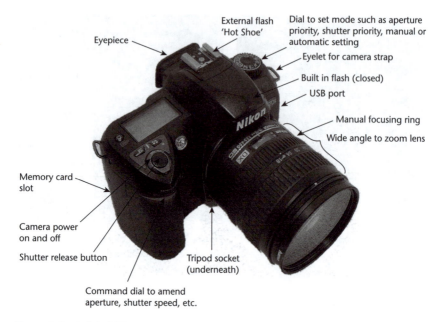

External flash 'Hot Shoe'

Dial to set mode such as aperture priority, shutter priority, manual or automatic setting

Eyepiece

Eyelet for camera strap

Built in flash (closed)

USB port

Manual focusing ring

Wide angle to zoom lens

Memory card slot

Camera power on and off

Shutter release button

Tripod socket (underneath)

Command dial to amend aperture, shutter speed, etc.

Figure 3.2 A digital SLR camera

film to assist in the differentiation of ridges and furrows by the fingerprint expert.

The film speeds range from 25 ASA or ISO to 1000 ASA or ISO and faster and is indicated by a rating found on the film, which shows the film sensitivity to light. The ratings are indicated by the letters ASA (American Standards Association) or ISO (International Standards Organization); the bigger the number, the more sensitive the film is to light. The ASA/ISO number, usually found on the shutter speed dial, should always be set on the camera to prevent the film being over- or under-exposed to light.

In digital cameras, in place of the light-sensitive film, a photographic image is recorded onto electronic sensors, which respond to light; these are set in a grid pattern within the camera. The light, which falls onto this grid of electronic sensors, produces a pattern of electrical charges, which in turn are converted into a series of numerical values and stored in the camera's own memory or on a memory card. Langford and Andrews (2007) describe five commercially produced memory card types used by different manufacturers: compact flash card (most popular type), secure digital (SD) card, xD picture card, memory stick and smart media. The camera's own memory or that of the memory card can be easily reaccessed and the number values converted to present an image on an electronic screen; if required, this image can then be printed. Each value within the electronic grid within the camera relates to an element of the picture known as a pixel. The quality of the images produced relies on the number of pixels available, these being the smallest piece of information that can be recorded. The quality of an image produced by a digital camera of between 2.5 and 3.5 million pixels is comparable to that produced by a 35mm negative (Stroebel and Zakia 1993), but most contemporary digital SLR cameras well exceed this figure, such as the Nikon D70, having well over five mega pixels, and the Cannon EOS-1DS, achieving 11 mega pixels (Miller 2006). There is no doubt that digital photography is equal to if not exceeds the requirements established by the more traditional 'wet film' photography for its use in crime scene work.

It is also good practice for CSIs to use a tripod to photograph crime scenes as this both reduces their workload by leaving hands free to hold a flashgun or torch and minimizes the possibility of 'camera shake', which could lead to the scene being blurred and therefore incorrectly recorded.

3.2 Photographing a crime scene

Photography always comes first when examining a crime scene, recording everything as it was found. Care should be taken not to disturb or contaminate other evidence types when taking the comprehensive set of photographs, the details of which should be conscientiously written on the crime scene investigation report form. When photographing a crime scene, the photographs tell the story, in colour, without words. For example, if a single murder had occurred in an upstairs bedroom of a house, as a minimum the CSI will always photograph the outside of the house, entry through the door, up the stairs and into the room before even reaching the body. On entering the room, general photographs are taken from each corner, making sure they overlap, so that everything in the room is recorded; this is termed 'quartering the room' or 'sectioning the room'. The CSI may have to use a wide-angle lens to allow a small room to be photographed, but care should be taken as such lenses can distort the size of the images. Then the CSI will move in towards the body taking a second series of photographs to show everything that is immediately around the body before finally photographing the body itself along with specific pieces of evidence such as tied hands, a knife or ropes used in a hanging. Rohde (2000) divides the series of photographs that should be taken at a crime scene into '(1) overview, (2) midrange, (3) close-up', and I would totally agree with this description. Once the body has been removed, then a further mid-range photograph should be taken to show any evidence, such as blood-staining on a floor, which was underneath the body. Aerial photographs should also be taken at the scene of a murder to assist in the description of the location of the crime scene (IAI 1999). Having taken numerous aerial photographs of crime scenes, I would agree that they are of immense value, but they can also be taken at other types of incidents such as arsons, where one can see the damage to a roof, or road traffic accidents to see the layout of the vehicles and roads.

Often the photographing of crime scenes takes place at night or in poor lighting conditions. In these conditions flashguns need to be used to introduce extra light, so they must always be kept charged and at hand. The photographing of the scene of a fire can require immense amounts of extra lighting due to the black and charred nature of the surfaces absorbing light. On such occasions an experienced CSI may use two flashguns to illuminate and balance light on a subject.

In the USA it is even possible for specially trained CSIs, equipped with diving equipment and the appropriate watertight underwater housing for the camera, to be asked to photograph underwater crime scenes such as bodies and weapons dumped into lakes and rivers, although it is generally acknowledged that due to particles in the water visibility can often be poor for such photography (Becker 2006; Miller 2006).

3.3 Photographing the scene of a road traffic collision and/or a vehicle

The photographing of a scene of a road traffic collision should be completed as soon as possible after the accident has occurred, but after casualties have been removed and it is safe for the CSI to enter the scene of the incident. The incident may turn into a criminal investigation into offences such as 'causing death through reckless driving' or 'manslaughter' and as such should be treated as a crime scene.

Initially photographs are taken from a distance (at times over 100 metres away), looking along the road and locating all of the vehicles involved; this will be repeated for all the roads and junctions looking towards the vehicles. If the accident occurred at night, then it will usually be necessary for the CSI to return in daylight to complete these long shots. The camera should be fitted with a standard lens, as this will minimize distortion of the image, and it should be placed on a tripod, looking along the middle of the road. Under no circumstances should the CSI attempt to replicate what the driver saw as he or she approached the accident as it would be impossible to know where the driver's head was within a vehicle, which way the driver was looking, where the vehicle was on the road, etc. The photographs taken by the CSI are to record the scene accurately in order to inform and not influence both the coroner and any subsequent investigation.

Next, photographs will be taken showing the position of the vehicles, as they were when the CSI arrived. If the vehicles have been moved to facilitate the rescue of casualties, no attempt should be made to replicate the accident.

Any skid marks and related debris are also photographed; it may be necessary for a police collision accident investigator to mark the start and finish of the skid marks to facilitate their complete photography.

Then individual vehicles must be photographically recorded. As with rooms, the vehicle must be quartered by taking a photograph, if possible, from each of the four corners. Close-up photographs of damage, such as smashed windscreens and collapsed wheels, will also be required. The CSI will concentrate on recording damage caused either during the accident or leading to the accident and not damage caused by the emergency services, such as the removal of door pillars to reach casualties. It may also be necessary to photograph the interior of the vehicles, including the engine compartment and boot; extra light may have to be introduced to allow accurate and complete recording of the interior, which would best be achieved by using a flashgun. If close-up photographs are required of items within the vehicle or the engine compartment, possibly engine numbers and items inside the boot, then a flashgun will have to be used.

Aerial photographs are an excellent way of providing an overview of the accident. Most police forces now have available an aerial support unit who will gladly record the scene.

3.4 Photographing fingerprints, footwear marks, tyre tracks and instrument marks

The photographing of any visible fingerprints, footwear marks, tyre tracks and instrument marks requires time and the careful positioning of the camera. Initially a photograph is taken to record where the marks are on the ground, door or window frame. Then the camera (if a traditional 'wet film' camera, it should be loaded with black and white film to heighten contrast between dark and light areas) should be placed on a tripod, immediately over the mark and square to it. In order to assist in the positioning of the camera directly over the mark an angle setter (a form of spirit level) is placed on the mark, then on the camera which is then moved until the angle setter is parallel to the mark. As the CSI looks through the camera viewfinder, the mark should fill the frame in the camera. The fingerprints, footwear and instrument marks should have two scales, placed at right angles to each other level with the mark. A label should also be placed next to the mark detailing the name of the CSI, the date, location and identification reference number (see Chapter 2). The marks are photographed using a standard lens so that any distortion to the mark on the final print or digital image is minimized. However, in the case of fingerprints and instrument marks, the CSI will have to get very close to fill the frame; this can be achieved by using a diopter lens which can be added to the front of the standard lens. In effect, the diopter lens turns the standard lens into a close-up lens, thus allowing close-up photography to take place. As an alternative to attaching a diopter lens, if a digital camera is being used, it may be switched to the macro setting which will allow the lens to be focused very close to a finger-print or instrument mark.

As the camera will be very close to the mark, then the greatest depth of field setting that the camera and lighting conditions allow, such as f16 or f22, should be utilized. This is because the actual depth of field in relation to the point of focus is extremely shallow, due to the closeness of the article. So by increasing the depth of field, any part of the mark on a curved surface, such as fingerprints around a bottle, or impressed into putty, or the deep detail in a footwear mark, will be in focus on the final print.

Often oblique lighting from a flashgun is required to illuminate the mark, particularly if it is impressed into a surface such as soil or putty. Using a torch the CSI will look through the camera and move the torch around the mark and from the ground to the camera. When he or she can see the mark most clearly, due to the small shadows that will be cast in the mark, then he or she will hold and fire the flashgun from the same location.

Figure 3.3 How to set up a camera on a tripod ensuring the camera is parallel to the footwear mark, with two scales at right angles to each other and a flashgun

3.5 Photographing the victim of a crime or a suspect

A CSI may have to photograph injuries to murder victims at post-mortems or victims of assault in the police station or their own home.

At a post-mortem the CSI taking the photographs, along with his/her equipment, should always remain clean, not coming into contact with any contaminated surfaces or body fluids. Some police forces maintain 'mortuary kits' that never leave the mortuary, which contain the necessary camera equipment. Alternatively, equipment taken into a mortuary should be effectively cleaned on leaving with a suitable disinfectant. Using a camera with a standard lens and colour film the CSI must begin by taking a series of photographs of the body, both clothed and unclothed, ensuring the whole body is recorded. Then he or she will take photographs as directed by other CSIs, the Senior Investigating Police Officer or the forensic pathologist of points of note, such as lines of hypostasis and injuries to the victim. Injuries could include stab or gunshot wounds, damage to internal organs and even inside the body cavity. Photography of these injuries requires the addition of two scales placed at right angles to the injury. The CSI will take a photograph before adding scales and then a photograph with the scales. This demonstrates to any individual viewing the photographs that the scales have not been used to hide evidence and the addition of the scales helps a jury visualize the size of the injury. This is always challenging work but the results are rewarding. CSIs must always be aware of the surfaces around them, not leaning or standing in body fluids. Mortuary surfaces are usually clean and shiny and as such will reflect light from the flashgun easily. Due to the colour and reflective nature of skin it is very hard to focus on, so care must be taken. As with all CSI work there will only be one opportunity to take these photographs correctly.

Assault victims, perhaps after a Saturday night brawl, are often difficult to photograph as, try as they will, they cannot sit still. The CSI must quickly gain the victim's confidence by talking to him or her and explaining what he or she is doing before attempting to photograph the injuries. The injuries can be on any part of the body, so it is prudent to have a CSI photographer of the same gender as the victim. This is one of the few occasions when it may be better not to use a tripod while taking the photographs, as this allows the CSI to move with the victim. The CSI should make him or herself the tripod by standing with feet apart. A fast shutter speed, such as $1/500^{th}$ of a second, should be set on the camera in order to freeze any movement, but the fast shutter speed must be within the flash synchronization speed, and colour film is usually used. It is often difficult to focus on skin; asking the injured party to place his or her finger next to the injury and focusing on that may help to ensure that the injury is in focus on the final print. Using a flashgun to take the photographs will also assist in freezing any movement and illuminate the injury. But the CSI must be careful not to have the flashgun too close to the injury as its powerful light output may mask lighter bruising on the final photographic print. Setting the aperture to reduce the depth of field, such as f5.6, will allow the CSI to blur the background in someone's house so that the image in the photograph is concentrated on the victim's injury. If available, a telephoto lens rather than a standard lens should be utilized, as this will allow the CSI to be a little further away from the victim so as not to invade his or her personal space. The first photograph taken will be of the victim's face before taking any injury photographs. The injury must be placed in a context so bruising on a leg should have a photograph of the leg taken after the facial photograph before a close-up of the bruising both with and without scales.

A CSI may also be asked to photograph crime suspects, perhaps recording injuries to them or the clothing they are wearing at the time of their arrest. Occasionally a CSI may also be asked to photograph a parade to record how representative the parade is in relation to the suspect. The requirement for the photographic recording of parades is gradually being reduced with the introduction of Video Identification Parade Electronic Recording (VIPER).

The national VIPER bureau was opened in West Yorkshire in 2003 and the system is now in use across a number of police forces. VIPER requires suspects to have a standard electronic image of their head and shoulders recorded at their local police station, which is then sent online to the central bureau. The central bureau collates a CD or DVD of similar standard images, from their extensive database of images previously recorded from volunteers. After the suspect has viewed the image collection, in order to make any objections, it can then be viewed by the witness without the suspect being present.

3.6 Photographing a computer screen

When assisting in the investigation of cyber crime it may be necessary for the CSI to record photographically what is displayed on the screen of a computer. In order to achieve this, the CSI must fill the frame of the camera with the computer screen, then take a reflected light meter reading. The light emitted from the computer screen provides the only light used within this photograph; flashguns should not be used as they may mask some information on the screen. Priority is given to the shutter speed, ensuring that it is set at 1/15th of a second, then the aperture is altered until sufficient reflected light is received through the lens. If the shutter speed was set any faster, such as 1/60th of a second, then lines, termed 'noise bars' that create the picture on the computer screen, would be visible on the final photograph. The image on a computer screen must be recorded in colour.

3.7 Taking aerial photographs

As an operational CSI I was called upon on a number of occasions to take a series of aerial photographs from both police and military helicopters in order to record evidentially outdoor murder scenes, road traffic collisions and extensive fire scenes. Although police air support units now routinely have their own photographic equipment available within the helicopters, it is still worthwhile having some basic guidelines for when the opportunity arises to be involved in this type of fascinating photographic work.

The first use of an aerial photograph was from a hot air balloon in 1858 (Langer and Dunaski 2007). Today when we consider the use of aerial photography we immediately tend to think of helicopters, but a CSI should also consider, subject to satisfactory health and safety arrangements, the advantages of taking aerial photographs of crime scenes from other elevated positions above eye level such as specialist lifting apparatus operated by the council or fire service.

When taking aerial photographs from helicopters, it is imperative that health and safety is prioritized (such as listening to safety briefings before the flight and safety straps remaining fastened during the flight) and ensuring that commands by the aircrew are observed at all times.

There is no need to purchase specialist equipment to take good aerial photographs, in good weather with good visibility, a digital SLR (with a resolution of five megapixels or greater) fitted with a standard lens produces good results. The use of a zoom lens can accentuate vibration from the helicopter, after all, the image can always be enlarged when back on the ground. Also don't lean against parts of the helicopter's airframe as vibration may affect your final image, instead cradle the camera using the upper part of your body like a shock absorber. The pilot will position the helicopter appropriately on your direction in order for you to capture the image you require; on command of the aircrew you may open the cabin door to take the photograph. Always ensure the camera is attached to you by using the neck strap and no other loose items (such as the lens cap) can fall off during the flight. Just before taking the photograph use the camera's own through the lens metering system and set the fastest shutter speed possible, 1/500th of a second or faster, with the focus set to infinity. Take care not to get either the helicopter's rotor blades or landing skids in the photograph. On completion of taking the photographs, the cabin door should be closed.

The type of photograph usually taken from a helicopter to record a crime scene is termed low oblique. This is an image taken around a 40 degree angle from the vertical axis (Eller 2000) at a height around 500 feet. Such low oblique images cover a relatively small area, don't show the horizon and familiar landmarks, such as buildings, can be observed and recognized. This is as opposed to high oblique images usually taken around a 70 degree angle (Eller 2000), from the vertical axis at a height around 1000 feet, where the horizon can be seen and the relief of the land is visible. Vertical images are usually taken from fixed wing aircraft well above 2000 feet and look straight down providing scale to the photograph (Eller 2000).

3.8 Issues with digital photography

The use of digital cameras is an excellent means of recording a crime scene and evidence found within it. Digital cameras have the distinct advantage that the photographer can view the image recorded on a small screen set within the camera, enabling the CSI to ensure that the image has been recorded accurately. Digital cameras work in broadly the same manner as other conventional camera types. The photograph is taken by combining the benefits of focus, apertures and shutter speeds to record the image accurately. The difference is that an electronic array rather than film captures the images. This information is then converted into pixels and can be displayed on a screen. The image recorded can be electronically transferred between sites for the purposes of briefing or searching against databases, and although the initial outlay for digital photographic equipment and the associated computer hardware and software is high, the production of images is relatively cheap compared to traditional wet photography.

Some police forces are investing heavily in digital imaging equipment, purchasing SLR digital cameras while other police forces are holding back. The more expensive SLR digital cameras with large image recording ability, such as over 5 million pixels, have the distinct advantage over smaller cheaper cameras with only 3 million pixels, in that the image that is recorded is not compressed. Compression of the image results in information being removed to allow storage. The elimination of compression means that the image is not altered in any way by the camera. In other words what the CSI sees is what the camera records. It is also worth considering the format that is used by the camera to store the captured image. There are three formats used by digital cameras, RAW files, TIFF files and JPEG files. Both RAW files and TIFF files provide excellent image quality but are very large files to store both in the camera and when transferred to hardware within the police station. TIFF files have the advantage of being easier to print and edit, but both keep the image as when it was first taken. JPEG files use compression to reduce the storage space of the image, but the more the image is compressed, the more information is lost from the image and each time it is re-saved in this format some more information is lost (Miller 2006; Langford and Andrews 2007). It stands to reason therefore that the initial image recorded should be as accurate as possible, so although no format for the image file within the camera is prescribed, if hardware, software and operational needs allow, either RAW or TIFF files would be most appropriate. Added to this, prior to copying back at the police station, no image taken with a digital camera should be deleted as this may be seen as tampering with the evidence.

The main issue with digital cameras appears not to be the image quality but the security and integrity of the electronic image from the crime scene, through the investigative process, to the court. It would be relatively easy to enhance a digital image or remove an object from it. This would also be true of wet photography, but with wet photography the original negative would reveal how the image was initially recorded and thus highlight any alterations. In order to overcome the issue of digital image manipulation the Police Scientific Development Branch (PSDB 2002) suggests that an audit trail should be initiated immediately a digital image is recorded that will remain with the image from its beginning until its final disposal. Such a trail should include details of the case, description of images recorded, any downloading of the images, creation of master files, their storage, any access to them, copying of the image, viewing of the image, and their use in a court of law (PSDB 2002). In addition, I would also suggest that the first digital recording of an image, such as a footwear mark or fingerprint, should as soon as possible be burned in an uncompressed format to a writeable CD in a Write Once, Read Many (WORM) format, in effect creating a negative. Information about the date and time the CD was recorded and the details of the person making the recording should also be added. This master file will support the integrity of the image as it was initially recorded at the scene. Any future alterations or enhancements of the image should also be recorded in sequence as they are performed. Additional security features could be the encoding of the pixels; this would provide a numerical value for each and every pixel and/or the watermarking of images, perhaps with the police force crest, to illustrate ownership. There are a number of software packages available that will allow the viewer to track any alterations that have been made to the image.

The eventual utilization of digital photography throughout the investigation of crime scenes, linked to the possibilities of online, secure access to national databases, such as the fingerprint database Ident 1, can only be of benefit to the CSI and the whole police investigative team.

Appendix 3.1

List of photographic equipment available to a crime scene investigator

- Single lens reflex (SLR) camera body (either digital or traditional 35mm film 'wet film' type)
- Standard lens (varies with manufacturer of digital cameras or 50mm for a 35mm 'wet film' type)
- Wide-angle lens (28mm)

- Telephoto lens (120mm)
- Flashgun with synchronization cable
- Ring flashgun
- Light meter
- Cable release
- Tripod
- Angle setter
- Two scales
- Memory card or traditional 'wet film' (both colour and black and white)
- Spare batteries

Taking care of your camera equipment

- Have the camera regularly serviced by a qualified technician.
- Avoid getting the camera wet (consider covering the camera with a polythene bag with a hole for the lens when using in the rain).
- Never drop the camera and keep it clean.
- The lens should only be cleaned with a lens cloth.
- The lens cap should always be replaced on the lens when not in use.
- The camera should always be put away when not in use.

Self-assessment questions

Answer the following questions without reference to the chapter:

1 How fast does light travel?

2 What size is a standard lens for a Nikon FM 2?

3 Which of these apertures would provide the best depth of field on the final print: f5.6 or f22?

4 Which of these shutter speeds is more likely to freeze the movement of an object: 1/8th of a second or 1/500th of a second?

5 What is a compact flash card?

6 What does 'quartering a room' mean?

7 When using traditional 'wet film', is colour or black and white film preferable for photographing fingerprints?

8 In relation to digital photography, what is compression?

9 At approximately what angle from the vertical axis are low oblique aerial images taken?

10 When should an audit trail begin when using a digital camera?

4 Trace evidence: fibres, glass, hairs, paint and soil

As part of the day-to-day routine of a crime scene investigator, examinations are made at scenes that reveal trace evidence that on face value appears limited in its usefulness. However, the recovery of these evidence types can lead not only to the detection of one crime but the linking of a number of different offences. A colleague of mine was commended by the Chief Constable as he had recovered paint samples from a large number of burglaries that were eventually linked by a forensic scientist to paint smears found on a single crowbar in the possession of a suspect. Trace evidence, such as fibres, glass, hairs, paint or soil can provide very useful evidence.

4.1 Fibres

Fibres can be broadly divided into two categories: natural or man-made. Naturally occurring fibres can derive from animals, such as wool or silk, or plants such as flax or cotton (which accounts for nearly half of worldwide fibre production). Man-made fibres, such as viscose, can be regenerated from natural polymers, or created from synthetic polymers produced for the purpose, such as polyester (Greaves 1995).

Fibres can be deposited from the offender's clothing at the crime scene or taken away from the crime scene on the offender's clothing. For example, in Northern Ireland, a vehicle that had been privately bought was used in a shooting. Fibres recovered from the suspect's clothing matched fibres deposited in the vehicle by the previous owner from whom the vehicle had been bought and consequently provided a link between the suspect and the scene (Marshall and Armstrong 2002).

Recovery and comparison

Fibres can be recovered from crime scenes using two methods. Large clumps of fibres stuck on broken windows or doors can be picked off using new tweezers that have not been contaminated with other sources of fibres. These clumps can be placed in a paper wrap then sealed in a polythene bag and labelled. However, if the fibres are at the point of entry and the weather is less than ideal, then the removal of fibres with tweezers may lead to some of them being blown or washed away. Consideration should always be given to using the second method of recovering fibres from the crime scene using clear adhesive tape. The sticky side of the tape should carefully be pushed onto the fibres; this can be repeated several times until all of the fibres are removed. The tape should then be placed onto a clear sheet of plastic before being sealed in a polythene bag and labelled.

The same method of lifting fibres with clear adhesive tape can also be used to recover fibres deposited on vehicle seats by the offenders. Such fibre tapings must systematically cover the whole seat of the vehicle using several pieces of adhesive tape. This must include the headrest, seatbelt and fabric on doors. Each seat should be treated separately and hence packaged and labelled as separate samples.

Fibre taping is also the generally accepted method of recovering fibres from a deceased naked body.

Surfaces at the crime scene that easily shed fibres, such as a thick pile carpet or a fluffy car seat, may deposit fibres onto the offender. Control samples of these will be taken by the CSI. Generally the best method to recover a representative sample of the fibres present is to recover the actual item, such as an off-cut of the carpet or removable car seat cover. This is securely packaged in a brown paper sack. If it is not possible to recover the whole item, then a representative sample of the fibres may be plucked from the surface using new tweezers. If this is also impossible, then fibre tapings will suffice.

The number of fibres deposited or taken away from the crime scene by the offender depends on a number of variables (Pounds and Smalldon 1975):

- the number of times a garment came into contact with the area;
- the force of the contact: more pressure would increase the number of fibres transferred;
- the nature of the surfaces coming into contact with each other.

Fibres transferred are usually short with most viscose or polyester fibres being less then 5mm in length (Kidd and Robertson 1982).

Once transported to the forensic laboratory, a forensic scientist will meticulously examine the fibres recovered by the CSI from the crime scene and identify any meriting further examination. These fibres are removed and mounted on slides for viewing under a microscope. The fibres on these slides will be compared against fibres removed by a different forensic scientist from the clothing of the suspect using similar methods but in conditions free from potential contamination by the original crime scene sample; these fibres would also be mounted on microscopic slides. These two groups of fibres will initially be compared visually for similarity before using a comparison microscope. Fibres under the microscope can be compared using white, ultraviolet and infrared light, as the differing light conditions will reveal different aspects of the fibres, such as the internal structure. For larger items of fabric, a forensic scientist may be able to comment on the likelihood of garments being torn apart or cut (perhaps with the blade of a knife). The dyes can also be abstracted from the fibres and compared using chromatography. A forensic scientist will also comment on the concentration and number of fibres on samples, such as the number and locations of particular fibre types which may appear on separate items of clothing worn by two individuals involved in an assault on each other.

The high level of concentration required to search for and compare fibres has led to several attempts to develop an automated 'fibre finding' system, with some limited success.

Hair and fibre evidence in the investigation into the murder of Sarah Payne

In the summer of 2000, 8-year-old Sarah Payne was abducted and murdered, her body was eventually discovered and identified using DNA. In 2001, Roy Whiting was put on trial for the murder. A shoe had been found that had a large number of fibres stuck to a Velcro strap of the shoe. On examination of the shoe by a forensic scientist, some fibres were found to match Sarah's sweatshirt and others matched a red sweatshirt found in Whiting's van. Fibre evidence provided a link between Sarah and the shoe and the shoe with the van. However, during the trial doubt was raised as to how a hair from Sarah had been deposited on the red sweatshirt found in Whiting's van.

A large number of items from both the crime scene and Sarah's house had been recovered by the police and sent to the forensic science provider for examination. On examination of some of the samples, forensic scientists found a number of hairs stuck to the outside edges of the adhesive sealing some of the crime scene sample bags. These samples had been recovered, packaged, sealed and labelled but then placed on the floor of Sarah's home by the investigator. It is from the floor that the extraneous hairs could have been picked up and then fallen onto other samples during their transport, storage and examination. At the trial it was suggested by the defence that this is how a hair had been transferred from Sarah's house to Whiting's red sweatshirt.

In court the forensic team admitted that contamination of the red sweatshirt with a hair could have taken place during the forensic examination at the laboratory with a hair falling from the adhesive or another source, but this was very unlikely as the evidence from the scene, suspect and victim are examined in different rooms. Accurate notes made by the scientist of what was initially visible and the procedures they carried out would support this. Supported by other forensic evidence, such as the fibres, Roy Whiting was found guilty of murder. However, this case study illustrates how easily contamination, or the suggestion of contamination, can take place, and the importance of robust evidence recovery and examination procedures.

4.2 Glass

Glass found at a crime scene can come in various forms, ranging from broken bottles used during an assault, broken headlamp glass at a road traffic collision to broken windows at a burglary. We will concentrate on window glass, as a broken window is often the means of entry to a burglary, but the principles are the same for all glass types. Window glass is made up of sodium, calcium silicate containing around 70 per cent silica and small amounts of other metallic oxides such as magnesium (Walls 1968). Different glass contains different amounts of silica and other metallic oxides. The most prevalent method for manufacturing window glass is the float process where the raw materials are heated and the molten glass is drawn out onto a bath of molten tin allowing uniform thickness and bright surfaces. Patterned and wired glass for windows are manufactured by heating the raw materials and then drawing the molten glass through rollers that are adjustable for thickness (Caddy 2001).

When an object, such as a hammer, impacts a window, fracture lines run out from the point of impact; these are called radial cracks. When the window can flex no further, concentric cracks form which link the leading edges of the radial cracks. As these concentric cracks occur they throw extremely small pieces of glass (usually 0.5mm or smaller) a distance of up to 3 metres back towards the object and/or person breaking the window. This backward fragmentation of the glass can place evidence from the crime scene onto the offender.

Recovery and comparison

The CSI must recover a representative control sample (usually six pieces) of glass from around the frame of each and every broken window. It is always preferable to recover glass from the frame rather than the floor, as the glass on the floor may have been there from a previous breakage (however, it is important to consider the presence of other evidence types on glass found on the floor such as footwear marks). The inside or outside of the glass recovered from the frame should be marked using a permanent marker (FSS 2003).

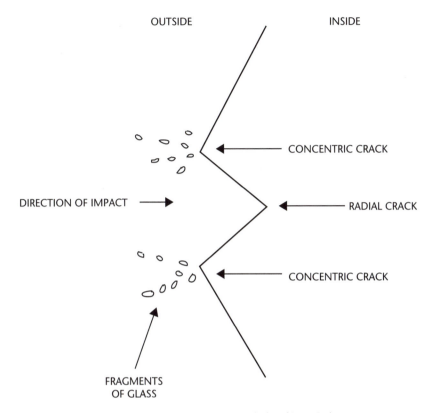

Figure 4.1 Backward fragmentation: cross-section of a breaking window

This will allow the forensic scientist to replicate the radial and concentric cracks, if there was any doubt as to which side the window was broken from. The control glass sample will then be packaged in a solid container such as a box to prevent further breakages, and possible injury when others handle the sample.

If a suspect or suspects are later arrested, it is possible that they may have fragments of glass on them from the backward fragmentation. A police officer who was not involved with attending the initial incident (as cross-contamination could take place) should take hair combings from the suspects as small fragments of glass may have landed in the suspects' hair. Then while the suspect stands on a large sheet of paper on the floor to catch any fragments of glass which may fall from them, their outer clothing should be recovered, and packaged as separate items. Then along with the control glass sample taken by the CSI from the crime scene, the clothing (and large paper sheet stood on by the suspect) should be submitted to the forensic science provider.

The amount of glass fragments, if any, present on the suspects and their clothing will vary. This is dependent on the number of times the hair and clothing have been washed, the amount of activity that has occurred, the texture of the hair and garments and the amount of time that has elapsed since the window was broken.

The location of the glass is significant. Meticulously the forensic scientist, a chemist, will recover any glass from the hair combings and the clothing. Research conducted by Lambert et al. (1995) suggests that if glass matching the control sample could be located within the hair combings of a suspect, then this would provide significant evidence for the investigation, whereas matching glass located in shoes may not be as significant. Glass from the hair combings and visible on the clothing will be picked off and in order to ensure all the glass is recovered, the clothing will be either vacuumed (Caddy 2001) or shaken over an alternative collection device such as a funnel. Any glass recovered will be compared with the control glass sample the CSI took from the crime scene. Initial comparison will be done microscopically, measuring the thickness of the glass and looking at the sharpness of the edges. Then, using the glass refractive index measurement equipment (GRIM), the forensic scientist may take a refractive index measurement of the glass samples. Alternatively the forensic scientist may compare the densities of the samples by floating them in liquids of known density. Finally a chemical analysis of the samples will reveal their chemical composition. If samples appear to have originated from the same source, then rarer glass, such as from stained glass windows, will provide better evidence than common glass found in many shop windows.

4.3 Hairs

The human body is covered with approximately two million hair follicles with over one hundred hairs being shed from the head alone every day (Robertson 1999). Therefore it stands to reason that an offender or victim may deposit hair at the scene of a crime. The CSI may also be required to recover a sample of head hair from either the offender or live victim for the purposes of comparison.

Recovery and comparison

Once located, hairs can be recovered from crime scenes using two methods. A hair stuck on a broken window or door can be picked off using new tweezers. The hair should be placed in a paper wrap then sealed in a polythene bag and labelled. However, if the hair is at the point of entry and the weather is wet and/or windy, then the removal of a hair with tweezers may lead to it being lost as it could be blown away by the wind or washed away by the rain. Consideration should always be given to using the second method of recovering a hair from the crime scene using clear adhesive tape. The sticky side of the tape should carefully be pushed onto the hair. The tape should then be placed onto a clear sheet of plastic before being sealed in a polythene bag and labelled. This is also the generally accepted method of recovering an extraneous hair from a deceased naked body in order to avoid the hair being lost in transit from the scene to the mortuary.

If the CSI recovers a hair from a crime scene with a root attached, then a DNA profile may be obtained. If no root it present, then a mitrochondrial DNA profile may be considered (see Chapter 6).

If a control sample of head hair is to be taken by a CSI from a suspect or live victim for the purposes of comparison, then each individual head hair should be plucked by hand. This will avoid damaging the structure of the hair or breaking it off while plucking with tweezers. The sample, numbering at least 25 individual hairs from across the head, should be placed in a paper wrap, then sealed in a polythene bag and labelled. If a sample of hair is required from any intimate part of the body, such as in a rape case, then the hair sample should be taken by a forensic medical examiner or forensic nurse. A forensic pathologist should always take a sample of hair from the body of a deceased victim. It is quite possible that the CSI will be involved in packaging these samples.

Hair is examined by a forensic biologist employed by a forensic science provider. Using a high-powered microscope the biologist will examine the length of the hair, then the appearance of both the hair and root (if present) as this may give an indication as to the racial origin of the hair and from where it originated on the body. Damage to the tip of the hair is examined, perhaps due to a recent hair cut, before an assessment is made of the colour. Then the diameter of the hair, any pigments present and the construction of each individual hair is carefully noted. This is then repeated with the control sample of hair taken from either the suspect or victim.

Hairs can also be examined by a forensic toxicologist for the presence of drugs. As the hair grows, it is 'fed' by the bloodstream so the level of drugs present in the hair will reflect the amount of drugs present in the bloodstream at any moment in time since it began its growth.

4.4 Paint

Paint is used to protect and decorate surfaces from window frames and doors to cars. The paint is usually applied several times and may also have an undercoat or primer at its base. Once dry, this paint can be chipped off and transferred from the crime scene to the hair, clothing or tools of a suspect. The transfer of paint usually occurs when an instrument such as a screwdriver or crowbar is used to force entry to the premises or car. Alternatively, a car involved in a hit and run collision may leave paint on the victim.

Recovery and comparison

Disturbed paint still attached to the window frame at the scene of a burglary will be carefully cut away by the CSI using a new scalpel blade, and must provide a representative sample of all of the layers present down to the bare surface. It is always preferable to recover paint still attached to the surface rather than paint that may have been blown or walked onto the floor of the crime scene. This paint sample should then be securely packaged in a paper wrap and then sealed in a polythene bag. At the scene of a road traffic collision, debris with paint attached should be collected and securely packaged (often in new boxes). Samples of paint should be taken from the damaged areas of each vehicle involved ensuring that the CSI uses a new scalpel blade to cut through all of the layers down to the bare metal. This paint sample should then be securely packaged in a paper wrap and then sealed in a polythene bag.

The hair of a suspect should be combed into a paper wrap to remove any paint present in his/her hair. The suspect should then stand on a large sheet of paper on the floor to catch any fragments of paint which may fall from them; their outer clothing should be recovered, and packaged as separate items. The hair of a victim should also be combed and their outer clothing securely packaged. These samples should then be transported to the forensic science provider.

A forensic chemist will examine the hair combings and clothing to remove minute traces of paint often less than 1mm in size (Caddy 2001). The sample from the suspect or victim and the sample recovered by the CSI from the crime scene will initially be compared using a microscope. This will enable the forensic chemist to compare the colour of the paint, its shape as well as its layer structure. If both of these match, then a chemical analysis of the paint will allow a more detailed comparison of the source from which they have originated.

If, as may be the case in a hit and run collision, the vehicle has not been found and examined by a CSI, then paint recovered from a victim may still be examined by a forensic chemist. Reference databases can be interrogated to identify the make and model of the vehicle involved and the year or years when that particular paint was applied.

4.5 Soil

A sample of soil recovered from the crime scene can be compared against soil found on the footwear of a suspect or on the tyres, underside and wheel arches of vehicles involved. Soil is made up of mixtures of minerals, organic matters, air and water and can be broadly divided into the three categories of sand, silt and clay. Samples of pollen mixed in with soil samples have been instrumental in proving many cases.

Recovery and comparison

When recovering a control sample of soil from a crime scene, several samples should be taken from the point that is believed to have been the location of the offence and from around the immediate area, the locations of which should be accurately photographed to show the relationship to the crime scene and notes made. These samples of soil should be packaged in separate brown paper sacks (FSS 2003). However, I would suggest that if recovering a soil sample from underneath a vehicle, a large sheet of brown paper laid beneath the wheel arch or underside will allow all of the soil to be easily collected as it is scraped off using a sterile tool such as a scalpel. This sheet should then be folded as if a large paper wrap, sealed and then packed in a brown paper sack. Footwear marks recovered using the technique of casting should remain with the soil in contact with the cast to provide a sample of the soil which has been in direct contact with the footwear; this should also be packaged in a brown paper sack. Steck-Flynn (2005) suggests that it is also possible to collect soil samples from inside premises or the footwells of vehicles; this could be achieved by sweeping the area with a new small brush into a paper wrap (which should then be sealed in a polythene bag) or using a specially designed portable vacuum cleaner. When a suspect is arrested, the footwear he or she is believed to have worn when committing the offence should also be packaged in a brown paper sack.

Once transported to the forensic science provider, a chemist will examine the soil samples from both the suspect's shoes and controls from the crime scene. After a visual examination to ascertain the presence of other evidence types in the soil (such as hairs and fibres), the chemist will sieve the soil samples in order to examine and compare the sizes of the particles. The particle size is dictated by its mineral content, with sand particles being up to 2mm in diameter, silt less than 0.06mm in diameter and clay particles being less than 0.002mm diameter (Brady 1990). Then the varying content and density of sand, silt and clay in each sample can be ascertained by the rate at which the samples settle when suspended in water. Examination of the chemical content of the sample of soil will reveal little difference in the chemical make-up of the sand and silt but the clays hold minute quantities of chemicals such as calcium, potassium and sodium. Thus the examination of soil will reveal distinctive physical and chemical characteristics (Brady 1990). The addition of 'contaminants' to the soil such as fertilizers, pollen or diesel may further enhance its distinctive characteristics, to link a sample from a suspect or vehicle to a scene.

Self-assessment questions

Answer the following questions without reference to the chapter:

1   What are the two categories of fibres?

2   What are the two methods of recovering fibres?

3   Which three variables affect the number of fibres deposited or taken away from crime scenes?

4   How large may the pieces of glass be that would be thrown towards someone breaking a window?

5   How many pieces of glass should be recovered by a CSI as a control sample from a broken window?

6   What does 'GRIM' stand for?

7   Which would provide better forensic evidence for an investigation: glass found in the soles of shoes or glass found in hair combings?

8   If a forensic chemist were to compare fragments of paint recovered from both a crime scene and a suspect, what would he or she examine?

9   What is the minimum number of head hairs that should be plucked for a control sample?

10 In which type of packaging should a CSI place samples of soil?

5 Impressions: footwear marks, instrument marks, glove marks and tyres

Impressions left by individuals' footwear, the instrument used to break into a building, the gloves they were wearing and the tyres of the vehicle they used to get away can all leave unique and identifiable impressions, many of which are recovered daily by a CSI.

5.1 Footwear

Offenders will always leave footwear marks at the scene of a crime; the challenge for the CSI is to locate them. The earliest known use of footwear marks left at a crime scene was during the latter part of the eighteenth century, when an unusual boot mark was found next to a body. A man was later traced with the same unusual mark on his boot; this evidence led to his conviction for murder. Green (2007) suggests that footwear as a source of evidence is at times not used to its full potential within contemporary policing, as once recovered from both crime scenes and potential suspects footwear evidence could be used to provide excellent intelligence to link crimes committed by the same individual and provide evidence for arrest and prosecution.

Footwear marks will not always be immediately visible so great care should be taken when approaching the scene. A good source of light and an enquiring mind will assist in their location. The location of the footwear marks will reveal to the crime scene investigator information such as the way the offender entered and exited the scene, where the offender has been in the scene and the minimum number of people involved. CSIs may also identify a link between other scenes they have been to that revealed the same type of footwear mark.

There are two types of footwear marks that may be located: impressed marks and surface transfer marks. Impressed marks will usually be located on the way into or out from the crime scene, having being impressed into any sand, soil or snow present. Immediately after discovery they should be covered to protect them from further damage; although if footwear marks in snow are left covered for any length of time they will warm and melt. Initially the impressed footwear marks must be photographed close up (see Chapter 3) before being cast, using a casting medium such as Denstone KD or Crownstone; these plasters are both strong and fine enough to record small detail in the impression. When mixed with the correct amount of water in a polythene bag, the casting medium can be carefully poured into the footwear impression, where it will harden. This allows the crime scene investigator to recover a copy of the impression. As the cast begins to set, the CSI will scratch his or her identifying mark and date into the top of the cast. The cast will take approximately 30 minutes to set sufficiently for it to be recovered but may take up to 48 hours to set totally. Using this type of casting, medium footwear impressions can successfully be recovered from under several centimetres of water. If footwear marks are to be recovered from the snow, then, after the footwear make has been photographed but before casting, the footwear impression should be sprayed with 'snow print wax'. This will seal the snow from the exothermic reaction that occurs as the plaster sets. Once recovered, the footwear impressions should not have the sand or soil removed as this not only protects the cast in transit but also provides a particulate control sample that has been in direct contact with the shoe. The casts should be packaged in a box.

If the offender has stood on a piece of paper while walking through the scene, it may be possible to recover an indented impression of the footwear on

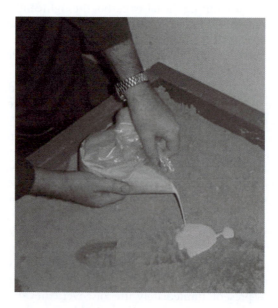

Figure 5.1   Pouring the casting medium into an impressed footwear mark

the paper. The paper should be carefully recovered from the crime scene and packaged to avoid any further indentations. Then, using an ESDA (electrostatic detection apparatus), the paper is placed on a brass plate and held there using a piece of clear film and a vacuum pump. The brass plate is then charged with a high voltage and toner is poured over the surface. The toner is attracted to the electrically charged brass plate and sits in the indentations in the paper, revealing the footwear impression.

Surface transfer marks will be located if the sole of the offender's footwear has been contaminated with anything from dampness to dust. Typically such footwear marks will be found on broken glass, window sills or tiled floors. Initially the surface transfer footwear marks should be photographed (see Chapter 3). If the item bearing the footwear mark can be recovered, such as on a piece of broken glass or magazine, then this will provide the best evidence. However, if it cannot be recovered, such as on a window sill, then the crime scene investigator first needs to decide if the footwear mark is dusty or has been wet then dried. If it is dusty, then the surface transfer footwear mark can be recovered using a portable dust lifting kit such as an ESLA (electrostatic lifting apparatus) or a pathfinder. These use a static electric charge to attract the dust onto a black film. Once recovered, the ESLA film should be photo-graphed as soon as possible and ideally stored flat in a box although rolling of the ESLA film is acceptable (Bandey 2008). After the use of the ESLA any remaining dust on the surface can be recovered using a gelatine lift which should also be stored in a box (Bandey 2008).

Figure 5.2 Photograph of ESLA/pathfinder recovered from a dusty footwear mark

If the footwear mark has been wet and then dried, it may be enhanced with the use of fingerprint powders. A contrasting coloured powder should be chosen. Generally granular black and white powders should be used on rough surfaces and flake aluminium or gold powder should be used on smooth non-porous surfaces. Once enhanced, such marks should once again be photographed before being lifted using either gelatine lifts for the granular powders or clear fablon lifts for the flake powders. Any gelatine lifts recovered should be photographed as soon as possible as they could lose some footwear detail over time, and stored in a box (Bandey 2008); clear fablon lifts should be placed on clear acetate for storage.

5.2 Samples from the suspect

If someone is arrested for an offence where footwear impressions have been found at the scene by the CSI, then the shoes of the suspect will be taken away as evidence and submitted with the crime scene footwear photograph, cast or lift for comparison by a footwear specialist. As a result of the Serious Organised Crime and Police Act (2005), it is also possible to overtly copy the footwear of those arrested for the purpose of intelligence. This can be done using 'Printscan', a commercial product that relies on vegetable extracts producing an inkless copy on a sheet of specially prepared paper, or alternatively the soles of the footwear could be photocopied.

The soles of footwear change over time; new damage is created as stones and glass are walked over and the sole of the shoe is worn down. So although the shoes of the most likely suspect are taken away for comparison, it is possible, even if they are the shoes that were worn at the crime scene, that a match will not be made to the crime scene mark.

5.3 Comparison of footwear

Most police forces in England and Wales screen to check if the footwear they are submitting to the forensic laboratory is likely to match the mark from the crime scene. The systems in use range from a manual comparison by an experienced crime scene investigator to the use of computerized systems such as SICAR6 (Shoeprint Image Capture and Retrieval version 6) which can interface with reference footwear collections such as those held on the SoleMate database. In 2007, the Forensic Science Service launched a secure online national footwear database in order to allow the comparison of footwear marks recovered from crime scenes to copies of footwear taken from individuals who had been arrested nationally. Whichever system is used as a screen, the footwear and the mark from the crime scene must be submitted to a specialist, a trained footwear examiner who is usually a forensic chemist, for comparison and provision of expert evidence at court.

The footwear specialist will make test marks from the suspect's shoe, often mimicking the way the crime scene mark was made, before making a visual comparison of the evidence. The comparison can take place by placing the test impression next to the suspect impression and, using measures, both can be compared, or alternatively a transparency of the known footwear is superimposed over the suspect footwear mark, allowing a direct comparison (Bodziak 2000).

The footwear specialist will make comment on the size and patterns present on both the sole of the suspect's shoe and the impression recovered from the crime scene. This would be followed by a comparison of the degree of wear present, for example, the shoe wearing on one side more than the other, and finally a search for corresponding accidental damage marks visible on both sole patterns. These damage marks are caused by the contact of the footwear with the ground and stones, sticks, etc. damaging the sole. As the footwear is worn, the damage features change over time which can lead to the obliteration of some marks and the creation of new ones. Identification of matching damage features on both soles can lead to the footwear specialist uniquely linking the shoe from a suspect to a mark left at the crime scene; however, such a match does not link the suspect to the scene, only the shoe. As footwear is worn, the foot of the wearer moves about within the shoe making indentations and impressions; so-called 'Cinderella analysis' aims to cast the inside of the shoe to demonstrate how the wear inside the shoe can be attributed to a specific person.

The evidence provided by the footwear specialist may range from being supportive to an investigation, such as confirming that the shoe is of a similar pattern and size to the crime scene mark, to providing conclusive evidence to link the shoe to the crime scene mark. The conclusive link can be achieved by the specialist identifying unique corresponding damage marks on both the shoe and the mark from the crime scene. There is, however, no set standard for the identification of a footwear mark; it is purely the judgement of an experienced footwear specialist, who will express such evidence of opinion in court if required.

5.4 Instrument marks

On arrival at the crime scene the CSI must ascertain where the offender entered the premises, and whether a tool was used to gain entry. Offenders who use a tool such as a screwdriver, pliers or drill to gain access to a property may leave levering instrument marks on the window or door they have forced, cutting marks on the wire they have cut or drilling marks on the frame they have drilled.

The CSI photographs any instrument marks to show both their location and detail. If the whole instrument mark can be recovered, such as two ends of a piece of cut wire, then this must be done. The CSI should ensure that the damage caused by the offender's tool is marked, so the laboratory knows which mark it should be examining, and then protected from further damage by packaging in a solid container such as a box. If the instrument mark cannot be recovered, such as in a window frame, then it may be cast. A variety of commercially produced soft putty-like casting mediums such as Microsil, Xantropen or Provil are used to cast the mark. These are applied liberally to the mark to provide strength to the cast. Most of the casting mediums dry in a matter of minutes. They are then carefully peeled from the surface and packaged in a solid container to prevent damage.

Occasionally offenders will leave the instrument they have used to force entry at the crime scene. This is photographed *in situ* then carefully recovered, with the end of the instrument being wrapped in a clean sheet of paper and then packaged in a solid container. There may be paint or metal fragments present on the end of the instrument that will be caught in the sheet of paper if they fall off. This paint or metal, as well as the instrument itself, may be linked to other crime scenes.

5.5 Comparison of instrument marks with tools

Instrument marks have the potential to link a particular tool conclusively to a crime scene. Old tools are far more likely to provide conclusive evidence as they have damaged and worn edges and ridges; although some of the damage is transient, other damage will remain on the tool. The forensic scientist makes test impressions of the suspect tool in a soft medium such as lead. These test impressions of the tool and the crime scene instrument marks, usually cast by the CSI, can be compared visually using photographic enlargements, although comparison is usually performed using a comparison microscope. Comparison microscopes allow both the impressions to be magnified over a thousand times and viewed together via an eyepiece or a monitor (Walls 1968).

5.6 Glove marks at crime scenes

When gloves come into contact with any surface such as a window or car door, then they will leave an impression. The impression can be in a visible contaminant on a surface, such as dust or oil, or a contaminant on the glove, such as water or sweat, which will leave a latent mark when transferred to a clean surface. Such glove marks, if carefully recovered, can reveal individual characteristics that can be identified (Lambourne 1975).

Any glove marks found must be initially photographed close up, as if they were fingerprints, before any attempt is made to recover them. Then, if they are visible in dust on a surface, using an ESLA followed by a gelatine lift should ensure their recovery. If they are in oil, then, unless the CSI can recover the actual item the glove mark is on, they cannot be recovered. If the glove mark is latent, it is likely to appear during the fingerprinting of the scene using fingerprint powders. The glove marks should be powdered carefully, as it is possible that the latent marks are fragile due to the limited amount of water or sweat that has been deposited by the glove. After photography the glove mark is lifted using gelatine lifts for granular powders and fablon lifts for flake powders.

5.7 Comparison of glove marks

Glove marks recovered from scenes of crime can be divided into four main categories: (1) leather or vinyl; (2) fine fabrics such as cotton; (3) coarse fabrics such as wool; and (4) rubber and latex (Lambourne 1975). Differences in the manufacturing process, such as the tightness of the weave on fabric gloves or the textured patterns on the rubber gloves, will allow an initial comparison by a specialist. Then damage caused to the gloves such as scars on leather gloves, holes in fabric gloves or worn pattern on rubber gloves can uniquely link a glove mark left at the crime scene to a glove recovered from a suspect.

The CSI should also consider the possibility of locating latent fingerprints inside both rubber and latex gloves on either the inside of the fingers or where the gloves have been held to be pulled on. These are best developed in a laboratory where there have been numerous successes in locating latent marks (Pressly 1999; Rinehart 2000). These successes have been achieved using chemical processes, such as dipping parts of a latex glove in ninhydrin. The ninhydrin reacts with the amino acid deposits in the fingerprint and, when dry, stains the amino acids purple, revealing the fingerprint.

5.8 Tyres

As vehicles are used in a high proportion of crime it stands to reason that tyre impressions are often left at the scene of the crime. As with footwear marks, in order to locate tyre impressions the CSI needs a good light source, often shone at an oblique angle, and an enquiring mind. Tyre marks can be impressed into a medium such as sand, soil, or even human tissue; alternatively a tyre contaminated with debris such as dirt, water or blood can transfer an impression to a surface such as a road, cardboard or broken glass.

Before the tyre impressions can be recovered, they are initially photographed in their surroundings in order to locate them with reference to the rest of the scene. Following this they must be photographed close up (see Chapter 3) along their entire length, or at least the equivalent to one full revolution of the tyre. Once photography is complete, tyre impressions in sand or soil should be segmented into manageable sections. Then, in turn, each section must be cast, using a casting medium such as Denstone KD or Crownstone. These commercially produced plasters are both strong and fine enough to record small detail in the tyre impression. When the powder is mixed in a polythene bag with the correct amount of water, it can be gently poured into the impression where it will harden, allowing the crime scene investigator to recover a copy of the impression. As it begins to set, the CSI should scratch his/her identifying mark and date into the top of the cast. The casting medium will take approximately 30 minutes to set sufficiently for it to be recovered, but may take up to 48 hours to set completely. Using the same type of casting medium, tyre impressions can successfully be recovered from under several centimetres of water by sprinkling the powder into the impression, allowing this to harden before pouring in more casting medium which will displace the water and set. The same procedures for recovery and packaging apply as if dealing with footwear impressions. Recovery of tyre impressions from the snow can also be achieved in the same way as dealing with footwear impressions.

As an operational CSI I was amazed to see tyre marks on the skin of a murder victim who had been run over by a vehicle several times. Tyre impressions on a human body should be initially photographed before being re-photographed using ultraviolet light, as this may reveal bruising and hence more tyre detail beneath the outer layers of the skin.

Tyre marks that have been transferred to a surface must initially be photographed to locate them in the scene before close-up photography along their entire length, or at least one full revolution of the tyre. If possible, the actual item containing the tyre impression, such as the piece of cardboard or glass, should be recovered. If this is not possible, then, after photography, tyre impressions in dirt may be recovered using the ESLA (electrostatic lifting apparatus), the results from which should be photographed as soon as possible. Any dust remaining on the surface should be recovered using a gelatine lift.

If the tyre mark that has been wet then dried is on a surface that is suitable to powder, such as fragments of glass on the floor at the scene of a ram raid or cardboard in a garage, then it may be enhanced with the use of fingerprint powders. A contrasting coloured powder should be chosen; generally flake aluminium or gold powder should be used on smooth non-porous surfaces such as the glass and granular magnetic powder on the cardboard. Once the tyre marks have been enhanced, they should be rephotographed before being lifted using clear fablon lifts for the flake powders and gelatine lifts for the granular powders. Tyre marks in blood, particularly on moveable objects, may be revealed using high intensity light sources or a variety of chemicals.

5.9 Test marks from suspect vehicles

When taking test impressions from a suspect vehicle, the tyres should not be removed as the location of each tyre on the vehicle may also provide evidence. There are two alternatives for the copying of the tyres. The vehicle should first be loaded to simulate the weight of the vehicle on the road, then each tyre could be driven through mud for a complete revolution. The resulting impressions would then be photographed and cast as if it were a crime scene. Alternatively each tyre could independently be inked as if it were a fingerprint, loaded and then rolled for one complete revolution onto plain paper such as wallpaper backing.

5.10 Identification of tyre marks

If the suspect vehicle has not been located, then a forensic examination of tyre marks from the scene of a crime can reveal intelligence that may be of use to the investigation, such as the brand of the tyre. To assist in this identification process a reference database, such as Treadmate, can be used to search known manufacturers' makes of tyres. If multiple tyre marks have been recovered by the CSIs, then on examination by the tyre specialist establishing the outer, inner and centre ribs of the tyre, even the wheelbase of the vehicle can be revealed. This combination of intelligence and different tyre brands makes a particular vehicle identifiable by the police.

If the vehicle has been located, when comparing tyre impressions, the tyre specialist looks for two categories of characteristics: those that are specific to the particular type of tyre, such as the brand and mould, and those characteristics that are accidental, such as cuts and tears.

Comparing both the test mark and the crime scene mark, actual size and side by side or overlaid, the specialist will first identify if the tyre marks are of the same brand. This will be achieved by comparing features such as the shape of the rubber portions of the tread that provide the wear surface of the tyre and groove shapes that are in the tread to help shed water. Next the expert will look for mould characteristics. Each mould used to cast tyres has slight and different irregularities. These irregularities will be reproduced in every tyre from that particular mould. The search for these irregularities will help eliminate tyres that have not come from the same mould but are of the same brand. Finally the specialist will search for accidental characteristics. Such accidental characteristics may have been caused by normal wear to the tyre such as around the circumference or depth of the tread. In addition, accidental characteristic damage may be visible, such as cuts made by sharp objects or stones that are trapped in the tread, causing an obstruction to the tyre impression.

There is no set standard for the identification of a conclusive link between a test tyre mark and a crime scene tyre mark; it is purely the judgement of an experienced tyre examiner who will express such evidence of opinion in court if required.

Self-assessment questions

Answer the following questions without reference to the chapter:

1   What will the location of footwear marks by the CSI reveal?

2   What are the two types of footwear mark that can be located at a crime scene?

3   What should a CSI scratch in the top of a footwear cast before it dries?

4   What piece of equipment would be used to recover a dusty footwear mark from a crime scene?

5   ESDA would work on what type of surface trodden on by an offender?

6   What are the three types of instrument marks that may be found at a crime scene?

7   How should a CSI package a screwdriver found at a crime scene?

8   How should a CSI recover a glove mark in dust?

9   What is the minimum length of an impressed tyre mark that should be photographed and recovered by the CSI?

10 Which two categories of characteristics would a tyre examination specialist compare?

6 Deoxyribonucleic acid (DNA) and body fluids

6.1 The background to DNA

In 1869, Friedrich Miescher discovered a section of DNA and noted that it was linked to our genetic make-up, but its significance at that time was not fully understood. Studies continued on the structure and use of DNA throughout the first part of the twentieth century. Then, in 1953, James Watson and Francis Crick suggested a model for DNA that is generally accepted as being the discovery of its structure (Portugal and Cohen 1977).

DNA is a double-stranded molecule, its structure resembling a ladder. The sides of the ladder are made of nucleotides. The nucleotides are made up of a sugar linked to a phosphate and a base. There are four different bases – adenine, cytosine, guanine and thymine. It is the sequence in which these bases are arranged which constitute our genetic code.

Normal human beings have 46 chromosomes in each cell, half of which we have inherited from our biological father and half from our biological mother. So our DNA is different from everybody else's, except an identical twin (Jeffreys et al. 1985).

Prior to the mid-1980s, blood found at a crime scene would only have been grouped into the types A, B, AB and O by the forensic scientist analysing the chemicals present in the blood and using sub-groups such as rhesus. This was based on the ideas of Landsteiner who in 1900 suggested that people could be separated into specific groups based on whether they were A, B or O blood types (Goodwin et al. 2007). Thus the blood could not be identified as coming from a particular individual. Therefore the evidence that the blood grouping produced was not conclusive but could be used to eliminate people from the enquiry who did not have the same blood group as that found at the scene.

Then, in 1985, Professor Alec Jeffreys from the University of Leicester suggested that DNA 'fingerprints' were specific to an individual and could therefore be used as a means of identification, including testing for 'parenthood' (Jeffreys et al. 1985). Jeffreys proposed the use of a multilocus probe (MLP)

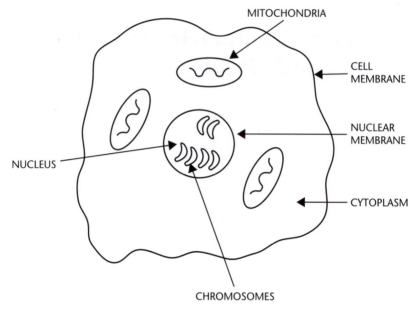

Figure 6.1 Structure of a cell

technique that the Forensic Science Service hoped could be used at every forensic laboratory. Jeffreys' technique examined a section of DNA molecules that were contained in the nuclei of cells. He created a chart for comparison (known as a profile).

Jeffreys' profiling technique was first put to the test in 1986. Two murders had occurred near to Jeffreys' laboratory in 1983 and 1986, in which the victims, both schoolgirls, had been raped before they were murdered. The main suspect for the two rape murders was profiled using Jeffreys' technique and cleared of leaving the DNA evidence, in the form of semen on the victims' clothing. The murders were now undetected and a mass screening ensued, in which every male in a certain age group within the area had a blood and saliva sample taken. After samples from 4582 men had been taken, none of them matched the DNA recovered from the crime scene. During a conversation in a pub it came to light that a local, Colin Pitchfork, had persuaded a colleague to present himself as Colin so that he would not have to give a blood sample. This was communicated to the police and when Pitchfork was arrested and a blood sample taken, his DNA profile matched those from the crime scene. In 1988, Pitchfork admitted both murders and received two life sentences (Fridell 2001).

The MLP process, although successful, relied upon the sample being rich in DNA and in good condition, unlike many of the stains found at crime scenes that could be days or even years old. The process was also unsuitable for the inclusion of results on a computerized database.

Next came the single locus probe (SLP) technique. Initially developed by ICI, then taken up by the mainstream forensic science providers, this process really advanced DNA technology (Martin et al. 2000). It looked at four pre-selected sites on the DNA and was far more sensitive, being able to differentiate between mixed stains.

In the early 1990s, polymerase chain reaction (PCR) techniques were developed that enabled scientists to amplify material from small amounts of DNA (Martin et al. 2000). Such DNA samples could be as small as a billionth of a gram (Nickell and Fischer 1999). Technology moved on swiftly to use short tandem repeat (STR) techniques. STR utilizes a number of preselected sites and all of the benefits of PCR techniques to come up with a computerized system that can be included on a database. The Forensic Science Service established a norm for STR, looking at six preselected sites and the sex determination site of the DNA. This became known as second generation multiplex (SGM). Technology has once again advanced to look at ten preselected sites and a sex site; this process, named SGM+, produces a DNA profile with the likelihood of someone having the same profile as up to 1 in one billion. It is also occasionally possible for 'adventitious hits' to occur, this is when an individual is misidentified by a DNA profile.

In 1995, the Forensic Science Service established the first ever national DNA database. The database contains the DNA profiles of people suspected, charged or convicted of criminal offences, even after acquittal (Criminal Justice and Police Act 2001) and the profiles of DNA samples recovered by CSIs from crime scenes. The Criminal Justice Act (2003) allowed DNA samples to be taken from individuals when they are first arrested and then placed and retained on the national DNA database. In December 2008, this was challenged in the European Court of Human Rights after two males, one who had his case dropped, and the other who was cleared, had asked the police to remove their DNA profiles from the database, and the police had declined to do so. The European Court held that this was in breach of their Human Rights and as such their profiles, and potentially those of over 850,000 others who had never been convicted of an offence, should be removed from the database (Travis, 2008). In November 2009, the Home Secretary announced new policies for the retention of DNA on the national database, which include: the deletion after six years of the DNA profiles of anyone arrested but not charged or convicted of a recordable offence, the deletion of the DNA profiles of 16-year-olds and 17-year-olds arrested but not charged or convicted of a serious offence, and the deletion after three years of the DNA profiles of all other juveniles arrested but not convicted of an offence. Retention of the DNA profiles of juveniles convicted of all but the most serious of offences remained for five years, along with the indefinite retention of the DNA profiles of adults convicted of a recordable offence and the profiles of juveniles convicted of a serious offence (such as murder or rape). In addition, all the samples used for the DNA analysis (such as blood or mouth swabs) should also be destroyed. DNA profiles taken for investigations relating to terrorism or national security can be retained beyond the six-year period with a periodic review of the need to continue to retain the profile (Johnson 2009).

Using the national DNA database, profiles of individuals can be compared against crime scene profiles and vice versa. If it is believed that a police officer (or CSI) has inadvertently contaminated a DNA sample (such as by coughing or sneezing near the crime scene sample), then their DNA profile can be eliminated by using the Police Elimination Database, which holds in the region of 100,000 DNA profiles of police officers and operational civilian staff. Using initially STR technology, in its first four years of operation the national DNA database held well over 700,000 samples from those convicted of offences and was achieving 700 matches every week (Martin et al. 2000). The growth of the national database continues to accelerate; by 2009, the database held the DNA profiles of nearly 4.6 million individuals and in the region of 300,000 crime scene profiles. It is possible that within the UK at any one time there are approximately 2.6 million active offenders, and it is hoped that eventually the profiles of all such active criminals will be included on the national DNA database (Home Office Science Policy Unit 2003). By 2001, SGM+ had become the standard process operated by the UK Forensic Science Service for samples to be included on the database.

Continuing research and development have led to further advances in recovering DNA from the crime scene, including its recovery after individuals have touched surfaces, perhaps leaving both a fingerprint and DNA (sometimes referred to as 'contact trace DNA'), and after fingerprint powders or chemical staining techniques have been used to develop fingerprints or footwear marks in blood (Bellefeuille et al. 2003). First introduced in 1999, but not routinely used in the examination of crime scenes, the low copy number (LCN) DNA process is extremely sensitive and can recover profiles from very small sources of DNA, such as those found on watch straps or jewellery. However, this sensitivity can cause issues as the process will also identify profiles from pre-event and post-event deposits of DNA (such as a shop assistant handling a watch or the finder of a piece of lost property). The sensitivity and reliability of evidence achieved using the LCN DNA process was questioned in the 2008 trial of a man accused of committing the bombings in Omagh, Northern Ireland, during 1998 which led to the deaths of 29 people. For a time the LCN process was suspended as a tool in the investigation of crime. The LCN process continues to be both time-consuming and expensive and as such is only used for the most serious of criminal cases. A more recent related development is DNA boost, a technique developed by the Forensic Science Service which enables mixed, poor quality or partial DNA crime scene stains to be enhanced before being interpreted. Mitochondrial DNA has been used in casework since 1992. Inherited along the maternal line, mitochondrial DNA analysis can obtain results from material such as teeth and bones. It was used to discover if nine skeletons found in Russia were the remains of the last Russian royal family (Kimber 2000). However, the results offer poor discrimination of around 1 in 100, and the profiles cannot be searched against the national DNA database. It is also possible, using familial searching, to suggest that an offender is likely to be related to an individual who is recorded on the DNA database but a complete match is not obtained to link the DNA from a crime scene to a person on the database (Goodwin et al. 2007). The Forensic Science Service has used third generation multiplex (TGM), which examines 12 sites of the DNA, for paternity tests.

In the USA, a number of DNA databases have been in use since the early 1990s in both local and state-wide law enforcement organizations. In 1994, the DNA Identification Act was passed, allowing the establishment of a national DNA database which commenced with a number of US states and by November 1998 all 50 US states were linked to the FBI's national Combined DNA Index System (CODIS) which by 2009 held over 6.5 million DNA profiles from offenders and 250,000 crime scene profiles (FBI 2009b). Williams and Johnson (2008) describe an initiative by Interpol to establish a truly international DNA database, but with a few notable exceptions, inputs have been very limited and a number of challenges continue to exist in relation to the compatibility of member states' DNA technology, the appropriateness of legislation to share information, concerns over who has access to the database and although no-one would question the value of sharing information and intelligence, the value of such a tool to everyday law enforcement must be limited.

6.2 Using advances in DNA technology to review murder cases

In September 2000, Ian Lowther was found guilty of the murder of 38-year-old Mary Gregson and sentenced to life imprisonment, 23 years after the murder had taken place.

In 1977, Mary Gregson had been walking along a canal towpath near Bradford in West Yorkshire, when she was sexually assaulted and violently murdered. The following day her body was found in a nearby river. During the investigation into her death a sample of semen was recovered from her clothing. This sample was grouped according to blood type, as at the time DNA processes were unavailable. Although a large number of individuals were interviewed, no one was convicted of the crime.

Developments in DNA technology over the following 23 years supplied a tool that allowed a re-examination of evidence from the case. Using low copy number DNA, a profile was obtained from the semen stain on Mary Gregson's clothing. A mass screen, taking DNA buccal swabs from individuals questioned during the initial investigation, led to a successful match with the DNA profile from the semen stain.

In February 1982, Sean Hodgson was found guilty of the murder of the 22-year-old barmaid Teresa De Simone in Southampton in 1979. At the time of the conviction, DNA evidence found at the scene was found to be of the same blood group as Sean Hodgson, who also confessed to the murder. In 2008, at the request of Sean Hodgson's legal team, the evidence in the murder case was reviewed, including the analysis of the DNA evidence from the scene using techniques not available in the early 1980s. A DNA profile was obtained on the 29-year-old crime scene sample that was found not to match a DNA profile taken from Sean Hodgson who was subsequently released after serving 27 years in prison (Lander 2009). The murder case was re-opened and at the time of writing continues to be investigated.

Both of these cases demonstrate the success of using modern technology for the examination or re-examination of DNA evidence.

6.3 The identification and recovery of DNA at the crime scene

DNA can be found in many forms at a crime scene, from the obvious sources of blood and semen, to less obvious sources such as saliva on facemasks or cigarette ends.

Blood

In order to locate traces of blood, a good light source, a keen eye and an enquiring mind are required, as the CSI may not always be searching for red blood on a white background. Apparent blood located at a crime scene can indicate much more than just a DNA profile. By analysing the bloodstain pattern it may provide us with a whole host of information. Bevel and Gardner (2002) suggest that by analysing the blood pattern, the CSI or forensic specialist may ascertain certain information to assist the investigation.

Information elicited from an examination of blood at the scene and on the suspect or victim may include any of the following:

- The direction from which any force was applied obtained by an examination of the direction the blood was travelling when it hit a surface. The tail of the blood splashes, termed 'cast-off', indicates this: the tail points in the direction the blood was travelling.

- The angle at which it hit the surface, indicated by the way the blood runs.
- The amount of force involved. The harder the victim was struck, the smaller the splash on the surface.
- The type of instrument used in the attack.
- The minimum number of blows struck. Two lines of splashes or cast-off indicate that the victim was struck at least three times, the first blow breaking the skin and bringing blood to the surface.
- The relative positions of the injured party and suspect, indicated by the location of the splashes and the size of the spots of blood. Blood dropped from a height usually makes a larger spot.
- Whether objects have been moved around the scene after the attack, indicated by areas not covered in blood spots, splashes or smears when the rest of the surrounding area is.
- In what sequence the events occurred, indicated by separate blood patterns lying on top of each other.

Analysis of such bloodstaining may be done by a forensic biologist or suitably trained and experienced crime scene investigator. However, before any examination takes place, the scene should be photographed with colour film so that the bloodstaining is recorded and can be examined at a later date.

Figure 6.2 Blood spots dropped from different heights: note the crown pattern on the edges

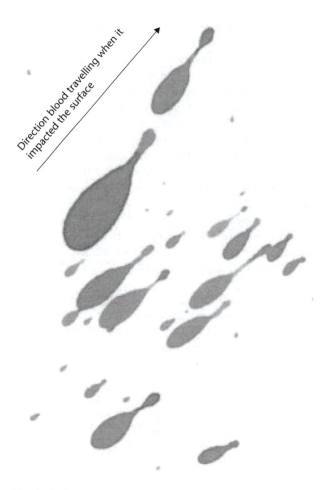

Figure 6.3 Blood splashes or cast-off: note that the direction of travel of the blood as it hits the surface is indicated by the tail of the splash

There are a number of presumptive blood testing kits available to distinguish apparent blood from other sources of red stains such as brown boot polish or coffee. One example is leucomalachite green (LMG). A drop of LMG and a drop of hydrogen peroxide added to a small filter paper that has been rubbed across the apparent bloodstain will turn green if blood is present. Another example, kastle mayer (KM) turns pink in the presence of blood. The tests rely upon the presence of an enzyme in the sample called peroxidase. Such tests are only presumptive, as false positives can be obtained from rust and plant extracts.

Once the presumptive blood test has demonstrated that the sample is

Figure 6.4 Blood smear: as if an article covered in blood has brushed against the surface

likely to be blood, then the sample must be recovered. A sample of blood recovered from a crime scene has a greater than 80 per cent chance of revealing the DNA profile of the offender. As a general rule, the best evidence will be obtained by recovering the whole item. Whether it be a bloodstained carpet, shoe or shirt, the item should be recovered. If it is still wet, it should be packaged in a polythene bag for transportation to a secure and uncontaminated area where it can be air-dried before being repacked with its original packing in a brown paper sack. Alternatively if the article is already dry, it can be immediately packed into a brown paper sack. The items should then be stored in a secure dry area before being sent to the forensic service provider for extraction of DNA.

If it is not possible to recover the actual item but the blood is on a vertical surface, such as a window frame, it may be possible to scrape the blood directly into a folded paper wrap. This wrap must then be overpacked in a polythene bag and placed in a secure dry store area before being sent to the forensic service provider for extraction of the DNA.

If it is not possible to recover the whole item or scrape the blood, then the final option is to swab the blood; this is the most common method of recovering blood from a crime scene. Using plain sterile swabs moistened with sterile water, a control swab of the background must first be taken adjacent to, but not in contact with, the bloodstain. This swab is used to eliminate any contamination that may be on the surface. Then a swab is taken of the bloodstain. These two swabs are packaged together and as they are wet, should then be frozen, as air drying them may present the risk of contamination of the sample. They should be transported to the forensic service provider in the frozen state for the extraction of the DNA.

Figure 6.5 Swabbing blood

Semen

Semen is a strong source of DNA and its presence at the scene of a sexual assault can do much to confirm or refute the victim's and suspect's story as to the sequence of events. A visual examination with a good source of light may reveal crusty white stains on a surface which could indicate the presence of semen. If so, these should be photographed. However, the only reliable method of locating semen is for a forensic biologist or specially trained crime scene investigator to use acid phosphatase. Working methodically around a scene such as the rear seat of a car, wetted blotting paper is used to draw some of the water-soluble constituents found in semen from the car seat. This is then sprayed with acid phosphatase, which creates a colour change to purple if semen is present. If semen is present, then the car, or the car seat packaged in brown paper, is forwarded to the forensic service provider for extraction of the DNA. If the semen stain is on an immovable surface, such as a window ledge, then plain swabs moistened with sterile water can be utilized to recover the stain; these should then be frozen prior to transportation to the laboratory. If a condom is recovered at a crime scene, it is imperative that a knot is tied in the top as vaginal material may be recovered from the exterior of the condom, and with semen on the inside this could provide invaluable evidence. A condom should be packaged in a solid container and then frozen.

A victim of a rape or sexual assault should be tactfully handled by an appropriately trained medical professional, ideally at a Sexual Assault Referral Centre (SARC) where there would be an integrated approach to survivors of rape and sexual assault providing medical care, the recovery of forensic evidence and support. A CSI may provide guidance on the recovery of samples but would not take them. The survivor should not wash or drink prior to samples being taken and these samples should be recovered by an appropriately trained medical professional. Samples may include the clothing (such as underwear) of the survivor, along with plain sterile swabs taken from the vagina, anus and mouth as appropriate. These should be securely sealed and frozen.

The likelihood of a semen stain revealing a DNA profile is high at nearly 70 per cent.

Saliva

DNA can be found within the buccal cells contained within the saliva. DNA can therefore potentially be located on any item that has been bitten, chewed or spat on. The likelihood of buccal cells being present in the saliva on items depends on the length and strength of contact of both the saliva and the item with the inside of the mouth. If the sample is recovered correctly, then there is in the region of a 40 per cent chance of the sample revealing a DNA profile. Any items that may have saliva and hence buccal cells on them should initially be photographed at their location in the scene. Then items such as a facemask should be packaged in a brown paper sack and stored in a secure dry store. Cigarette ends should have any ash knocked off, then be packaged in a container so that they will not be crushed. This is so that the forensic scientist can comment on the likelihood of the cigarette end being walked into a crime scene or stubbed out at the scene. If the cigarette end is dry, it should be stored in the secure dry store; if wet, it can be frozen. The samples will then be transported to the forensic service provider for extraction of the DNA.

6.4 Sample from the suspect

There are three types of samples from a suspect that can be taken for DNA profiling. Occasionally under the legislative conditions of the Police and Criminal Evidence Act (1984) a healthcare professional, such as a doctor, can take a blood sample; 5ml of blood are taken and placed in a container coated with a preservative called EDTA. This sample is then frozen prior to transport to the forensic service provider. Second, and by far the most common form of taking a sample of DNA, is by the use of a mouth swab sampling kit. As a non-intimate sample, as defined by the Criminal Justice and Public Order Act (1995), these samples may be taken by a police employee, often a civilian detention officer working within a police custody suite. Two swabs are scraped down the inside of the cheeks, buccal cells that are present on the inside of the mouth are collected, and these are then frozen and stored. The swabs containing buccal cells, once transported to the laboratory, will reveal a DNA profile of the donor. Finally, and rarely, plucked hairs with roots can be taken as an alternative to the mouth swabs, as the roots will also reveal a DNA profile. Both the mouth swabs and the plucked head hair samples are entered onto the national DNA database for the purposes of intelligence only. If a hit is made with a DNA profile from a crime scene on the database and the suspect is arrested, a further DNA confirmation sample must be taken in the same manner.

The process of using mouth swab sampling kits has proved very successful and it has been extended to provide an elimination database of police employees in case they inadvertently leave their DNA at a crime scene. Also, kits have been made to conduct mass screens that have proved successful in identifying DNA left at the scene of a crime.

6.5 Comparison of the samples

In order to be profiled, the DNA sample must contain a cell with a nucleus, which can be extracted from the crime scene stain. This can sometimes be very challenging with some samples, for example, semen can be mixed with other cells present (Goodwin et al. 2007). This is done by using enzymes and solvents to remove the elements of the stain that are not required. Traditionally the clean DNA would be placed on a gel. Then, by introducing an electrical charge (electrophoresis), the molecules of the DNA would be encouraged to move along the gel, the lighter molecules travelling faster and therefore further. This gel can then be fixed. Finally X-ray film would be added to the process onto which a bar chart of a section of the DNA would be produced. This system is now automated. Once a DNA sample is received at the laboratory, DNA is extracted from the sample and purified, then the amount of DNA is measured before it is diluted to a standard concentration. The DNA is then multiplied until there is sufficient for analysis; the fragments of DNA are still separated on a gel before they can be interpreted to form the profile that can be included on the national DNA database (LGC 2003). If this were to be repeated with the sample from the suspect, then a comparison between the two DNA samples could be made.

Once the two mouth swabs containing buccal cells taken from the suspect have arrived at the forensic science laboratory, the swabs are separated. One of the swabs is placed in deep freeze for future reference while the other is processed to obtain a DNA profile. The DNA profile of the suspect is then placed on the national database where it can be searched against outstanding crime scene stains and other profiles in case the suspect has given false details. As the database is only used for intelligence purposes, any hit against either crime scene stains or other entries will require a second sample to be taken from the suspect for confirmation and production at court.

When crime scene stains arrive at the forensic science laboratory, they are processed and any resulting DNA profile is placed on the national database where it can be searched against the profiles of suspects and linked to other crime scenes.

Self-assessment questions

Answer the following questions without reference to the chapter:

1   What does DNA stand for?

2   What four bases make up DNA?

3   When was DNA first used in the UK during the investigation of a crime?

4   When was the first national DNA database established?

5   Using SGM+ how likely is it for two people to have the same DNA profile?

6   What does LCN stand for?

7   In what should a CSI package dry bloodstained items?

8   How should swabs of apparent blood be stored?

9   What is the only reliable test for locating semen?

10   What three samples can be taken from a suspect to obtain a DNA profile?

7   Fingerprints

It has been suggested that the likelihood of two people having matching sets of fingerprints is many millions to one, therefore this makes fingerprints an effective and cheap way of detecting crime. My interest in the identification of individuals using fingerprints, palm prints and footprints stems from my work as a fingerprint examiner within a fingerprint bureau. I searched marks recovered from crime scenes by crime scene investigators in an attempt to establish who had left them at the scene. It takes a studious and observant person with an eye for detail to become a fingerprint examiner (also known as latent print examiner). The training is a long process, taking over three years to reach expert status, but it can be a very worthwhile and fulfilling career.

7.1 The background to fingerprints identification

The use of fingerprints as a form of identification can be traced back through the ages, with their first appearance on early Chinese documents and hand-made Japanese pots. The first recognition in the West was in 1684 when Nehemiah Grew presented a paper to the Royal Society in London. The paper described the patterns made from ridges that appeared on the hands and the feet. In 1823, Professor Johannes E. Purkinje at the University of Breslau in Germany published a thesis in which he described nine individual pattern types. But neither Purkinje nor anyone before him suggested that fingerprints could be used to identify individuals.

In 1880, Dr Henry Faulds, a surgeon working in Japan, published his research. He initially examined finger impressions left in pottery, then the fingers of a Gibraltarian monkey, and then naturally progressed to studying the fingerprints of humans. He noted that sweat from the skin left faint oily latent (invisible) deposits on surfaces. Using ink and paper he took fingerprint impressions from those who worked around him and suggested that a lens could be useful to examine these. He noted different patterns, suggesting that these could be used for classification purposes (Faulds 1880). From conducting original experiments, rubbing away the outer layers of the skin and observing how they slowly regrew to the original pattern, Faulds suggested that the fingerprints were persistent. He was arguably the first European to suggest that fingerprints could be used to identify criminals.

Faulds' publication led to a response from Sir William Herschel. As an administrator and magistrate in the Hooghly Province of Bengal, India, Herschel had repeatedly taken fingerprints over a 20-year period. In one incident Herschel insisted that every prisoner in a chaotic Indian jail placed his fingerprint after his name. This created order from the chaos; no longer could someone else be paid to serve a sentence on a prisoner's behalf or claim that he had not previously been in prison (Thorwald 1965). He also noted how the fingerprints were consistent and never changed. In 1877, he had written to his superiors setting out his findings that all fingerprints were different and constant and suggesting that a register of criminals' fingerprints should be established. His letter was never acted upon or published and only came to light when Faulds' findings were published.

Faulds went on to seek support from the naturalist Charles Darwin, who in turn referred him to his cousin, Sir Francis Galton. Galton developed an interest in using fingerprints as a means of personal identification. Conducting research on pattern types and their prevalence, he estimated the probability of one human possessing the same ten fingerprints as another human as many billions to one. In 1888, Galton described in a public lecture, written up in the publication *Scientific American*, the features of fingerprints as a means of identification (Galton 1888). Having developed his work, in 1892, Galton published a textbook called *Finger Prints* in which he set out a means of classification of fingerprints and the identification of individual features. Galton later acknowledged the work of Faulds but regarded Herschel's work as more significant.

A civil servant, Sir Edward Henry, was working in the Indian Province of Bengal. Henry had inherited Herschel's work and, as an advocate of the ideas of Galton, he led a team, including two native sub-inspectors Azizul Haque and Hem Chandra Bose, who simplified Galton's approach to identification. The team developed a classification system, during which the importance of the work conducted by Galton and others before him was duly noted (Henry 1934). Henry also experimented with the ideas of Alphonse Bertillon's system of anthropometry.

In 1893, the then Home Secretary, Lord Asquith, set up a committee under the leadership of Charles Troup to examine the subject of identification and misidentification of recidivists. The Asquith Committee reported in 1894. It recommended using anthropometry, limiting the number of Bertillon's measurements to five, and that the ten fingerprints of every offender should be taken according to Galton's system (Thorwald 1965). As a result of this, a registry was established at New Scotland Yard collating both Bertillon's measurements and fingerprints. This combined system was found to be less than satisfactory and in 1900 Lord Belper led another committee. Hearing evidence from Henry, the committee recommended the adoption of the use of the fingerprint system to record criminals. In 1901, Henry became an assistant commissioner with the Metropolitan Police in London and a fingerprint bureau was established using his system of classification in the same year.

In 1902, the first recorded use of fingerprint evidence was given in an English court. A burglary had occurred in Denmark Hill, London. Investigation at the scene revealed a fingerprint on a freshly painted surface. This fingerprint was identified as belonging to Harry Jackson, who had previously been in prison. The court was convinced of his presence at the burglary due to the fingerprint evidence and hence Jackson was sentenced to several years' imprisonment (Thorwald 1965).

By the 1930s, the Henry system of classification of fingerprints had been accepted worldwide with over 50 fingerprint bureaux using the system. In 1932, the fingerprint bureau at New Scotland Yard held over half a million sets of fingerprints and annually was making over 20,000 fingerprint identifications (Henry 1934).

One of the first mass screens using fingerprints to identify a murderer was during the summer of 1948. A young child, June Anne Devaney, was abducted from her cot in Blackburn Hospital and later found murdered in the hospital grounds. At the scene of the abduction detectives found fabric impressions and a number of fingerprints on a Winchester bottle (Tullett 1981). The senior investigating police officer ordered that copies of the fingerprints recovered from the crime scene be sent to all of the police fingerprint bureaux in the UK. Additionally the fingerprints of all males aged between 14 and 90 resident in the Blackburn area were to be taken (Tullett 1981). This mass screen was to have positive results when after several months of painstaking work the fingerprints of Blackburn resident Peter Griffiths were found to match those from the Winchester bottle. Along with the fingerprints, other forensic evidence such as fibres and blood, and a confession, led to Peter Griffiths being found guilty of the murder of June Anne Devaney and he was hanged in November 1948.

Many cases have been proved in a court of law on the basis of fingerprint evidence, but one case often referred to as an example of the importance of accurate note taking by the CSI and the possible perils of relying on fingerprints as a sole form of evidence to prove a case is that of the legal appeal made by the Chief Constable of Avon and Somerset Constabulary v Jest (1985). The defendant (Jest) had been charged with an offence of taking a motor vehicle without the owner's consent. The defendant's left thumbprint had been recovered from the internal rear-view mirror of the stolen vehicle; however, the appeal court held that although the thumbprint would place the defendant in the vehicle, it did not demonstrate that he had stolen or used the vehicle.

7.2 The detection and recovery of fingerprints

When we talk about fingerprints, we tend to ignore other parts of our body that have raised ridges. The skin has two main layers: the epidermis (the outer tough protective layer) and the dermis (the inner layer). Around 5 per cent of the skin area of a human body has these raised ridges, similar to those found on our fingers. These raised ridges, formed accidentally during the development of the foetus, are called friction ridges and cover the whole of the inner surface of the hand and the underside of the soles of our feet.

The ridges tend to run parallel to each other, bending and turning to form the patterns distinguished by Faulds, Herschel and others. But the ridges are not continuous; they break to form the ridge characteristics identified by Galton. The dips between the ridges are called furrows. Friction ridges have three biological functions. First, as the name suggests, friction ridges create friction, enabling us to hold smooth objects such as drinking glasses. Second, the dermis section of the ridges contains extra nerve endings resulting in a heightened sense of touch. Third, the raised ridges also raise up extra sweat pores. There are over 550 sweat pores per square centimetre in the ridges found on fingers (Siegel et al. 2000); these allow the skin to cool by the discharge of sweat. The sweat is made up of approximately 98.5 per cent water and the remaining 1.5 per cent is made up of amino acids, chlorides, fats, sugars and urea. However, the amount of each constituent is not a constant, changing from individual to individual and day to day.

The structure of the ridge system

With the almost constant flow of sweat from the friction ridges, when someone puts their bare hand, or other body part, onto a surface, they can leave a tell-tale mark. Although we will refer to fingerprints, please remember that the same will apply to any area of friction ridging.

There are two types of fingerprints that are likely to be left on a surface: visible and latent (invisible). Visible fingerprints can either be impressed into a soft medium such as putty or grease, or alternatively they may be surface transfer marks, for example, a fingerprint contaminated with blood will leave another mark in blood the next time it touches a surface. Latent marks will only be found through further examination.

When examining any scene in order to locate fingerprints, it is of paramount importance that a thorough and logical visual examination is initially carried out with a good source of artificial light. The angle of the light source should be continually altered in order to cast shadows at different angles, as this will increase the likelihood of locating the fingerprints. If it is necessary to move items, then they should be handled with care. Items should always be

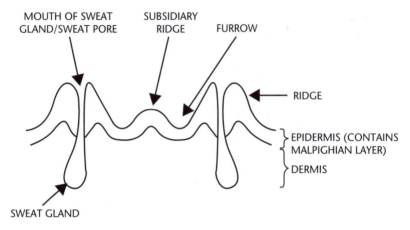

Figure 7.1 Structure of the ridge system

held the least likely way anyone else has held them, for example, holding a bottle on the top and bottom rather than around the neck or waist. As fingerprints are located, then brushing to add fingerprint powder should follow the pattern of the ridges as this will assist in developing the latent fingerprint. Brushing across the fingerprint may distort or damage some of the features of the ridges. As photography is a non-destructive process, any visible fingerprints should be photographed, ideally at actual size using black and white film (see Chapter 3). After photography other processes may be used in an attempt to improve or further record the fingerprint. For example, fingerprints in blood may be enhanced with the use of a number of chemical processes.

Latent fingerprints found at crime scenes are generally searched for with the use of fingerprint powders. There are two main types of powder: granular and flake. Ground granular graphite powder was first used towards the end of the nineteenth century to locate latent fingerprints. Today granular types of powder are usually either black or white and are made up of large spherical grains. The powder is applied to the surface using a soft animal hair brush in a gentle brushing motion. Single grains of the powder will adhere to secretions from the fingers and once fingerprint ridges have been found, the shape of the fingerprint pattern must be followed with the brush so that the brush does not move across the ridges and possibly damage the fingerprint. The fingerprint that has been revealed must then be photographed with a scale and a label detailing the minimum details of the name of the person who found the fingerprint, the date, location and identifying mark. This granular type of powder was never designed to be lifted off the surface with adhesive tape, as the grains of the powder may move if compressed under the tape. However, in the 1930s, the method of using gelatine-coated photographic paper that must first be fixed, wetted then warmed before applying to the latent fingerprint allowed its recovery (Bridges 1942). This technique has recently been refined to allow the use of thicker gelatine lifts that can be placed directly onto the fingerprint. The best results will be obtained if these are initially warmed by the hand; this will enable lifting of the fingerprint, but must only be attempted after photography.

Flake powders came into general use in the 1970s; the most common type is aluminium, although other types, such as bronze or gold coloured powders, which are actually brass flake powders (Bandey 2007), are also available. It is recommended that the powder is applied with what is commonly referred to as a 'Zephyr' type brush that is twirled, enabling a very light contact with the surface, such as glass, being examined (Bandey 2007). As the powder is flat in construction, the first layers of the powder will have maximum contact with secretions on the surface from the fingers, and then as the brush once again passes over the initial layers of the powder, additional layers will stick to the flat surface. Flake powder was designed to be lifted and as such, using low tack adhesive tape, the upper layers of the powder can be lifted from the surface and adhered to a piece of clear plastic. This should immediately be endorsed with the minimum details of the name of the person finding the fingerprint, the date, location and identifying mark. If the fingerprint lift was on a vertical surface such as a window frame, then the fingerprint lift should also be marked with a gravity arrow pointing down in order to help later interpretation as to how the fingerprint may have got there. Some crime scene examiners also add further information to their lifts such as offence type and thumbnail sketches depicting location of the fingerprint.

There are also a number of magnetic powders available that contain iron. These powders are applied with the use of a magnetic wand. Available as either granular or flake powders, these can provide better results on articles, such as magazines and writing paper, that would be unlikely to yield a result with conventional powders. Magneta flake powder is very popular for examining dark but textured surfaces such as vehicle steering cowlings. The results are photographed or lifted depending on the choice of granular or flake powder. Trials have been conducted in several police forces to electronically record fingerprints and then wirelessly transmit them to a fingerprint database for comparison and identification; such trials have had some success.

When deciding what type of powder to use, it is advantageous to look first at the surface to be examined. Generally, smooth and non-porous surfaces, such as windows, highly glossed wood or enamel ornaments, are the best surfaces on which to use flake powder. On lightly grained surfaces, such as non-gloss painted window surrounds or surfaces that may be damaged by using lifting tape, such as car body work with flaking paintwork, it would be best to use granular powder. The fingerprint powder selected should be a colour that contrasts with the surface being examined. The ability of a latent fingerprint to

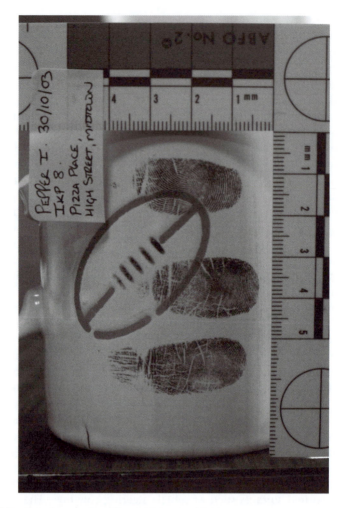

Figure 7.2   Granular powdered fingerprints on a drinking mug

attract fingerprint powders should in no way be used as a basis for suggesting the freshness of the print, as there are many environmental factors that may affect this (Midkiff 1993).

If the fingerprint is either visible in a contaminant such as blood, or latent on a surface such as paper, which cannot readily be powdered, then the fingerprint may be developed using chemical processes. Specialist laboratory staff working within the Fingerprint Development Laboratory (FDL) will often conduct these processes.

The Home Office Police Scientific Development Branch (PSDB) based at Sandridge, England, has a number of scientists and police officers who develop

Figure 7.3 Twirling a Zephyr brush

the best processes for the development of fingerprints. If fingerprints were found in blood, then PSDB would recommend a visual examination and then photography. Following this, a fluorescence examination will be conducted, followed, depending on the surface, by diazafluoren-9-one (DFO), ninhydrin, amido black, and physical developer (PSDB 1998).

Some constituents found in fingerprints and substances that may have contaminated them fluoresce if exposed to the correct source of light from either a laser or high-intensity light source such as a quasar. A laser operates on one wavelength of light and is very intense, whereas a quasar operates across a band of wavelengths and the light produced is therefore less intense but more versatile. This method can be used either at the crime scene or in a police laboratory by appropriately trained staff. If fingerprints are found using fluorescence, then they should be photographed. If the fingerprint, let's say in blood, is on a porous surface, such as raw wood, then it should be treated with a working solution of DFO, which is heated and then examined using fluorescence. Any fingerprints found should then be photographed. Ninhydrin should be used next in the sequence of examining the porous surface for a fingerprint in blood and may equally be used on a non-porous surface. Having passed the article through a working solution of ninhydrin, it should then be humidified before fluorescing and photographing any fingerprints. It should be noted that the use of ninhydrin might damage the recovery of DNA

Figure 7.4 Fingerprints, powdered, lifted and documented at crime scene

evidence. Next, a working solution of amido black can be applied to either porous or non-porous surfaces. This will stain proteins present in blood or other body fluids a blue/black colour, then any fingerprints found should be photographed. Finally, immersing the item in a working solution of physical developer allows this aqueous reagent to react with parts of the sebaceous sweat (PSDB 1998). Once again, any resultant fingerprints should be photographed.

A number of other chemical processes are available within a laboratory environment to assist in the recovery of fingerprints. For example, the use of superglue fuming on non-porous surfaces such as firearms and the plastic from the insides of vehicles has had a great deal of success. The article for examination is placed within a humidified chamber. Superglue is heated to approximately 1208C; the superglue vapour then polymerizes on latent fingerprints. Vacuum metal deposition can be used to find latent fingerprints on smooth non-porous surfaces such as polythene bags by allowing metal particles to adhere to the constituents of fingerprints within a vacuum chamber (PSDB 1998). Sticky-side powder is a simple and cheap method of locating fingerprints on the sticky side of adhesive tapes. The use of chemical processes to recover fingerprints is potentially limitless. Attempts have even been made to chemically recover latent fingerprints from the skin of victims, with varied success.

7.3 The taking of fingerprints and palm prints

Fingerprints and palm prints can be taken for a number of reasons. These include the identification of an individual for the police, the court, immigration services and other law enforcement agencies. They are taken for comparison against unidentified marks recovered from crime scenes and then to prove the identification of a crime scene mark at court, for inclusion in a fingerprint collection, to identify a previously unidentified body, and to eliminate an individual from an enquiry. The fingerprints taken in the custody suite of a police station will often be taken by civilian detention officers or police officers. Fingerprints taken for elimination and other purposes may be taken by a CSI.

Good quality fingerprints are required in order to reveal as much information as possible in the fingerprint pattern. This will aid identification whether done manually or via a computerized system.

The finger and palm prints are taken by one of two methods: either electronically using an IT system called 'Livescan' or on a 'tenprint' form. Whether taken electronically or using ink on a tenprint form, the details of the donor, such as name, date of birth, gender and date taken, should be completed prior to commencing the printing.

Most police forces use a 'Livescan' system, which allows the electronic scanning of fingerprints when someone is arrested, which leads to immediate access and comparison against a fingerprint database. Once each of the fingerprints has been carefully scanned by the donor (person under arrest) pushing each finger with even pressure onto the glass plate, which is in effect a flatbed scanner, the fingerprints can be launched to check an individual's identity against the fingerprint database. Response time from scanning of the fingerprints to the verification of identity can be as quick as five minutes if the Livescan operator helps narrow the search by selecting the appropriate search criteria such as gender. The Livescan verification results are reported to be in excess of 98 per cent plus accurate.

The Livescan inputted fingerprints can also be searched against unidentified crime scene marks. Although taking longer, the results will come back to the operator with any possible matches and a level of confidence (i.e. the likelihood of it being an accurate identification). This identification of crime scene marks does require a two-stage process: the first stage being an identification via Livescan and the second stage a comparison and identification in a fingerprint bureau by a fingerprint examiner. Since 2006, a number of police forces have also trialled hand-held fingerprint scanners (termed 'Lantern') which can be used by operational police officers to scan an individual's index fingerprint to check in digital real time an individual's identity when they have been stopped on the street. The 'Lantern project' was so successful that in

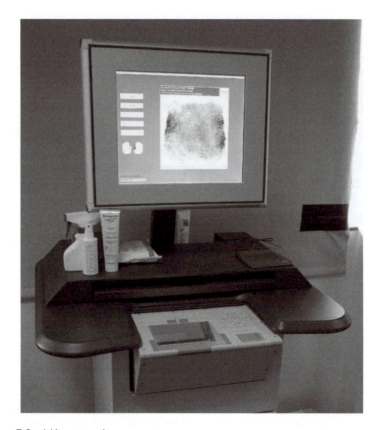

Figure 7.5   A Livescan unit

2008 the government launched a further project 'MIDaS' (Mobile Identification at Scene) which is hoped by late 2010 to allow all police officers to be equipped to scan fingerprints of an individual and check their identity against the national fingerprint database at a scene of an incident.

Fingerprints taken using ink will require either a pre-inked strip or an ink block that has an even layer of the ink rolled onto it. Starting with the right thumb, the fingers of the donor should be rolled from nail to nail on the inked surface. The ink extends below the first joint on the finger. Each finger is inked, then rolled from nail to nail in a single motion onto the ten print form, placing each finger in the correctly titled box. On no account should fingers be rolled backwards and then forwards across the box as this will create a double image and will hamper identification. After the rolled fingerprint impressions of both hands have been taken, then the plain impressions should be taken. The fingers of each hand should be placed together, inked and then in one motion placed together on the base of the tenprint form; both thumbs should also be done together. These 'plain' impressions are taken to ensure the rolled impressions have been recorded in the correct boxes on the tenprint form (Bridges 1942). The plain impressions may also reveal useful information for the fingerprint expert on the tips and below the first joint of the finger.

If the donor has fingers missing or extra digits (polydactylism), notes should be made on the tenprint form accordingly, and all digits should be printed.

Palm prints should also be taken on the back of the tenprint form. The palms of the donor need to be coated in ink, ensuring that the whole palm area from the wrist to the fingers is covered. The heel of the palm should be placed on the tenprint form, then rolled down and back to ensure the whole palm is recorded.

If a deceased person of unknown identity cannot be identified by the usual means, such as recognition by a relative, then a CSI may be asked to take the fingerprints of the deceased at a mortuary. Once the fingerprints are recovered, the procedure is to search the fingerprints of the deceased against local and national records of fingerprints in the hope that the person has had his or her fingerprints taken when alive. Alternatively if it is believed that the deceased came from a particular house, then a comparison can be made with latent fingerprints recovered from personal items within the house.

The recovery of fingerprints from a deceased person presents its own unique problems. The hands are likely to have rigor mortis but could also be macerated, perhaps having been immersed in water for a considerable time; alternatively they may be desiccated having been exposed to the dry air for some time. The hands may also have been burnt, damaged by trauma or may be decomposing. If the body has been stored in a refrigerator within the mortuary, it will also be damp as it comes back to room temperature; if the body has been in long-term storage, it should have been kept at −14° centigrade (Interpol 2009b) so will take some time to come to room temperature.

The rigor mortis can be overcome by gently massaging the hand and manipulating the tendons until the hand opens sufficiently for fingerprints to be taken. Special care must be taken when manipulating hands that have suffered other damage, such as that described, as the skin on the fingers may crumble or break off.

If there is any possibility that the skin on the fingers may be damaged while attempting to recover a set of fingerprints, then the pattern on each finger should be photographed. If the hands are not damaged, then it is possible to use fingerprint ink to recover a set of ten prints by inking and rolling each finger in turn onto a tenprint form as usual. If the fingers cannot be rolled onto a tenprint form due to damage, perhaps burning, then it is still possible for the CSI to recover the fingerprint. Wearing two light coloured latex

FINGERPRINT FORM

Surname:		Classification:	
Forename(s):			
Alias/Maiden Name:		Unique Reference No: (in pencil)	
Nationality:		Impression Taken by:	
Date of Birth:		Name, Rank/Number	
Sex: Male / Female / Unknown		Force:	Date:
Offence:		Prisoner's signature:	
Place of Offence:			

1-RIGHT THUMB	2-RIGHT FORE	3-RIGHT MIDDLE	4-RIGHT RING	5-RIGHT LITTLE

1-LEFT THUMB	2-LEFT FORE	3-LEFT MIDDLE	4-LEFT RING	5-LEFT LITTLE

LEFT HAND		THUMBS		RIGHT HAND
		LEFT	RIGHT	

Classified by:	Checked by:

Health and Safety
Forms contaminated with blood or other body fluids should be appropriately sealed

Figure 7.6 Tenprint form

FINGERPRINT FORM

Comments:

RIGHT PALM

LEFT PALM

Health and Safety
Forms contaminated with blood or other body fluids should be appropriately sealed

gloves over the top of each other and after inking the finger of the deceased, the inked finger of the deceased is placed in the palm area of the CSI's double-gloved hand. The outer pair of gloves can then be removed and the fingerprint cut out and mounted onto a clear plastic sheet.

Another method for the recovery of fingerprints from a deceased requires the fingers to be completely dry; this may be accomplished with regular wiping. Granular or flake fingerprint powders can then be brushed onto the ridge pattern of the fingers before being lifted off with either white sticky labels or lifting tape and stuck onto clear plastic sheets. Each label or lift should be marked with the details of which finger and which hand it has been recovered from.

Whichever method is used to recover the fingerprints of a deceased at a mortuary, it is imperative that the CSI conforms to health and safety requirements (see Chapter 13). All fingerprints recovered in such situations should be sealed in a polythene bag and disinfected or autoclaved.

7.4 The identification and classification of fingerprints

Once the fingerprint has been recovered from the crime scene, or perhaps on an article recovered from a scene that has been chemically treated in some way to reveal latent fingerprints, it will be forwarded to the fingerprint bureau for comparison against fingerprints from recorded offenders.

In each and every case the fingerprints (or partial finger, palm or foot prints) recovered from the crime scene will be analysed, compared, evaluated and verified (ACE-V) by the fingerprint examiner. During the first stage of the ACE-V process, analysis, the fingerprint examiner assesses the different levels of detail that would assist in the possible identification of the fingerprints. Then while completing the next stage, comparison, the examiner will compare the different levels of detail with similar fingerprints, such as ridge characteristics or accidental scars, in order to identify the detail that does match and the detail that doesn't. The fingerprint examiner must continually evaluate his or her findings in an effort to reach the conclusion that the fingerprints are the same, different or inconclusive. Once the fingerprint examiner has reached a conclusion, then verification or analysis by a second and third examiner of the fingerprints must be completed. In the United Kingdom since 2001, there has been a non-numerical standard for fingerprint identification, in other words there is no minimum number of points of similarity between fingerprints that the fingerprint examiner must identify to demonstrate that two fingerprints match.

During the initial analysis stage of the examination of the fingerprint and then in order for the fingerprint examiner to identify a fingerprint when comparing the mark recovered from the crime scene with fingerprints from recorded offenders, he or she will examine several layers of detail. First, the examiner will decide to which of the general pattern groups the fingerprint recovered from the crime scene is likely to belong; this is termed Level 1 detail, but cannot, however, be used as a means of positive identification alone. Then the ridge characteristics will be identified, such as ridge endings, bifurcations and accidental scars; this is termed Level 2 detail. Then finally Level 3 detail is highlighted, such as location of the sweat pores, the size and shape of the ridge edges, etc. Some fingerprint examiners also study the shape, location and individualization of sweat pores as a specialism, this is termed poroscopy. All of this information is utilized by the fingerprint examiner when making fingerprint identifications and, equally important, deciding when fingerprints don't match. Every fingerprint identified by a fingerprint examiner goes through a series of checks by his or her peers.

A basic understanding of how fingerprints are classified and identified is of importance to CSIs. This will aid their recognition of the fingerprint patterns so that they can do the best they can to recover the complete, undamaged fingerprint by adding fingerprint powder while brushing in the direction of the pattern. This will lead to the minimization of damage to the different levels of fingerprint detail that may be available to assist in the identification by the fingerprint examiner.

Pattern groups

There are three main pattern groups for fingerprints: arches, loops and whorls, but these groups can be further divided. Each fingerprint, with the exception of arches, has at least one core and one delta.

The delta and core

Table 7.1   Fingerprint pattern groups

Arch	Loop	Whorl
Plain or tented	Plain, converging or nutant	Plain whorls, elongated whorls, twinned loops, lateral pocket, composite

Plain arch

In this pattern the ridges run in one side of the fingerprint and out the other without making a backward turn or recurve. There are no deltas (Henry 1934).

A plain arch

Tented arch

In this pattern the ridges run in one side of the fingerprint and out the other but in the centre they make an upward thrust creating the appearance of a tent. There are no deltas (Henry 1934).

A tented arch

Plain loop

In this pattern the ridges flow in from one side of the finger and some of them make a backward turn, or recurve and exit the finger on the same side as they came in. These patterns have one core and one delta. There are two types of plain loop: radial, where the ridges that recurve start and end on the same side of the hand as the radial bone (the thumb side), and ulnar, where the ridges that recurve start and end on the opposite side.

A radial loop on a finger of
the right hand

An ulnar loop on a finger
of the right hand

Converging loop

In this pattern the ridges flow in from one side of the finger and some of them make a backward turn, or recurve, and exit the finger on the same side they came in, but some of these ridges converge into the centre. These patterns have one core and one delta.

A converging loop

Nutant loop

In this pattern the ridges flow in from one side of the finger and some of them make a backward turn, or recurve, and exit the finger on the same side they came in, but during the recurve the ridges bend downwards. These patterns have one core and one delta.

A nutant loop

Plain and elongated whorls

In this pattern the ridges make concentric circles, which may be elongated, with at least one complete 360-degree circuit (Henry 1934). These patterns have one core and two deltas.

A plain whorl

An elongated whorl

Twinned loop

In this pattern the ridges entering from opposing sides form two loops that embrace each other. These patterns have two cores and two deltas.

A twinned loop

Lateral pocket

In this pattern the ridges forming the loop-shaped patterns enter from the same side and one of the loops is bent sharply downwards providing a pocket into which the second loop is encompassed. This pattern has two cores and two deltas.

A lateral pocket

Composite

In this pattern the ridges combine to form two or more of the other types of pattern (Henry 1934). This pattern has three or more deltas.

A composite

Classification of fingerprints

Using the tenprint form and utilizing a system of pattern group identification a fingerprint examiner can, if required, produce a sequence of numbers and letters to classify the fingerprint form. This would assist in narrowing the search parameters when attempting to search manually through a large collection of fingerprints, some of which would contain over one million sets of tenprints, which would have been filed using the same number and letter system. The system of classification relies on the accurate recognition of the pattern group plus further observations that break down the classification into primary, secondary and tertiary features. There are a number of variants of the system of classification first devised by Henry and his team. The variants and sub-classifications used are often dependent on choices made within each separate fingerprint bureau. Detailed here is a simple classification system, which is used in a number of fingerprint bureaux and has been adapted from the classic Henry system of classification.

For the primary classification, the patterns are grouped together and given a numerical value or not. Plain arches, tented arches, plain loops, converging loops and nutant loops are grouped and given no value while plain whorls, elongated whorls, twinned loops, lateral pockets and composites are grouped and given a value. The values vary depending on which finger shows the pattern.

In order to construct the primary classification the values of the whorls on the fingers of the right hand are added together, then 1 is added to the total. This value forms the top half of a fraction. Then the values of the whorls of the left-hand fingers are added together, and 1 is added to the total. This value forms the bottom half of a fraction.

In order to construct the secondary classification, a symbol is used to denote the pattern group that appears on the right forefinger, forming the top half of a fraction, and the pattern group that appears on the left forefinger forms the bottom half of the fraction. The symbols are: plain arches (A),

Table 7.2 Values of whorls on different fingers

Right hand				
16	8	4	2	1
Thumb	Fore finger	Middle finger	Ring finger	Little finger
Left hand				
16	8	4	2	1
Thumb	Fore finger	Middle finger	Ring finger	Little finger

tented arches (T), plain loops are subdivided into ulnar loops (U) and radial loops (R), converging loops and nutant loops both have trends towards either ulnar or radial loops so are given the symbol (U or R). Plain whorls, elongated whorls, twinned loops, lateral pockets and composites are grouped and given a symbol (W). Any arch patterns, which appear on the thumbs or middle fingers of either hand, should be marked in the secondary classification with a small (a).

In order to construct the tertiary classification, ridge counting and ridge tracing must take place on the right forefinger and middle finger to form the top half of a fraction and on the left fore and middle finger to form the bottom half of the fraction. If the pattern on any of these fingers falls into a loop category, then the number of ridges which separate the delta from the core should be counted. If the ridge count is between one and nine on the forefinger and between one and ten on the middle finger, then each digit is given a symbol of (I) or inner. If the ridge count is 10 or greater on the forefinger and 11 or greater on the middle finger, then each digit is given a symbol of (O) or outer. If the pattern on any of the fingers falls into a whorl category, then the lower ridge which forms the delta on the left of the pattern should be traced across towards the right-hand delta; each time a ridge ends the tracing should drop down onto the next ridge. When reaching the other delta, if the ridge falls in front of the other delta, then this is given a symbol of (I) or inner; if the ridge meets the other delta, then this should be given a symbol of (M) or meeting; if the ridge falls outside the other delta, then this should be given a symbol of (O) or outer. If the pattern groups are not the same on the right fore and right middle or left fore and left middle (i.e. the right fore is a loop and the right middle is a whorl), then the symbols should not be placed along-side each other in order to avoid confusion. Routinely the forefinger pattern group will take precedence and the unmatching pattern group on the middle finger will be replaced by a dot (.). Patterns which fall into the arches group cannot be ridge counted or traced and should therefore be marked with a dot (.).

The classification is completed with the addition of the ridge count, if available from the right little finger. If no ridge count is available from the right little finger, then this may be substituted with that from the left little finger but this should be marked with a bracket.

If presented with the series of fingerprint patterns on the form in Table 7.3, then the primary classification would be 17 on the right hand plus the one that should always be added and eight on the left hand plus the one that should always be added. The secondary classification would be an ulnar loop on the right hand with a whorl proceeded by an arch on the left hand. The tertiary classification would be an inner count and an outer count on the right fore and middle fingers and an inner tracing with a dot on the left fore and

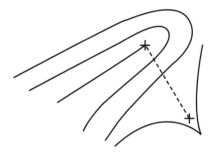

Figure 7.7 Ridge counting (loops). Number of ridges that cross an imaginary line between the delta and the core, in this case three

OPEN DELTA

CLOSED DELTA

Figure 7.8 Ridge tracing (whorls)
Starting on the lower limb of the delta work left to right, always dropping to the lower limb of a bifurcation or lower ridge until level with the right-hand delta, in this case an inner tracing.

Table 7.3 A classified tenprint form

Right hand				
Whorl (with a meeting tracing)	Ulnar loop (with a ridge count of four)	Ulnar loop (with a ridge count of twelve)	Ulnar loop (with a ridge count of four)	Whorl (with an inner tracing)
Thumb	Fore finger	Middle finger	Ring finger	Little finger
Left hand				
Arch	Whorl (with an inner tracing)	Ulnar loop (with a ridge count of three)	Ulnar loop (with a ridge count of nine)	Radial loop (with a ridge count of ten)
Thumb	Fore finger	Middle finger	Ring finger	Little finger

middle fingers. The classification would be completed with a ridge count of ten from the left little finger.

The classification for the form would be written as:

$$\frac{18 \quad \text{U IO (10}}{9 \quad \text{aW I.}}$$

If fingers are missing, then when classified they should be made the same as the preceding finger but with the possible alternatives also marked on.

Galton details

Sir Francis Galton noticed that the ridges on the fingers did not run in lines without breaking, and he identified a number of ridge characteristics to aid the identification of the fingerprints. There is some dispute among fingerprint experts as to whether there are two types of ridge characteristics (ridge endings and bifurcations) or the six ridge characteristics as listed in Figure 7.9.

In order for a fingerprint found at a crime scene to be identified as belonging to the inked fingerprints taken from a suspect, the ridge characteristics, rather than just the pattern, are used. Since 1924, a 16-point standard had been used in the UK (Knowles 2000). In order for an identification to be made for production at court, 16 ridge characteristics on one finger would have to be

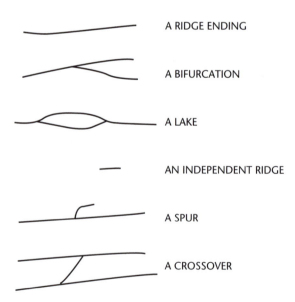

A RIDGE ENDING

A BIFURCATION

A LAKE

AN INDEPENDENT RIDGE

A SPUR

A CROSSOVER

Figure 7.9 Ridge characteristics

shown to be in the same position and sequence on both the crime scene mark and suspect's fingerprints. However, since 2001, this has no longer been necessary. The fingerprint expert now makes a judgement on which characteristics match and which do not, and presents this evidence of expert opinion to a court of law.

When comparing the fingerprints, looking for the ridge characteristics, a fingerprint examiner will use a fingerprint glass or comparator to magnify the image to make the comparison easier.

Figure 7.10 Using a comparator

7.5 Computerized systems of identification

Since 2006, all 43 police forces in England and Wales plus forces in Scotland have had access to the Ident1 national fingerprint database, this being extended to include the UK Border Agency in 2008. This superseded the National Automated Fingerprint Identification System (NAFIS). Ident1 is a commercially produced computerized fingerprint identification system which allows local police forces online access to a national database of the fingerprints and palm prints of those arrested. The retention of fingerprints taken from a person arrested should adhere to the same guidelines as those set for DNA by Johnson (Johnson 2009) (see Chapter 6). The database consists of in excess of 7 million 'tenprint' sets of fingerprints, nearly 5 million palm prints and a collection of approximately 2 million finger and palm marks recovered from crime scenes (NPIA 2009). The Ident1 system allows the national verification of tenprints integrating with the Livescan system, the ability to search tenprints and palm prints against outstanding scenes of crime marks, and the searching of scenes of crime marks against the tenprint and palm print database identifying thousands of crime scene marks annually. The search of crime scene marks against the tenprint database aims to have a response within 20 minutes of launching the mark on the system, with a list of possible matches being produced. The likelihood of the first name on the list being a successful match ranges between 70 per cent and 90 per cent. It is then up to the fingerprint examiner to make a comparison.

Conceived in 1923, the Federal Fingerprint Bureau was intended to hold records of individuals convicted across the United States of America (Henry 1934). Now the Federal Bureau of Investigation (FBI), which has successfully operated an Integrated Automatic Fingerprint Identification System (IAFIS) since 1999, holds national fingerprint records. With over 55 million sets of tenprints, search and response times for marks submitted to the IAFIS are approximately two hours, with the aim to develop the system to include other identifiable data within IAFIS such as palm prints and other biometric information (FBI 2009a). The IAFIS also operates the facility of remote access to search the database live via a laptop, such as at the scene of a disaster. Individual police departments across the USA also operate their own computerized fingerprint databases.

The near future holds the possibility for crime scene investigators across the UK to record fingerprints at the crime scene electronically and, as with Livescan, forward them for immediate searching of the appropriate fingerprint database, thus leading to the swifter identification of offenders.

Self-assessment questions

Answer the following questions without reference to the chapter:

1 What are the three biological functions of friction ridges?

2 What does 'latent' mean?

3 What are the two main types of fingerprint powders?

4 Which type of fingerprint powder would work best on a drinking glass?

5 Which chemical process provides good results when examining firearms for fingerprints?

6 What are the three main fingerprint pattern groups?

7 How many deltas does a plain whorl fingerprint pattern have?

8 What is Livescan?

9 What is poroscopy the study of?

10 What is the name of the national fingerprint database used across England, Wales, Scotland and the UK Border Agency?

8 The investigation of a fire scene

While working as an operational crime scene investigator (CSI) I took a particular interest in the investigation of the scenes of fire. The investigations were usually dirty, sometimes dangerous, but always intriguing to examine. The scenes I examined ranged from the total destruction of multi-million pound warehouses and the death of individuals in accidental fires to damage caused by fireworks being pushed through letterboxes.

Deliberate ignition, often referred to as arson, occurs frequently in England and Wales. For the 12 months up to the end of March 2008 the fire service across England reported over 187,000 primary and secondary fires that had been caused deliberately and across the United Kingdom there were 500 deaths in fires (Communities and Local Government 2009). It is a challenge for the CSI, sometimes in company with a fire brigade investigator or forensic chemist, to identify evidence to recover from such fire scenes.

8.1 Ignition of fires

In order for a fire to combust, it requires heat, fuel, oxygen and a source of ignition. Research conducted by the London Fire Brigade discovered that nearly half of all unintentional fatal dwelling fires were ignited by the careless disposal of smoking materials such as cigarettes (Holborn et al. 2003). If a fire, once ignited, is to continue to burn, the elements of heat, fuel and oxygen must be linked in a chain termed 'the triangle of fire'; those wishing to extinguish the fire must attempt to break the chain by removing one of the three elements.

Once burning, the fire will consume all in its path. The heat from the fire will move from room to room or surface to surface by conduction, convection or radiation, or indeed a mixture of all three. Conduction is the transfer of heat through a solid medium such as a metal pipe. Convection occurs when the air is heated and rises as it expands, perhaps reaching the ceiling of a house, which it then rolls across, igniting other mediums, such as posters and lampshades as it goes. Finally, radiation is the heat transferred in straight lines being absorbed by another medium, such as furniture, until it too ignites.

All forms of heat transfer were present in the Bradford City football stadium fire in 1985. This fire, which was broadcast live on television due to the earlier football match coverage, spread through the stand and wooden roof in less than four minutes. Heat was conducted along the metal supports for the stand, convection led to the heat rising and igniting the roof and radiation transferred heat forward. This fire led to the deaths of 56 people, injuries to several hundred and the destruction of the large covered stand.

8.2 The role of the agencies involved in the investigation of a fire

Investigators from a number of agencies may be involved at the scene of a non-accidental fire. These could include CSIs from the police service, fire investigators from the fire and rescue service, forensic scientists and forensic pathologists. The fire and rescue service has responsibility for the extinction of any fire. Home Office Circular 1/2006 indicates the roles and responsibilities of a number of the agencies involved in the investigation of non-accidental fires, generically referred to as deliberate fires. The Fire and Rescue Services Act (2004) provides authority for the fire and rescue service to investigate causes of a fire. If the fire did not occur accidentally, then the police service are solely responsible for the investigation of any crime and the reporting to the coroner of any death that occurred as a result of the fire.

The fire service groups fires into primary and secondary categories. Examples of primary fires are those which occur in occupied buildings or large structures, vehicles or are of high financial loss. At such fires, after their extinction, the fire and rescue service will preserve the scene as far as is possible, noting any unusual phenomena, dispatch a senior fire officer to control the scene, report the fire to the police and notify a specialist fire investigator. The police will attend the scene and liaise with the fire and rescue service and if either party suspects a crime, it will be recorded as such and specialist investigators (such as a CSI and forensic scientist) will be requested to attend to conduct an investigation in liaison with the fire and rescue service fire investigation officer. If a death or serious injury occurred as a result of a fire (regardless if a crime has been committed or not), a police supervisor will always attend. Secondary fires are those that occur in derelict buildings, on grassland or in rubbish bins. Often a senior fire officer and the police do not attend these scenes, but information and intelligence about trends and patterns should be gathered and shared between both the fire and police agencies (Fire and Rescue Service Circular 2006).

On arrival, the CSI gathers information by liaising with the fire service and police officers at the scene, then, assuming the fire has been extinguished, takes over responsibility for the preservation of the scene. The CSI should stand back and take a good look at the scene itself, consider whether there is a point of forced entry, and whether the scene appears to extend beyond the boundaries of the burnt structure, to include, for example, footwear marks, tyre marks or abandoned vehicles and clothes. When in possession of as much information as possible the CSI enters into a discussion with the investigating police officer to ascertain whether the expertise of a forensic scientist might be required during the examination. The main role of the CSI extends to the identification, recording, recovery and packaging of forensic samples and their subsequent integrity and storage. The CSI must consider their own health and safety and the health and safety of those around them at all times (see Chapter 13).

Most fire services have full-time Fire Investigation Teams (FIT). These consist of investigators who are fire officers with an excellent knowledge of and experience in fires and who have received specialist investigator training. Their primary role is to investigate the cause of the fire and if necessary provide evidence in a court of law; they will also assist the police by providing evidence of the origin, growth and decay of the fire. In some areas, arson task forces have been established as partnerships between the fire and rescue services investigation teams and police investigators in order to jointly investigate deliberate fires and reduce such occurrences, particularly in areas which have a high incidence of deliberate fires.

At the request of the police a forensic scientist, a chemist, will also attend the fire scene. The scientist will interpret the scene and identify locations for the recovery of fire debris samples by the CSI for later analysis at the laboratory. If a death has occurred in the fire, then a forensic pathologist will also attend the scene at the request of the police. The pathologist will gather information from both the fire service and police prior to conducting a preliminary examination of the body at the scene. Such an examination may provide information relating to the pathologist's findings, such as unburnt areas of skin, during the subsequent post-mortem examination at the mortuary. As such, bodies should not be moved until the forensic pathologist has visited the scene.

8.3 Is it a deliberate ignition?

There are many reasons why a fire may be ignited, such as the careless disposal of a cigarette, accidents when using a cooker or standing too close to a heat source such as a heater (Holborn et al. 2003). But there are a number of reasons why a CSI may suspect arson. On arrival at the scene the CSI should gather as much information as possible from those police and fire officers around them – after all, the fire fighters will have been to more fires than the CSI. The fire fighters or police may indicate that there have been a number of fires at the location, the same person has been seen hanging around a number of times, fire appliances have been tampered with (such as sprinklers turned off), or someone stands to benefit from the fire. Cooke and Ide (1985) suggest a number of reasons why a CSI may suspect arson. They suggest there may be multiple areas where fires were ignited, called seats of fire. Once excavated they can show deep-seated burning where the fire has been alight the longest and may also reveal preparation for the fire such as matches or screwed up paper. The unusual arrangement of furniture perhaps piled around the seat of the fire is suspicious. Articles dear to the arsonist may have been removed from the building for safe keeping prior to the ignition of the fire. There may be a wildly ridiculous claim as to what has been destroyed in the fire or obstructiveness, or evasiveness, on the part of the occupier of the fire-damaged premises. The fire may have been set to cover up and destroy evidence of another crime such as a murder or theft. If the fire had been very severe, developing rapidly and spreading through a property, this indicates that an accelerant may have been used.

An accelerant is anything that speeds up the growth of the fire. Although usually associated with liquid fuel, such as petrol or paraffin, an accelerant could equally be straw or newspaper. A liquid fuel accelerant will typically leave a pool burn on the surface on which it has been burning. As the vapour from the liquid fuel burns, it creates a pool or halo shape on the surface.

When attempting to locate the seat of the fire, there are a number of clues that may assist the CSI. Low burning where the floor is most damaged and high burning where the ceiling is most damaged may help locate the seat of the fire. But the CSI should be careful in jumping to conclusions as some

Figure 8.1   A ceiling fire just before a flashover occurs

materials may burn more quickly than others and at different temperatures or they may be affected by draughts or fire fighting. Burn patterns are classic indicators, with the 'V' pattern burn having the seat of the fire at its base. Glass and plastics melt towards the heat produced by the fire; light bulbs will often explode on one side in the path of the advancing fire indicating a direction of travel (DeHaan 2007). These so-called thermal indicators can be of immense use in locating the seat of the fire. Smoke damage may travel away from the fire so will help in its general location. Specially trained fire and rescue service hydrocarbon detector dogs may be used to assist investigators in determining if liquid accelerants such as petroleum-based products (which contain hydrocarbons) were present at a particular location within the scene of a fire (Fire and Rescue Service Circular 2006).

Glass lying flat on a floor, clean on the side next to the ground but with smoke and debris on the other side, may indicate that it was broken before or immediately after the fire started; window glass on the top of debris would indicate that it was broken during the fire fighting. Broken window glass on the exterior of the building may indicate a 'flashover' has occurred. This is when all the combustible surfaces in a confined fire almost simultaneously ignite and the fire spreads very rapidly to engulf the space, thus causing a massive and sudden change in the heat applied to the window glass. Depth of charring to wood can be a rough guide to assist in establishing the length of time a surface has been exposed to the fire in relation to other areas (DeHaan 2007). I would agree with DeHaan and note that there are numerous variables that can affect the depth of the char, such as the type of wood, the amount of heat to which it is exposed and other constituents such as paint or varnish on the wood. Using depth of char to establish the seat of a fire should be viewed with caution.

A chemical or biological reaction within a hay stack or pile of coal can lead to a rise in temperature and spontaneous combustion of the material; in effect, it appears to burst spontaneously into flame. Spontaneous human combustion has been recorded as far back as the seventeenth century but with little or no hard evidence to support its occurrence. The current scientific explanation is that the body supplies fuel for a fire in the form of body fat and an external source of ignition, such as a heater, is required to ignite the body fat initially leading to a chain of events that creates the triangle of fire. In effect the body acts like a candle with a wick, the flame being focused on the exterior of the body. A body burnt in a fire, caused by whatever means, is not usually completely destroyed often leaving traces such as pieces of bone (DeHaan 2007).

8.4 Recovery of samples by the CSI

Initially the CSI should thoroughly record the scene both photographically and diagrammatically; video is an excellent tool for recording the scene for possible future reconstruction as it records in low light conditions and provides the viewer with a 360-degree view. Then the CSI, in conjunction with other specialists present, will recover samples of the debris at the seat (or seats) of the fire or alternatively at the lowest point of burning. Each of the debris samples of 1–2kg in weight should be checked that they do not contain any items that may puncture the packaging, and should then be placed in large nylon bags. Nylon bags are used as they retain any accelerant vapours from the debris better than polythene bags. When packaging a sample, the nylon bags should be about half-filled with debris and then the other half of the bag should have some air left in it; the opening should be twisted and bent over before being sealed with a plastic tie, sellotape or string in such a way that will not allow any of the air to escape. As a general rule, any items from either the scene of a fire or from a suspect (such as shirts, trousers, shoes and socks) which require checking for the presence of a liquid accelerant should also be packaged in nylon bags in the same manner. Any liquid accelerant left at the scene, such as in the base of a petrol bomb, should be collected in clean solid containers, such as glass or metal and then packaged in a nylon bag. Any petrol bomb fragments should also be packaged in a solid container (such as a box) before being placed in a nylon bag. It is also good practice to exhibit a nylon bag or container from the same manufacturing batch to prove that no accelerants were already in the packaging material prior to recovery of the sample for analysis.

When recovering samples, care must be taken by the CSI not to contaminate the evidence. It is essential that clean, protective outer garments (including hand and footwear) are worn, tools used to recover samples are thoroughly clean (some police forces use disposable shovels) and samples recovered from the scene are transported as soon as possible to the forensic science provider.

8.5 Examination at the laboratory

A forensic chemist will examine the debris for the presence of liquid accelerants, such as petrol or paraffin. The air left in the nylon bags containing the debris is the source for the check for these accelerants. If the debris is carefully warmed, some vapours from the accelerant will rise into the air caught in the bag, albeit in minute amounts. The same is true if a solid container is heated, allowing the vapours to rise. A sample of this air is drawn off and placed in gas chromatography apparatus, which will split the vapour down into its component parts and produce a graphic display of its composition. The graphic displays can then be compared with those for known liquid accelerants. The debris is then searched in controlled laboratory conditions with good lighting to identify any item or part of an item that may have caused the fire, such as a lighter or cigarette end.

It is possible that the item that has ignited a fire is never found. This happened during the investigation into the King's Cross underground station fire in 1987. A fire was initiated and spread rapidly along one of the escalators, engulfing the whole concourse in less than 14 minutes, leading to the deaths of 31 people and the injuring of many more. After numerous tests by forensic scientists, including the construction and burning of scale models, it was concluded that the fire was probably initiated by the careless disposal of a lighted match, although it was never found. The match is believed to have fallen underneath an escalator, igniting grease and other accumulated debris; the fire was then drawn up the escalator by the flow of the air, igniting other flammable materials as it went, until the whole ticket hall was engulfed (Fennell 1988).

Self-assessment questions

Answer the following questions without reference to the chapter:

1   What does a fire require in order to continue to burn?

2   Describe how the heat from a fire will move by conduction.

3   What is the role of the police service at the scene of a non-accidental fire?

4   What is the first thing a CSI should do on arrival at the scene of a fire?

5   What is an accelerant?

6   What clues may assist a CSI in locating the seat of a fire?

7   If a piece of broken glass was lying flat on the floor with smoke on the upper side and was clean on the other, what might this indicate?

8   How much should debris samples recovered from the seat of a fire weigh?

9   In what should fire debris samples be packaged?

10 What should the CSI always ensure remains within the packaging for the debris sample?

---

9   Firearms

The use of all types of firearms in the commission of crime has been prevalent across the world for many years. In 1900, the *Buffalo Medical Journal* published an article providing details of firearms-related injuries and how bullets could be identified. This was followed in 1912 by a professor in the University of Paris developing the basic principles for the examination of cartridge cases and bullets (Warlow 2005). On 14 February 1929, seven men were murdered in a garage in Chicago, USA. Forensic examination of firearms evidence, in the form of cartridge cases and bullets, recovered from the scene and the victims of the 'St Valentine's Day Massacre' eventually linked machine guns found in a suspect's house to the killings (Herzog and Ezickson 1940).

Today the use of firearms in the commission of crimes in the United Kingdom continues to be of concern to both the police and general public, although statistics suggest that crimes involving firearms are decreasing. During the 12 months ending in June 2008, the Home Office (2008b) supplementary note reported 9,306 crimes involving firearms (although these figures exclude air weapons) which led to 48 deaths and 374 serious injuries; this is compared to a similar period of firearms offences in England and Wales during 2001/2002, which led to 97 deaths and 558 serious injuries (Flood-Page and Taylor 2003). Crime scene investigators can come into contact with a range of firearms themselves, or components of them, along with cartridges and bullets at scenes ranging from murders to burglaries. Alternatively the CSI may be requested to recover evidence from individuals to prove, or disprove, firearms have been handled and discharged. I became involved in numerous firearm incidents ranging from someone committing suicide by shooting themselves with a shotgun to police officers being shot at in the street with a self-loading pistol.

Whichever firearms evidence type is being recovered, the safety of the CSI and his or her colleagues is of paramount importance, otherwise tragic consequences can occur. In January 2003, Scott Russell Spjut, a forensic specialist in the USA, was examining an AK-47 rifle for fingerprints when it fired, fatally injuring him (Charlton 2003). This is a tragic lesson for us all:

get someone who is trained and authorized to make weapons safe to do so, but still always treat a firearm as if it is loaded and never point it towards anyone.

9.1 The structure of firearms, cartridges and bullets

When we hear the word 'firearm' we tend to think of modern rifles, submachine guns, self-loading pistols and revolvers. However, there are other types of weapons such as shotguns, airguns, CS canisters, older style guns that use blackpowder (such as flintlocks weapons) or even firearms disguised as mobile telephones with several rounds of ammunition, that can all be equally deadly. The Firearms Act (1968) with amendments in 1997 defines a firearm as 'a lethal barrelled weapon of any description from which any shot, bullet or other missile can be discharged' (English and Card 1996). The Firearms Act also includes other prohibited weapons, whether complete or in parts, such as assault rifles, rocket launchers, mortars or equipment used to disperse toxic gases. The Violent Crime Reduction Act (2006) implemented new legislation to help deal with firearms-related crime, including measures to control replica firearms, such as making it harder to convert new replica firearms to fire real ammunition and controlling their sale and increasing the age for buying air weapons, along with the implementation of minimum sentences for courts to impose for specific crimes involving firearms.

Excluding air weapons, the most common firearms used in the commission of crime are handguns, although Hale et al. (2006) also identified other more specific firearms, such as the MAC 10 submachine pistol (which can fire over 1000 rounds a minute), being available to those involved in crime. There are a range of sources of handguns (and other firearms) available to the criminal in the UK. These range from those bought or hired on the 'grey market' of old military weapons and souvenirs, to those re-activated or imported. Firearms amnesties could perhaps provide an indication of the number of guns that may still be in circulation; such an amnesty was implemented as a result of the 1996 Dunblane School murders in Scotland where 16 school-children and their teacher were shot dead. This amnesty led to the handing in of 142,000 handguns, in the region of 60,000 handguns short of those the police estimated were legally held (Malcolm 2002), while Goodchild and Lashmar (2005) suggest that up to four million illegal firearms may be available to potential offenders across the UK. It is therefore unclear how many handguns are currently in illegal circulation, what type they are, or even where the handguns actually come from (Martis 2005). It is even possible to illegally hire a handgun and then return it to the illegal armourer after it has been used (Malcolm 2002), the costs of which are around £200 to hire a handgun which had been previously used in crime to £1400 for a new and unused one and about 50p per round of ammunition (Hale et al. 2006).

Although I shall mainly use handguns as an example to describe the structure of firearms, cartridges and bullets, the general principles for the recovery of evidence and its examination are similar for other types of weapon.

Handguns can be divided into the three distinct groups: single shot pistols, revolvers and self-loading (sometimes referred to as semi-automatic) pistols. Single shot pistols are the design from which all modern pistols have evolved and today are primarily used for target shooting. Revolvers have a circular cylinder that usually contains six or seven cartridges; the action of the person either pulling the trigger or cocking the hammer causes the cylinder to revolve to the next cartridge. Self-loading pistols use some of the energy when a cartridge is fired to eject the spent cartridge case and reload the pistol from a magazine that can hold up to 20 such cartridge cases.

Self-loading pistols and revolvers can come in numerous shapes and sizes. The SIG Sauer P226 self-loading pistol, designed in the 1980s and to date in the region of 500,000 manufactured, weighs 750 grams, is 196mm long and carries a 15-round magazine, whereas a Smith and Wesson Model 686 famous Magnum revolver weighs 1400 grams, is 351mm long and carries six rounds in a cylinder (Jones and White 2008).

Ammunition is made up of separate parts. The case, usually made of brass, contains the primer and the powder and on the end is the bullet. When the firing pin from the handgun strikes the section of the cartridge case containing the primer, it causes a small flash which ignites the powder. As the powder burns, it turns to gas, which is confined in the cartridge case, which in turn is confined in the barrel. In a short space of time the bullet, made of lead or a lead alloy, which is stuck like a bung in the end of the cartridge case, is pushed out and along the barrel. From the trigger being pulled to the bullet exiting the end of the cartridge case takes just over 0.009 seconds (Hartink 1996).

Just like pistols and revolvers, ammunition comes in various shapes and sizes. The calibre of the weapon refers to the approximate size of the bore of the weapon's barrel. It can be described in inches or millimetres and is usually stamped on the base of the ammunition such as .38 referring to .38/100 of an inch or 9mm.

Shotgun cartridges are slightly different in their construction and consequently may leave other evidence at the crime scene. A shotgun cartridge usually has a case which is constructed of brass at the base and plastic casing. Within the base of the cartridge is the primer, which when hit by the firing pin, ignites the propellant which will then force a piece of wadding (often plastic or card) down the barrel pushing the multiple pieces of lead shot in front of it until both the shot and wadding exit the end of the barrel. Thus, at the crime scene, the CSI may be able to locate the lead shot, wadding and the shotgun cartridge.

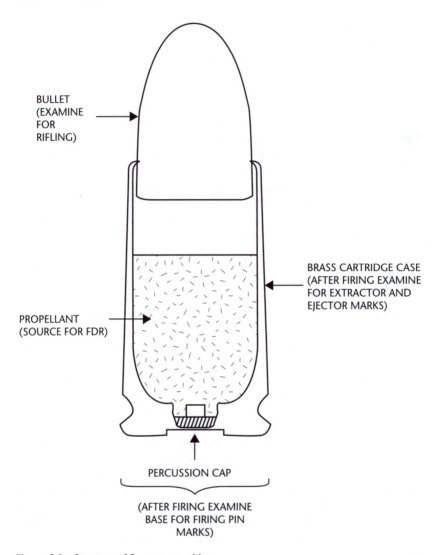

BULLET
(EXAMINE
FOR
RIFLING)

BRASS CARTRIDGE CASE
(AFTER FIRING EXAMINE
FOR EXTRACTOR AND
EJECTOR MARKS)

PROPELLANT
(SOURCE FOR FDR)

PERCUSSION CAP

(AFTER FIRING EXAMINE
BASE FOR FIRING PIN
MARKS)

Figure 9.1   Structure of 9mm ammunition

Figure 9.2 Components of 9mm ammunition (Photo: Derek A. Kirkpatrick)

Figure 9.3 Components of a shotgun cartridge (Photo: Derek A. Kirkpatrick)

9.2 The recovery of firearms, cartridges and bullets

Firearms should always be made safe to handle by trained and authorized specialists. In the case of rifles, shotguns, pistols and revolvers, authorized individuals are likely to be specially trained police firearms officers or possibly forensic firearms experts, but in the case of mortars and rockets, for example, the appropriately trained specialists are most likely to be military personnel. As the firearm is being made safe to handle, if it is safe for the CSI to be present, the CSI should record either photographically or in note form the state the weapon was in when it was found. It would be useful for any subsequent investigation to know whether the safety catch was on or off, whether there was ammunition in the breech, etc. The CSI must comprehensively photograph the scene of the shooting (with and without scales present on marks made by bullets or shotgun pellets) and any victim and their injuries should also be extensively photographed. I would agree with Warlow (1996) who suggests that the use of colour film to record the scene photographically assists the firearms specialist in determining the difference between bloodstaining and black powder marks from the weapon. Accurate and meticulous surveying and mapping of the scene of a shooting can also be of immense value to an investigation and can lead to the reconstruction of the path a bullet took. For example, the plotting of a bullet fired from a handgun allowed detectives reviewing an unsolved crime from 1980, to show that an inclined pane of glass in a window could affect the trajectory of the bullet passing through it (De Kinder et al. 2002).

Ensuring that the authorized police firearms officer is wearing clean nitrile gloves, the CSI should ask for any magazines to be removed from the weapon and it should be shown to be safe for the CSI to handle (i.e. no round in the weapon). If it is believed that the firearm has been placed in someone's mouth, then the CSI may wish to take swabs for DNA from the barrel, before it is then tied, along with the magazine, carefully and securely in a box that has a plastic window in it. This is so that the contents can be viewed, for example, during a police interview, without opening the box. The box should then be completely sealed and labelled. Under no circumstances should fingers or pens be pushed into the barrel or the trigger as this is not only dangerous, but could damage evidence present within the barrel.

Wearing protective gloves and with the minimum amount of contact between the gloves and the cartridge case, the CSI should package each case separately into small plastic tubes; in fact, half a swab container fits smaller types of cartridge cases, such as .22. The small plastic tube should be packed with polythene to prevent the cartridge case moving around and damaging evidence such as its fragile markings made by the firing pin, ejector and so on. The plastic tube should then be placed in a polythene bag along with the gloves that were worn when it was recovered. The polythene bag should then be securely sealed and labelled.

As well as the evidence available directly from both firearms and cartridge cases (such as fingerprints), research has been conducted into the recovery of the shooter's DNA deposited on parts of the firearm, such as the butt and magazine or on the cartridge cases after they had been fired. The research, although limited in size, had a high degree of success in recovering DNA from firearms and some success when recovering DNA from cartridge cases (Szibor et al. 2000).

Bullets or shot from shotguns, if impacted into a surface such as a partition wall, should be carefully cut around, leaving a piece of the wall surrounding the bullet. This piece of wall containing the bullet should be securely packaged in a solid container, such as a plastic tube or box, so that it does not move around and damage unique marks. The package should then be sealed and labelled. Bullets or shot lying freely on a surface should be handled as little as possible and placed in a plastic tube or box padded with polythene. The tube or box should be sealed before placing in a polythene bag that should also be sealed and labelled. Shotgun cartridges also contain a wad, which surrounds the shot within the cartridge. When the shotgun cartridge is fired, the wad is pushed out of the barrel with the shot and can travel up to 8 metres in the direction in which the shotgun was fired. The shotgun wadding should also be searched for and recovered before being packaged in a solid container, such as a tube or box.

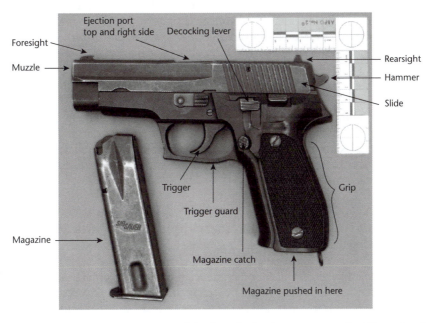

Figure 9.4 A SIG Sauer P226 9mm self-loading pistol and separate magazine (Photo: Derek A. Kirkpatrick)

9.3 The recovery of firearms discharge residue

When a firearm is discharged, residues from the bullet's propulsive charge, the primer, cartridge case and firearm itself are expelled from gaps in the gun's working parts. These particles, termed either firearms discharge residue (FDR) or gunshot residue (GSR), are deposited onto the person holding the weapon and any surfaces nearby. It is imperative that FDR is recovered from a suspect as soon as possible after the shooting took place; otherwise the residue may fall off or be washed off. The process of recovering FDR begins with the suspect having his or her head and any facial hair combed with a comb that has a swab woven through it to collect any particles caught in the hair. Then the face and hands are swabbed and fingernail scrapings taken. The washing and wiping of the face and hands by the suspect will reduce the time period over which FDR may be recovered from the skin up to a maximum of approximately six hours after the incident took place (Schwoeble and Exline 2000). However, clothing may retain FDR for considerably longer. The clothing of a suspect should therefore be recovered, ideally after swabbing of the skin has taken place, so that removal of the clothes does not remove from the skin the particulate material that constitutes the FDR. Clothing should be packaged in brown paper sacks. Other surfaces that may have been in contact with FDR, such as the skin of the victim, can also be swabbed.

CSIs who routinely come into contact with firearms, perhaps as a military reservist or at a gun club, would be advised not to be involved in the recovery of FDR. It is likely that a CSI with such interests will already have FDR on their hands, hair and clothing and would not wish to transfer such evidence to a scene or suspect.

9.4 Analysing the firearm, cartridges, bullets and FDR in the laboratory

Forensic firearm experts will attend crime scenes in order to provide advice and guidance to the investigative team, but the majority of their work is conducted within the laboratory environment. The study of firearm ballistics is often divided into three disciplines which are of course interrelated: internal ballistics is what happens within the firearm when it is fired and as the bullet travels down the barrel (such as marks made by the barrel on the bullet), external ballistics is concerned with the flight of the bullet (such as the trajectory), and terminal ballistics deals with what occurs as the bullet ends its flight impacting on a surface (such as a person's body) and the consequences of this (Pepper and Pepper 2009).

When a firearm arrives at the laboratory, a firearms expert will immediately check that the firearm is safe to handle and make a record of the details of the firearm, such as make and model, safety catches on or off, and visible serial numbers. Initially any other trace evidence types required from the firearm should be recovered by the appropriate specialist, such as blood from the barrel recovered by a biologist. The firearms expert will then swab the weapon to recover any firearms residue to demonstrate that it has been fired, although results will not indicate when the weapon was fired. The firearms expert can conduct test firings if controls of bullets and cartridges are required for comparisons with bullets and cartridges recovered from crime scenes. The weight required to pull the trigger is measured along with the effort required to put on or take off safety catches in case it is later suggested that the weapon went off accidentally.

When examined under a microscope, cartridges recovered from the crime scene may bear the markings of the calibre to assist in their identification. But even if the calibre is present, the firearms expert will still carefully take a number of measurements, such as width and length of the cartridge, before checking against known reference material. Marks made when the cartridge has been pushed into the chamber of the weapon, marks made by the firing pin, cartridge case extractor and ejector may also be evident to the expert. Such information and marks will assist in comparing control cartridges, test-fired from a known firearm using a comparison microscope, or identifying the type of firearm that had been used at the crime.

As a bullet travels down the barrel of a firearm it is forced to twist by the rifling, which is in effect a series of spirals around the length of the barrel. As the bullet twists, it has a copy of the so-called 'lands and grooves' of the rifling forced into the metal. The width and direction of twist of the lands and grooves can help identify the weapon from which the bullet was fired.

The National Ballistics Intelligence Service (NaBIS) was established in 2008 and operates a specialist firearms intelligence service from three state-of-the-art laboratories in London, the West Midlands and Manchester. Using laboratory equipment and the skill of the forensic firearms specialist, NaBIS staff can compare evidence obtained from crimes involving firearms against reference databases in order to link weapons used in the commission of such crime with other offences, people and places. In the USA, the Integrated Ballistic Identification System (IBIS) has been used since the 1990s to maintain comparison databases of bullets, cartridge cases and firearms used in crime, leading to many thousands of possible matches (Joyce 2007).

9.5 Crimes involving firearms: the Jill Dando and the Virginia Polytechnic murders

In April 1999, 37-year-old television presenter Jill Dando was murdered on the steps outside her London home. She had been shot with a 9mm pistol in the rear of her head and at close range. In May 2000, after one of the largest manhunts for years, Barry George was arrested and just over 12 months later was found guilty and sentenced to life imprisonment for the murder of Jill Dando.

Barry George lived near Jill Dando and had been a great fan. After criminal psychologists had identified traits of the likely offender, Barry George was placed under police surveillance. At the end of May, he was arrested.

After Barry George was arrested, specialist police teams searched his address and a selection of samples, including a coat, were seized. Later examination of the samples recovered from George's address by a forensic firearms expert in a laboratory found a single minute particle of firearms discharge residue, just over 11 microns in size, in the pocket of George's coat. This particle was found to be very similar to FDR containing comparable portions of chemicals, such as lead and barium, to that recovered from the hair of Jill Dando. A cartridge case had also been found at the crime scene and the FDR found in Barry George's pocket could also have come from the cartridge case. The gun used in the murder, believed to be of a calibre of 9mm, has never been found.

The evidence from the FDR, along with fibre evidence that linked Barry George's trousers with Jill Dando's coat, led the jury to decide on a guilty verdict in July 2001. After several appeals against his conviction, a retrial in 2008 led to Barry George being acquitted of the murder. At the retrial it was acknowledged in court that the minute FDR found on the deceased could have come from alternate sources (as could the fibre evidence) and Barry George could not be positively identified by witnesses. In August 2008, he was released and the murder case of Jill Dando now remains open.

On 16th April 2007, at Virginia Polytechnic Institute, USA, a student, Seung-Hui Cho, committed mass murder. Using two handguns, both with erased serial numbers, in two separate incidents less than two hours apart, Seung-Hui Cho shot and killed 32 people and injured many more before finally committing suicide. A team of CSIs were involved attending the crime scene and the mortuary to photograph and recover a range of forensic evidence from cartridge cases and footwear marks to bullets and a suicide note in an effort to aid the investigative team positively identifying both the offender and the victims and to demonstrate that Cho was responsible for the shootings.

Self-assessment questions

Answer the following questions without reference to the chapter:

1 How should a CSI always treat a firearm?

2 Other than airguns, what type of firearm is most commonly used in crime?

3 How does the Firearms Act (1968) describe a firearm?

4 In which type of packaging should a CSI place a firearm?

5 In which type of packaging should a CSI place a cartridge case?

6 How should bullets impacted in a wall be recovered?

7 What does FDR stand for?

8 What is the approximate maximum length of time FDR will remain on the skin?

9 What four types of marks will the firearms expert compare between test-fired cartridge cases and cartridge cases recovered from a crime scene?

10 What is NaBIS?

10 Terrorism, mass murder and disaster (major incidents)

Terrorism, mass murder and disaster appear to be very separate types of event where a CSI may be required to attend. However, all these incident types are likely to have a number of common features, these being the large-scale loss of life, the requirement to recover evidence from the scenes and victims, along with a multi-agency response. These types of incidents can be broadly defined as:

- Terrorism

  The Terrorism Act (2000) defines terrorism as the use or threat of use of any action to influence Government or intimidate the public, or to advance a cause which is political, religious or ideological. An example of a terrorist incident would be the attacks on the London transport network in July 2005, causing the deaths of 52 people plus the four bombers, injuring many hundreds and paralysing London's transport network.

- Mass murder

  'When a number of murders are committed in one event in a single area or location' (Pepper and Pepper 2009). An example of a mass murder was the August 1987 shooting of 16 people in the Berkshire village of Hungerford by Michael Ryan.

- Disaster

  An unexpected natural or manmade event which causes significant loss of life, damage and destruction and usually requires combined responses from a number of agencies. An example would be the December 2004 tsunami in the Indian Ocean which caused the deaths of several hundred thousand people and affected many millions.

Across the United Kingdom, acts of terrorism, mass murder or disaster are generically termed by the emergency services as 'major incidents' and it is the response of the CSI to such events on a worldwide basis which will be discussed in this chapter.

10.1 Dealing with a major incident

The immediate and overriding responsibility of all of the emergency services at a major incident must be the saving of life. To this end the fire and rescue services along with the ambulance service are given priority within a scene to rescue survivors and treat casualties, with the police service assisting with the facilitation of the rescue phase. As with a major crime scene, if possible, two cordons are established to control entry and exit from the scene of the incident through specified entry and exit points. The inner and outer cordons are the barriers in the form of natural edges (such as field boundaries) and barrier tape put in place by initial responders from the fire and rescue service along with the police, to create a controlled area for rescue and to contain the incident. Recommendations for the radius of an inner cordon vary significantly with regards to the type of incident and its location, however, guidance exists from the Association of Chief Police Officers and the National Police Improvement Agency (ACPO/NPIA 2009) who propose, for example, an inner cordon of 1000 metres radius for a vehicle-borne explosive device. The outer cordon is put in place by the emergency services to provide an area which is safe to work within and to keep the general public away from the scene. If there has been a chemical, biological, radiological or nuclear explosion (CBRNE), then the police take overall responsibility for control within the whole scene (ACPO/NPIA 2009) and decontamination sites will be established for survivors, rescuers and victims.

After the rescue phase, then the police take over responsibility from the fire and rescue services for control of the scene of the incident in order to retrieve physical evidence (including the deceased) from the scene and conduct an investigation. It is at this point that CSIs will become involved both at the scene and at the mortuary where the deceased from the major incident will be transported for post-mortem examination. A Senior Investigating Officer (SIO) is appointed by the police with responsibility for the investigation (which could of course lead to the uncovering of criminal offences such as murder or corporate manslaughter). At the scene of the incident a Scene Evidence Recovery Manager (SERM) may be appointed to oversee the recovery of the deceased and associated evidence for identification purposes by the Disaster Victim Identification (DVI) team which will include CSIs, police search advisors, trained police searchers and specialists as required (such as a forensic medical examiner) (ACPO/NPIA 2009).

The scene of the incident within the inner cordon is segmented into manageable zones to allow a line search (by trained police searchers), which will be supported by the CSI providing photography and video/digital recording at the scene, along with advice and guidance (and on occasions hands-on dealings) in relation to packaging of evidence and the identification through unique numbering and then recovering of the deceased or body parts. Other forensic specialists will also provide support to the line search such as a forensic medical examiner (who is required to certify death) and forensic science specialists as required (such as those with expertise in the examination of explosive devices). The methodical search and evidence recovery from the scene of the incident can take an enormous amount of time.

After the deceased have been recovered from the scene of the incident, then they should be taken initially to a temporary holding area for documentation to be completed before being transported to the mortuary or temporary mortuary, which would usually be established in a secure area near to the incident to deal with the large number of bodies to be processed. At the mortuary CSIs will also work with the mortuary DVI teams of police officers and specialists who will follow internationally recognized procedures for the recovery of evidence from the deceased, such as using radiography and the taking of dental impressions. The CSI will be involved in taking photographs of the deceased, such as the full body with and without their unique number, full head/facial, tattoos and scars and specific injuries, etc. identified by the forensic pathologist, along with the recovery of fingerprints, palm prints and footprints after the post-mortem has been completed (Interpol 2009b). In the USA, the Federal Disaster Mortuary Operational Response Teams (DMORT) can be utilized to perform the task of establishing and running such a temporary mortuary facility to deal with mass fatality incidents.

Dealing with such major incidents raises a host of health and safety issues, from the provision of the appropriate personal protective equipment to dealing with individual responses to the traumatic events. Specialist health and safety advice should always be sought. Those involved with the incident should be monitored and supported during and after the event.

10.2 Terrorist incidents

Chemical, biological, radiological and nuclear explosions

The law enforcement agencies and the general public throughout the world have become increasingly concerned about a terrorist attack using weapons that are chemical, biological, radiological or nuclear (CBRN) in nature. A number of CSIs across the UK and the USA have been trained and equipped to operate within a CBRN environment. They must be able to recover forensic evidence from such an incident involving CBRN weapons and also be able to decontaminate the packaged samples recovered.

An experienced CSI working in a large and busy UK police force states:

When dealing with terrorist incidents, you will have to search premises with great care. Chemicals and powders used to make devices may be secreted in kitchen cupboards, drawers, wardrobes, etc. Liquids are frequently mixed together to make dangerous cocktails.

(Anon., personal communication, 25 November 2009)

The CSI may also be involved in the recording and the recovery of samples from the location where the weapon was constructed. The equipment used to record photographically and recover such samples must also be carefully selected, as after use at a CBRN incident it must be decontaminated or destroyed. For example, it may be preferable to use an underwater camera at the scene as this can easily be decontaminated without damage and a tape recorder in a plastic bag will be easier to decontaminate than writing paper and pen.

Chemical and biological weapons have previously been used in terrorist attacks and the commission of crime. In 1993, terrorists bombed the World Trade Center in New York. The chemical sodium cyanide was incorporated into the bomb in the hope of creating sufficient cyanide gas to kill the occupants of the tower; fortunately the cyanide was destroyed in the explosion and consequent fire. The chemical sarin is many times more powerful than cyanide, with the ability to kill a human with one pinhead-size drop exposed to the skin. In March 1995, the Japanese 'Aum' cult mounted an attack on the Tokyo subway using sarin. Five cult members took 11 packages, each containing 600 grams of diluted sarin wrapped in polythene and nylon bags, onto the subway during the rush hour and then punctured the bags before making their escape and seeking the antidote (Tucker 2000). The vaporized sarin killed 12 and injured several thousand.

Biological weapons can be subdivided into four groups: bacteria (such as anthrax); viruses (such as smallpox); rickettsia (such as typhus), and toxins (such as ricin). In 2001, anthrax was used in a terror campaign, with a number of packages being sent through the US mail, resulting in the deaths of five people and the contamination of many others. There were also a large number of false alarms both in the USA and the UK with packages containing white powder. Such incidents cause massive disruption to normal everyday services. 'Survivors at a scene may be witnesses or offenders! They must [all] be evacuated as safely and as quickly as possible' (Anon., personal communication, 25 November 2009).

In 2001, an exercise was conducted in the USA simulating an attack with smallpox; the results of the exercise suggested a disaster with thousands of casualties. Micro-organisms, or rickettsia, such as typhus, can be transmitted by flea bites or larvae. In 1978, the toxin ricin was used to assassinate Georgi Markov, a Bulgarian journalist working in London. While waiting for a bus, Markov was stabbed in the leg with the tip of an umbrella. The umbrella had been tipped with a small pellet of ricin, which was injected into his leg and from which he later died.

Explosives

It is most likely that a CSI will come into contact with an improvised explosive device (IED) or a vehicle-borne explosive device which has either detonated or been made safe by military teams. The military across the United Kingdom operate Explosives Ordnance Disposal (EOD) teams who will attend scenes at the request of the police in order to deal with suspect explosive devices. Often the military will disrupt the package from a safe distance with a very high velocity jet of water. It is extremely unlikely that a CSI will come into contact with a live device.

High explosives (HEs) fall into three basic categories: military, commercial and home-made. Every HE is very powerful but relatively stable, requiring a strong force to initiate an explosion. High explosives range from the military Semtex formed into small blocks to home-made explosives packed into vehicles. Incendiary bombs are usually home-made and often unstable. Small incendiary devices have been used with some success in the past by the Animal Liberation Front.

Figure 10.1 The remains of parts of an explosive device after disruption

HE was used with dramatic effects in the 1988 bombing of Pan Am flight 103 over Lockerbie in Scotland. A single explosive charge packed into a radio/cassette player, within a bag and then within a metal baggage container in the hold of the Boeing 747 aircraft, detonated, causing the aircraft to disintegrate and fall from the sky. The crash resulted in the deaths of 259 people on the aircraft and 11 people on the ground with a consequent crime scene spread over several hundred square kilometres. Careful and painstaking search for and recovery of the evidence, which involved many agencies including CSIs, led to the eventual reconstruction of the events by the Air Accident Investigation Branch and forensic scientists, even identifying the exact location and make of radio/cassette player which contained the bomb.

An IED consists of five elements:

- the explosive charge;
- a means of detonating or igniting the bomb, such as a military detonator;
- a power supply, often in the form of batteries;
- a switch such as a watch;
- a container for the whole package which could be anything from a vehicle or suitcase to an envelope or audio cassette case.

These elements, which could also be in the form of a vehicle-borne IED, can be remotely detonated using electrical devices such as pagers or mobile telephones (Quirk et al. 2009).

If the IED has detonated or alternatively has been made safe by a military team, the area around the explosion/disruption should be subdivided into zones. The seat of the explosion, usually identified as a zone, is examined by a CSI and forensic scientist who together attempt to identify and recover what is left of the five elements that made up the explosive device. Specialist police teams search the other zones, which can extend hundreds of metres. As an experienced CSI describes:

> Each area is marked on a plan and numbered. A team of CSIs may be required to examine the zones, or they may work on their own, dependent on the scene and number of other scenes. It is important that each CSI understands their task and the zone that they will be examining. Evidence must be documented meticulously and recovered methodically.
>
> (Anon., personal communication, 25 November 2009)

Items recovered as part of the examination that are believed to have been in contact with explosives should be packaged in nylon bags which should then be sealed with sellotape and labelled. A specialist forensic science unit will later examine such items. The CSI should also consider the possibility of the presence of other more common forms of trace evidence such as hairs, fibres, fingerprints, and so on, which should be recovered and packaged in the normal way.

Explosive residue can easily be transferred from one person to another or one scene to another. The CSI must be extremely aware of the issues concerning cross-contamination and must take every step to avoid it such as:

- never dealing with both the suspect and the scene;
- wearing full protective clothing, such as one piece oversuit, gloves, overshoes, etc. while in the scene;
- using only new equipment while in the scene;
- thoroughly cleaning vehicles (especially tyres that may pick up minute pieces of debris) after leaving the scene;
- thoroughly showering on completion of the examination.

World Trade Center attacks, 11 September 2001

The attacks on the World Trade Center and the associated attacks on the Pentagon and in Pennsylvania by four large hijacked passenger aircraft led to the deaths of just under 3000 people. After being struck by the Boeing aircraft the two World Trade Center towers, each over 400 metres high (along with a smaller tower), all collapsed in a central location causing massive loss of life among both Trade Center workers and rescuers and making everyday items usually found within such a building unrecognizable. After the rescue phase had been completed and all fires extinguished, the many tons of debris was all transported from the scene of the incident to a nearby landfill site for methodical searching by teams which took a year to complete. Records from the Chief Medical Examiner (January 2009) in New York City show that of the 2752 people reported missing in the World Trade Center attacks, by using DNA, dental records, fingerprints, photography, personal viewings, X-rays, personal effects, tattoos and by other means 1626 victims have been identified but 9030 body remains recovered by methodical searching are still unidentified.

10.3 Mass murder

On 20 April 1999, two high school students, Eric Harris and Dylan Klebold, walked into Columbine High School, Jefferson County, Colorado, USA, armed with an array of weapons, intent on carrying out a planned mass murder. DeLisi (2002) suggests that the assailants intended to kill several hundred people using a plan which they had developed over a year. Over the next few hours the two Columbine High School students targeted and murdered 13 students and staff and injured many others with shots fired from a range of weapons (including a Tec 9 semi-automatic pistol, a rifle and sawn-off shotguns) and by using improvised explosive devices (home-made bombs) both within the high school and with a number planted outside to detonate during the attack (Sheriff, Jefferson County 2000). During the massacre the pair fired on the police and students running from the scene on numerous occasions; in response, law enforcement officers fired 140 × 9mm, shotgun, .45 and .223 calibre rounds (T.J. Griffin, personal communication, 16 October 2009). Eventually the inevitable siege was concluded by Klebold and Harris committing suicide.

The Sheriff of Jefferson County (2000) details how the extensive crime scene at Columbine High School was processed over a number of weeks by teams of investigators from a number of national law enforcement agencies, Sheriff's offices, Police Departments and the Colorado Bureau of Investigation who suggest that 'The processing of a mass crime scene is the same as any crime or suspected crime scene' (Griffin and Andrist 2000). A CSI, retired from the Colorado Bureau of Investigation and now working for Bevel, Gardner & Associates, involved with processing the crime scene commented:

> At Columbine, there were two types of scene teams. One type was what I'll call the already established teams. This included the FBI, the Bureau of Alcohol, Tobacco and Firearms (ATF), and the Denver Police Department (DPD). These teams were [staffed] by criteria established by their agency. These teams handled the exterior scenes (which included two of the student deceased victims and the parking lots with the shooters' vehicles with their bombs), some of the school interior, and the autopsies. The remaining five forensic teams were comprised of individuals from numerous law enforcement agencies ... (Multi-agency teams.) The duties common to all of these teams were at least one photographer, one person for evidence custody (not to be confused with evidence collection), someone drawing sketches and taking measurements, someone from the Colorado Bureau of Investigation (CBI), and a team leader.
>
> (T.J. Griffin, personal communication, 30 October 2009)

It is the scale and planning required to deal with such a mass murder crime scene that make these types of examination more challenging for the CSI. For example, investigations at the crime scene by the investigative teams led to in excess of 330 bullet and projectile holes being examined, 260 bomb and/or projectile fragments being recovered, along with 255 cartridge cases/shotgun cartridge cases, not to mention the 50 explosive-related items examined (Sheriff, Jefferson County, 2000). In the school library alone, a CSI team recovered 23 shotgun cartridges and 40 × 9mm cartridge cases (T.J. Griffin, personal communication, 16 October 2009).

> So how do you package a firearm to ensure chain of custody, prevent contamination of biological hazards associated with the firearm, have it in a sturdy container, and allow it to be viewed? The team took commercial firearm evidence boxes which were sturdy enough to hold the evidence, secured each firearm with plastic ties (or tie-downs), to secure the firearm in its box, tape a piece of clear, colorless plastic to the box lid and over the opening of the box, and place additional tape seals where appropriate.
>
> (T.J. Griffin, personal communication, 30 October 2009)

As when dealing with the leadership and management of the forensic examination of any major crime scene (see Chapter 11), after completing their involvement at the Columbine High School shooting, Griffin and Andrist (2000) reflected upon their experiences and provide some sound advice for dealing with an incident of mass murder. They suggest investigators should break down the processing of the crime scene into the manageable tasks and consider the needs in terms of:

- pre-planning for an event (such as agreeing mutual aid arrangements between law enforcement agencies);
- after being called out but before entering the scene (identification of roles and team membership);
- after the team has been formed (such as the standardization of roles and terminology);
- during the crime scene processing (such as assessing equipment needs continually);
- completion of the crime scene processing (such as reviewing processes used and identifying any omissions);
- conclusion (such as an evaluation of what worked and what could be done differently another time, plus the availability of critical incident debriefing).

10.4 Disaster

Indian Ocean tsunami, 26 December 2004

The tsunami of the 26 December 2004 was caused by an undersea earthquake in the Indian Ocean. Morgan et al. (2006) suggest that the final death toll from the tsunami was over 226,000 people with the largest numbers of dead from Indonesia (in excess of 165,000), but deaths from the tsunami were also reported from numerous countries around the Indian Ocean as far apart as Somalia, Sri Lanka and Malaysia. Foreigners within the region also became victims, for example, the Cabinet Office UK Resilience (2009) details how 10,000 UK nationals in the region were directly affected by the tsunami which included 151 deaths in the Maldives, Sri Lanka and Thailand.

With such an enormous death toll across such a large area, the international responses led to numerous agencies both from the host nations and those providing international assistance becoming involved in the humanitarian relief and eventual forensic identification of the deceased. Morgan et al. (2006) highlight that in Indonesia the military attempted to co-ordinate 42 different agencies, dealing with both body recovery and identification. Morgan et al. go on to detail how in Thailand a tsunami victim identification centre was established in partnership with Interpol and followed the Interpol DVI procedures to aid identification. Many nations, such as Australia, the UK and the USA, deployed forensic expertise (including CSIs) to assist with the identification process of the deceased.

Self-assessment questions

Answer the following questions without reference to the chapter:

1   What is the overriding responsibility of the emergency services at a major incident?

2   What is the suggested radius for an inner cordon when dealing with a vehicle-borne explosive device?

3   What does DVI stand for?

4   Which country operates a Federal DMORT service?

5   What does CBRN stand for?

6   What are the five elements that go together to constitute a bomb?

7   In what should items be packaged which are believed to have been in contact with explosives?

8   What techniques were used to identify victims of the World Trade Center attacks in 2001?

9   Approximately how many cartridge cases/shotgun cases were recovered from the Columbine High School shootings?

10 Approximately how many people are believed to have died in the Indian Ocean tsunami of 2004?

11 The leadership and management of the forensic examination of a major crime scene

11.1 Introduction

Along with the vital importance of forensic evidence to the investigative process, the forensic management of the investigation requires strong leadership and direction.

Police courses are run by several agencies in the United Kingdom on crime scene management. These have successfully raised common occupational standards.

11.2 Background to the forensic examination of a crime scene

When an incident is reported to the police via the telephone, the internet or in person, a police officer will attend to assess the incident in order to confirm what has happened. During the 12 months ending in March 2008, the Home Office (2008a) reported in the region of five million crimes being recorded by the 43 police forces in England and Wales; of these crimes, 12 per cent were burglaries, 19 per cent involved violence against a person and 1 per cent were recorded sexual offences. Kershaw et al. (2008) detail that of the recorded violent crime in 2007/2008 across England and Wales, there were 784 homicides and 620 attempted murders. The first police officer that attends the scene of a suspicious death (a death which is unexpected or cannot be explained) will make an assessment of what he or she has seen and then, after communicating their findings to other officers, decide what immediate action needs to be taken. In the case of an apparent suspicious death, which may have been suggested by the paramedics, doctors or the police themselves, the police officer would protect the scene by leaving the immediate location and ensuring that it is secure; this may be as simple as shutting the door. With assistance from other police officers, cordons would be established around the scene, usually using police barrier tape. Other police officers may be placed at strategic locations, such as entrances and exits, in order to ensure scene security. Usually two cordons are established: an inner cordon to preserve evidence, acting as a barrier against contamination taking place, and an outer cordon to keep the general public away. Access to the scene is limited to those who legitimately need to be there.

A record should be made of all individuals who enter the scene. The 'scene log' should include details of the person making the record, when individuals enter and exit the scene, who they are, why they are there and who gave them permission to be there, along with their signatures to avoid later confusion as to who was at the scene (ACPO 2000).

One of the first specialists to attend the scene of a suspicious death would be the CSI. When a major incident, such as a suspicious death (which may or may not turn out to be a case of homicide) is discovered, then a senior CSI will move from their daily role to be appointed as a crime scene manager (CSM) to lead the examination of the potential crime scene. The CSM needs to utilize his/her skills of leadership and management to lead a small team of CSIs to record and recover successfully all the available forensic evidence at the crime scene. Horswell (2000) suggests that the crime scene manager should have available a team of competent, and appropriately qualified investigators from a range of forensic disciplines. The type of murder scene examined could be a house which is easy for the police to secure, has limited access to possible suspects and has one deceased with apparently obvious signs of death. Such an incident occurred during January 2002 when a male victim was found stabbed to death in a house in the North of England. Alternatively, a crime scene could be mobile, with numerous suspects who may have had access to the crime scene in numerous countries, with the extended crime scene being extremely difficult to secure. Such a complex scene was uncovered with the discovery of 58 deceased Chinese nationals who had suffocated in the back of a lorry en route to Dover in the United Kingdom in 2000. Whichever the case, the crime scene investigation team, led by the CSM, is an extremely important element of a much larger team of individuals brought together to investigate the crime. It must always be borne in mind that the CSIs only get one chance to recover the evidence that may prove or disprove someone's involvement in an incident. This was demonstrated in the investigation into the murder of Stuart Lubbock by Essex police commencing in March 2001. Stuart Lubbock was found dead next to the swimming pool at the home of a television celebrity, and the subsequent investigation never identified the killer. An Independent Police Complaints Committee investigation into the conduct of the murder enquiry found that the crime scene had initially been thought to be only the swimming pool area and this was secured, but the whole house and swimming pool area were not cordoned and controlled by the police until later in the morning of the incident and evidence, such as a thermometer, was photographed but never seized (Hughes 2009).

The large team involved at such a major crime scene will vary according to the complexity and requirements of each investigation. The team could include specialists from the police service such as a senior investigating officer (SIO) who will take charge of the enquiry, crime scene investigators, police search advisers (POLSAs) and plan drawers. Forensic specialists from outside the police service could include a forensic medical examiner (FME) who would pronounce life extinct, a pathologist who will examine the body at the scene prior to transportation to a mortuary for a post-mortem examination and a forensic scientist, for their specialist knowledge and skills. Forensic scientists are available from a range of disciplines such as biology, chemistry, toxicology or firearms.

After initial examination of the crime scene other specialists may become part of the investigative team such as the Technical Support Unit (TSU) gathering covert intelligence and the family liaison officer (FLO) being the link between the family, victim and the police investigation.

The examination of a crime scene for forensic evidence is the responsibility of each police force's scientific support unit. A team of CSIs would attend each separate major crime scene led by a CSM. Crime scene managers have responsibility for establishing the extent of the crime scene and hence sometimes expansion of the cordon established by the first police officers attending the crime scene. Using their experience or information that has since come to light, CSMs may decide to extend the cordons to preserve further evidence such as tyre tracks or trails of blood. They must operationally lead and manage a team to conduct effectively all the scientific support aspects of the examination of the scene of the crime. Such aspects include the establishing of common approach paths (CAPs) as a point of entry and exit for all to use (this is usually the least likely route to have been taken by an offender and is often marked out using barrier tape), establishing a plan to ensure the scene is extensively recorded using video and photography, zoning the scene to facilitate the search for and recovery of physical forensic and fingerprint evidence, and the management of other specialists within the scene. On completion of the examination of the crime scene it is good practice for a CSM to conduct a 'walk through' of the scene with a fellow CSM as a measure of quality assurance and to ensure potential sources of evidence have not been overlooked. The CSM should also keep a policy log of decisions made in relation to the examination and why these decisions were made. CSMs should be experienced CSIs with in-depth knowledge of the principles and procedures required to recover forensic evidence effectively. It would be advantageous for the CSM to be both academically and vocationally qualified, holding at least a Diploma in Crime Scene Examination or related subject (ACPO/FSS 1996).

11.3 Leading the forensic examination of a major crime scene

Throughout history there are a number of leaders who stand out as being effective. From Napoleon leading his armies to conquer Europe to Churchill leading the nation to defend Europe, there has been a general belief that leaders were born rather than made. This is called the traits approach to leadership, where certain leaders demonstrate certain traits. Research suggests that successful leaders do have certain traits such as drive, a desire to lead and motivate others, honesty and integrity, self-confidence, the ability to evaluate information and relevant subject knowledge (Steers et al. 1996). But we all have traits that would be useful in a leader, such as being able to listen, communicate, make decisions and convince others.

The ability to lead and motivate a team to examine the scene of a crime effectively is of paramount importance. After all, there is only one chance to recover the invaluable evidence. An efficient crime scene manager must walk a tightrope when leading a team. This tightrope must have democratic traits at one extreme, allowing the team to exercise initiative, and autocratic traits at the other, when tasks need to be done, no matter how distasteful. If a CSM is to use the skills they most certainly possess in order to achieve

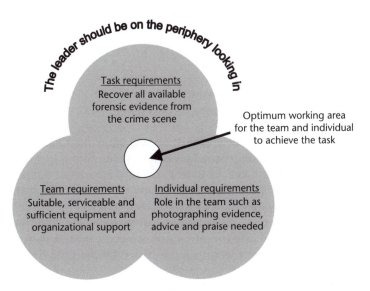

Figure 11.1   Role of the crime scene manager

Source: adapted from an idea of Adair (1984)

the most effective outcome, then two of the most useful models to be taught and understood are Adair's interaction of group needs and Maslow's hierarchy of needs.

The interaction of group needs leadership model (Adair 1984) allows the CSM to focus their attention in the area that is most required. Adair suggests that in order for the team to achieve its task, the leader must take on the responsibility of planning by gathering all available information and creating a plan for an achievable team task. The leader must then initiate the action by briefing, explaining, allocating tasks and setting standards for the team. As the task progresses, the leader must take control and move the team towards achieving its objective, constantly ensuring that standards are maintained and discussions are relevant. Throughout, the leader must ensure support for the team by encouraging, disciplining, developing team spirit and using appropriate humour to diffuse growing tension. Any new information must be passed on to the team and from the team to others with any changes to the plan being clarified. During the task, and once the task has been achieved by the team, the leader must evaluate performance and standards so lessons can be learned.

I would suggest that a good method for the CSM to use to evaluate team performance in order to learn lessons is to conduct a forensic after incident review (FAIR). Either on completion of a day's activities or on completion of the task, using a dry wipe board or flip chart either at the scene or back at the police station, the CSM should lead the team in an immediate concise debrief of the forensic process. The 'FAIR' should not be used to apportion blame but to answer four simple questions:

1   What did we set out to do?
2   What did we actually do?
3   How does this differ from our nominated task?
4   What lessons have we learnt for next time?

This effective method of timely evaluation will allow the CSM to ascertain whether or not the team understood his or her communication of the task. It will also allow all the individuals to feel as if they are part of the process of deciding how far they have gone in achieving the task and what they will require to do next time they have a similar task to complete.

By taking on the roles of leadership and management, the leader will ensure that the team is able to concentrate on achieving the task in hand. After the FAIR review the lessons learnt can be passed by the CSM to other colleagues and teams.

Using Maslow's model of the hierarchy of needs, the CSM must also take account of the motivational needs of individuals within their charge. Maslow's model of the hierarchy of needs is a series of building blocks that link together to create a pyramid, which helps to explain human motivation. At the base of the pyramid are physiological needs, such as food and shelter; the pyramid then grows to take account of an individual's need for safety, belonging to a group, and self-esteem. On reaching the top of the pyramid, an individual (or team) will self-actualize, reaching their full potential. Maslow suggested that an individual's needs influence the activities of that individual. For example, the hierarchy establishes the need for food and shelter as most fundamental. If the people are focusing on their hunger or the need to get out of the rain, they are not focusing on achieving the task for the team. The CSM can address both of these issues with regular meal breaks and the acquisition of a tent. At the top of the hierarchy is self-actualization: individuals are concerned with developing their unique potential, seeking tasks that are challenging and that will enable them to use their initiative (Steers et al. 1996). The CSM should be aiming to achieve this for the team, facilitated by training.

11.4 The body as the scene of the crime

At the scene of a murder, a body can provide a great deal of evidence that may lead to both the perpetrator and the cause of the death being discovered. Bodies should be treated, even if within a scene, as a separate and complete entity (and always with respect). Recovery of the body from the scene of the crime, which may take several days, should be carefully conducted, with evidence that may be lost in transportation being removed. Then the hands, feet and head should be covered in plastic bags to collect any further debris that may fall out of the hair or from under the nails. Next, the body is wrapped in clean plastic sheeting and a body bag (a comprehensive list for the processing of a body at the scene can be found in Appendix 11.1). Finally, the body should be escorted to the mortuary for a post-mortem examination to provide continuity of the evidence (in this case the body) for the court of law.

A Home Office forensic pathologist conducts the post-mortem examination in a suspicious death. Acting as an expert member of the investigative team, the forensic pathologist will conduct a visual examination of the whole body, often attending the scene to see the body *in situ*. As a CSI team member commented in relation to the 1999 Columbine High School Massacre (see Chapter 10) a team of forensic pathologists visited the crime scene.

> Five forensic pathologists performed the fifteen autopsies. Part of one day was set aside and all of these pathologists came to the school. This allowed each team and the pathologist who performed the autopsy for the deceased in that team's area to interact.
>
> (T.J. Griffin, personal communication, 30 October 2009)

At the mortuary, the forensic pathologist will note any injuries that are then photographed by the CSI. Lines of hypostasis (where the blood has settled in the body after death) may give an indication as to how the body was laid shortly after death. Rigor mortis, the locking of the muscles in the body after death, usually wears off after 24 to 36 hours, so may be used as a very rough guide as to the time of death (McLay 1990). The fall in body temperature, approximately 1.5° centigrade per hour (McLay 1990) may also assist in determining the time of death. However, factors such as the clothes worn by the victim, the outside air temperature or the immersion of the victim in water will affect such decisions on time of death. Also the possibility of contaminating the body and losing evidence while attempting to take, for example, a rectal temperature with a thermometer, should be considered by the investigative team before it goes ahead. In some cases specialist equipment, such as X-rays, may be used on the body to reveal bullets or bullet fragments, indicating a possible cause of death.

After a visual examination, the pathologist will take a number of samples from the exterior of the body, starting at the head and working down to the toes (a comprehensive list of samples taken can be found in Appendix 11.2). Samples such as hair and fingernails are recovered by the pathologist as his or her sample but are packaged by the CSI. Any samples to be taken for DNA analysis, such as splashes of an assailant's blood on a victim's body, should be recovered as soon as possible, as up to 50 per cent of mortuaries are likely to have other sources of DNA present on surfaces and instruments (Rutty et al. 2000). A blood sample is then taken by the pathologist from the femoral artery (in the thigh); this sample can later be examined for alcohol, drugs, etc. The pathologist then proceeds to cut through the chest and remove organs ranging from the lungs and heart to the stomach and kidneys for closer examination. For example, a closer examination may reveal a broken hyoid bone (found around the larynx) that could indicate that the deceased was strangled. Examination of the interior of the skull and the brain is usually left until examination of the body cavity has been completed. All of the organs are returned to the body, which is then made good. Throughout the process, a so-called 'dirty' CSI will be assisting the pathologist with the packaging and labelling of the forensic samples, with a second CSI taking the required photographs which can be anything from a bruise on the exterior of the body to a tear to an organ inside the body cavity.

Other specialists may assist the investigative team, depending on the circumstances of the incident. For example, a forensic odontologist may examine the teeth of an individual badly damaged in a fire in an attempt to provide identification, such as in the law enforcement siege and resultant fire that occurred in Waco, Texas, during 1993, leading to a number of deaths. A forensic archaeologist, a member of the Forensic Science Advisory Group (FSAG), may be able to locate buried remains. If a body has been attacked by insects after death, then the expertise of a forensic entomologist can assist the investigation by identifying insects and their stage of life cycle, helping to indicate the time and place of death. A forensic anthropologist could be used to examine bones recovered from a mass grave such as those found in Kosovo during 1999. Due to anatomical differences, examination of bones could determine gender of the deceased, for example, the pelvis of a male has an angle at its base of less than 90° whereas that of a female has an angle of more than 100° and has a smoother and lighter structure (Martini 2001).

The process of examining a body at a post-mortem requires constant close supervision and management. The CSM needs to organize the CSI team and the teams of experts to eliminate the possibility of evidence contamination and individual infection. This is achieved by ensuring that everyone is wearing the appropriate protective clothing and that procedures are meticulously enforced and documented. The CSM must also ensure that all the evidence is recovered in what can be a stressful and unnatural situation that may last many hours. New CSIs should be carefully monitored and supported throughout this process, ensuring that both their minds and hands are kept occupied. The body of the deceased should always be treated with respect.

11.5 A practical context

In order to explain the role of the CSM in a practical context I will use as an example a well-publicized scene that many can remember: the murders of Nicole Simpson and Ronald Goldman. In the early hours of the morning on 13 June 1994, both Nicole and Ronald were found dead outside a condominium in a Los Angeles neighbourhood. Nicole was found lying in a pool of blood. Later that night police went to the nearby home of Nicole Simpson's ex-husband O.J. Simpson. They could raise no one at the location, but on discovering what appeared to be blood on O.J.'s white Bronco car parked outside the premises, they climbed over the wall and found further blood leading up to the premises. They eventually raised O.J.'s houseguest and ascertained that O.J. had earlier flown from Los Angeles to Chicago on business. On looking around the grounds of O.J.'s premises police found a bloodstained brown leather glove that would eventually match a similar glove found at the murder scene (Nickell and Fischer 1999).

The bloodstained glove became a crucial piece of evidence. The blood on the glove was found to be consistent with that of the victims but the defence attacked the scientific evidence, suggesting that after the glove had been found, it had been contaminated and that the glove didn't fit O.J. The element of doubt had been raised with the jury and in 1995 O.J. Simpson was cleared of the murders of Simpson and Goldman.

Hypothetically, if this event had occurred in the United Kingdom, then steps would have been taken to ensure the effectiveness of the examination and maximum recovery of evidence. Initially the crime scenes would have been secured, cordoned and access controlled by the first police officers attending. Once called to the scenes the initial thoughts of the forensic investigators should be the possibility of cross-contamination between these varying crime scenes. It must be considered that there is the potential for minute traces of evidence, such as blood or fibres, to be transferred from one scene to another by an investigator's footwear or clothing, etc. The Simpson and Goldman murder scenario would have been broken down into five separate, but linked, scenes. The first scene would be where Simpson and Goldman were found, the second scene would be O.J.'s premises, the third would be the white Bronco car parked outside, the fourth and fifth would be the bodies at the post-mortem. Teams of CSIs each led by a CSM would be deployed to each of these separate scenes.

Using Adair's model, the CSM at each scene would focus on the task ahead, planning by deciding how many CSIs will be required, establishing the cordon around the extent of the evidence, and so on. The CSM would take into account the needs of the team in order to achieve the task of completing a systematic examination to recover all potential sources of physical and fingerprint evidence. For example, the team might require extra lighting, as they could be examining the scene during the hours of darkness, or should the team be allowed to rest and start in the morning? In consultation with the senior police investigating officer, the CSM would decide when to initiate the examination, as tired eyes can miss evidence. The CSM would set the expected standards for the scene such as the wearing of the correct protective clothing in order to protect the individual and prevent the likelihood of contamination. Such protective clothing would include new paper suits, overshoes, masks and gloves. Each individual wants to play a role in the investigation so each member of the forensic team would be allocated an area of responsibility ranging from scene photography to evidence recovery. As time progresses further into the morning, then the focus of the CSM may move from the task of processing the scene to the needs of the team such as rest periods or, using the ideas of Maslow, the needs of the individuals such as food and drink.

The CSM needs to be kept aware of developments in the enquiry that may alter the task for the team, and the team would be informed of any developments and changes to the plan. The recovery of a bloodstained glove at O.J. Simpson's premises should be communicated to the CSMs at the other scenes of the murder and the car, as this may well have led to such a glove being searched for at these locations. Once a task is completed, or the day's activities have ceased, then the CSM, using the FAIR method, should evaluate the team's performance with them and feed back to the team in a constructive manner. Lessons learnt should be communicated to other CSMs.

I am not suggesting that the process in the UK is perfect and things always go right, but an example of good practice occurred during the forensic investigation into the murder of Julie Paterson. In 1998, 32-year-old Julie Paterson disappeared from her home in County Durham. Several weeks after her disappearance a torso was found in a back lane in Darlington. A forensic investigation at the scene of this gruesome discovery involved a CSM leading a team of CSIs, a forensic scientist and a pathologist. Over a number of hours the team recovered forensic evidence, which led eventually to the identification of the torso as that of Julie Paterson. The house of the main suspect, David Harker, was raided by the police and examined by another team of CSIs led by a CSM; several other locations were also searched for the missing body parts. The whole complicated process was coordinated by a scientific support coordinator who was the adviser to the senior detective investigator. The teams were successful in their enquiries and in 1999 David Harker was found guilty of Julie's murder.

11.6 Coordinating the forensic examinations of major crime scenes

Standing away from the scenes, and often at the incident room established at a local police station, coordinating several linked crime scenes such as those in the O.J. Simpson or the Julie Paterson case, will be the Scientific Support Coordinator (SSC). In order to fulfil their role effectively, scientific support coordinators should possess appropriate knowledge and skills and demon-strate attributes of a good manager (ACPO/FSS 1996). A SSC needs to possess knowledge of the forensic processes involved during and subsequent to the examination of a crime scene, and know who has the other specialist skills that are required. Advice and guidance may be available to the investigative team via the National Crime and Operations Faculty (NCOF). Based at Bramshill in Hampshire, the staff of the NCOF have a good deal of experience in assisting with major investigations and also maintain a national database of experts available to assist in cases as wide-ranging as the sudden death of an infant, major disasters (calling on MDAT, Major Disaster Advisory Team) and the comparison of wood fragments. SSCs should not be involved at any of the crime scenes and therefore are not contaminated with evidence such as blood. They should act as a conduit through which information can flow between the scenes and to the investigative team and vice versa.

In complex enquiries a 'specialist advisor' (previously known as a 'Byford' scientist) can be appointed by the forensic science services, who may be used to assist the SSC and the investigative team by giving advice and guidance on forensic issues. Byford scientists were named after a report by Sir Lawrence Byford, who reported to the Home Office in the 1980s on the police enquiry into the Yorkshire Ripper cases and how a number of errors could be overcome. As an experienced senior forensic scientist, a specialist advisor will take a strategic view and assist in coordinating all forensic submissions to the forensic science provider. In England and Wales, laboratory forensic examinations are conducted on behalf of the police in the main by the Forensic Science Service but also by other forensic service providers such as LGC Forensics; the police service pay for these examinations. In Scotland and Northern Ireland, forensic examinations of items are conducted in laboratories more local to the forces.

The CSM leading the examination of O.J.'s white vehicle might have decided that in order to achieve the task the vehicle needed to be removed to covered premises in order to prevent any evidence, such as blood, being washed away by wet weather. This should be communicated to the SSC, who would be responsible for organizing the best means of recovery and storage premises for the vehicle. Any evidence later recovered from the vehicle would not automatically be forwarded to the forensic science provider, but, after consultation with specialists such as a Byford scientist, only the evidence most likely to advance the enquiry would be forwarded; the remaining evidence would be placed in secure and appropriate storage.

The team that examines the vehicle cannot be deployed to another related scene because of the risk of cross-contamination. In order to ensure this does not occur, the SSC would keep a simple matrix as to who has been to which scenes.

The SSC should also make use of Adair's leadership model by taking a strategic view. For example, the purpose of the task is to ensure that the maximum amount of forensic evidence is recovered from each of the scenes examined. Both the police detective teams and the CSI teams need to be kept informed of developments that may focus but not blinker their own work. The needs of the individuals, both the senior police investigating officer and the CSM, are that they get the best possible support and scientific advice.

Table 11.1 Example of a scene matrix

Crime scene investigator	Scene 1 Murder scene	Scene 2 House	Scene 3 Car
CSI J. Brown	X		
CSI I. Grey		X	
CSI J. White		X	
CSI R. Black	X		
CSI A. Green			X

11.7 The day-to-day running of the Scientific Support Department

In many police forces, at the outset of a major incident the scientific support manager (SSM) takes on the role of the scientific support coordinator (SSC).

If acting as the SSC, it is important for the SSM to ensure that the day-to-day work of the scientific support department examining the high levels of volume crime such as burglaries is not interrupted. Some police forces have over 150 operational CSIs spread across several divisions, making the reallocation of work achievable, but in smaller forces some have less than 20 CSIs; in this case resources are bound to be stretched to the limit. Using the process of 'mutual aid', forces can request assistance from other forces in times of crisis.

11.8 Conclusion

The leadership and management of any part of the forensic investigation of a major crime scene in the United Kingdom is a complex issue. It has several managerial tiers ranging from the crime scene investigators and crime scene managers who are operational at the scene to the scientific support coordinators and scientific support managers who are strategically facilitating both the investigation and the daily running of the crime scene investigation department. It is clear that the whole process requires strong leadership, creating a strong team, with good support and communication in both directions up and down the tiers. I believe that the use of formalized, comprehensive knowledge and skills training in leadership and management at a crime scene, supported by demonstration of occupational competence, has helped achieve these standards. Such knowledge and skills should be refreshed, updated and exercised on a regular basis. A thorough understanding of the demands of each other's roles within the forensic process will help in facilitating a successful crime scene examination. Once completed, the examination should be effectively evaluated, not in order to apportion blame but to learn lessons for the next time, which is sure to occur.

Appendix 11.1

Processes to be considered to maximize the recovery of evidence from a deceased body before a post-mortem examination

> *Task for a CSI
> ♥Task for pathologist

Before the body is moved

Photographs

- Required of the whole scene, including exterior location shots *
- Showing position of the body, usually taken using the technique of 'quartering' or 'sectioning' *
- Mid-range showing items in relation to the body, such as blood spatter *
- Close up showing the body and specific areas of interest, such as tied hands or bite marks *

Forensic evidence (the order in which this evidence is recovered may be dictated by circumstances)

- Tape areas of exposed skin for hairs and fibres of assailant *
- Swab for DNA evidence, such as saliva from obvious bite marks or LCN DNA *
- If the forensic pathologist attends, consider the recovery of evidence that may be damaged in transit to the mortuary such as:
    - clothing that shows specific blood spatter patterns * or ♥
    - a knife in the body ♥
- Intimate swabs for semen ♥
- Speculative swabs for firearms discharge residue (FDR) *
- Consider the use of plan drawers to locate the body exactly within the scene

Fingerprints

- Consider the use of intense light sources, such as QUASAR, to search for fingerprints on the body *

Package the body

- Place bags on hands, head and feet secured in place with adhesive tape *

- Cover the whole body in a sterile plastic sheet *
- Place the body in a body bag for removal from the scene *

After the body is moved
- Photograph where the body had been lying or sitting *
- Examine for any further forensic or fingerprint evidence that had been underneath the body *

This is not an exhaustive list and certain circumstances may require lateral thinking.

Appendix 11.2

Samples to be considered for recovery by the pathologist from a deceased body before, during and after a forensic post-mortem examination

*Task for a CSI
♥Task for pathologist

Before the body cavity is opened
- The body bag, plastic sheet and bags placed over the head, hands and feet must be retained * or ♥
- Photographs of both the front and back of the body clothed then unclothed *
- Photographs of any injuries, marks or other items of interest on the body *
- Swabs from any bite marks for saliva or other potential sources of DNA that have not been recovered at the crime scene *
- Evidence of interest, such as ropes used to tie hands ♥
- Combings taken from the hair on the head ♥
- Sample of head hair ♥
- Sample of eyebrow hair ♥
- Sample of facial hair (such as beard or moustache) ♥
- Swabs from the rear of the throat through the nasal passage ♥
- Swabs from the mouth ♥
- Sample of body hair ♥
- Nail clippings from fingers ♥
- Combings taken from the pubic hair ♥
- Sample of pubic hair ♥
- Swabs from the anus ♥
- Either penile swabs or vaginal swabs ♥
- Toenail clippings ♥
- Sample of blood from the femoral artery (in the thigh) ♥

After the body cavity has been opened
- Photographs as required by the forensic pathologist and investigative team *
- Sample of urine ♥
- Contents of stomach ♥
- Other biological evidential samples ♥

After the body cavity has been closed
- Finger and palm prints of deceased *
- Footprints of deceased *

This is not an exhaustive list and certain circumstances may require lateral thinking as to the samples to recover.

It should be remembered that the samples are recovered by the pathologist, packaged by the CSI and labelled as the pathologist's exhibit, with the CSI signing the continuity part of the CJA label to demonstrate that he or she has handled the sample.

Self-assessment questions

Answer the following questions without reference to the chapter:

1   At a major crime scene, which two types of cordon are put in place?

2   Who takes charge of a major police enquiry?

3   What percentage of the work of a CSI is volume crime?

4   Which non-police specialists may be involved in the investigation of a major crime scene?

5   The examination of which bone by a forensic pathologist may indicate that the victim has been strangled?

6   Which forensic specialist may examine teeth to assist in identifying a body?

7   Who coordinates the examination of several linked crime scenes?

8   What do the initials SSM stand for?

9   Who is available to provide advice and guidance during a major investigation and maintains a national database of expertise?

10   What would a 'specialist advisor' do during a major investigation?

12 Other sources of evidence for the crime scene investigator

12.1 Cyber crime

Computers and associated information technology (such as mobile telephones, PDAs and iPods) are being used in an increasing number of cyber crimes, ranging from simple credit card fraud and hackers breaking the security of national agencies to the grooming of young children for paedophile activities using internet chat rooms. As part of an ongoing enquiry a CSI may be requested to recover computer equipment for future forensic examination. Following one of the ACPO:7Safe (2007) guiding principles for dealing with electronic evidence, it is imperative that no action is taken by the police or CSI that changes information and data stored on the computer and other relevant devices. Access to the computer itself and stored information is only conducted by those who are competent to do so and are willing to explain their actions in a court of law. As Bryant (2008) describes, evidence located on computers, etc. is very fragile and just like traditional forensic physical evidence, it can easily be contaminated or lost. The presence of DNA and fingerprint evidence is possible on any IT equipment; however, care should be taken as the fingerprint powders in particular can damage the hardware and react adversely with electrical supplies.

Initially the CSI should photographically quarter (section) the room ensuring that everything within it is recorded. Then the computer and all of its peripheral devices should be photographed. If the computer is switched on and information is visible on the monitor, then this should also be photographed (see Chapter 3). An appropriately qualified computer forensic technician should then disable the computer. The CSI should not attempt to do this without specialist training, as it is possible that the owner of the computer has rigged the machine to delete all information if it is tampered with.

Once the computer has been shut down, the rear of the computer and peripheral devices should be photographed with the cables in place. Each cable, along with the port into which it is fitted, should be individually labelled before once again being photographed and then removed. This will allow the forensic computer specialist to recreate the exact set-up of the computer. All the computer hardware such as monitors, towers, keyboards and printers, etc., along with any other equipment such as computer disks or external hard drives, should be securely packaged and labelled in anti-static bags (often referred to as Faraday bags). Anti-static bags will help prevent the build-up of any static charge from electrical items, which may damage the information recorded on the computer or its related systems. Even so, care should also be taken by the CSI and other investigators not to place the recovered evidence against sources of static such as large speakers or other computers, or to damage the computer while being transported.

Once received by the forensic science provider, a computer specialist will 'ghost' the contents of the computer onto another system so that the original data are never tampered with or lost. Then, with careful examination, the use of specialist computer programs and patience, the forensic computer specialist can recover information from the system even if it has been deleted.

The forensic examination of mobile telephones can provide a host of information and evidence in relation to criminal activity. The forensic examination can range from the telephone, its own memory and SIM card memory to the network and receiving/transmitting stations used by a particular telephone. It is therefore imperative that mobile telephones are recovered for forensic examination. As a general rule ACPO:7Safe (2007) advise that mobile telephones should be switched off when found to prevent evidence being lost if a battery loses its charge and to prevent the telephone being remotely accessed to, for example, lock the mobile telephone. The phone should then be securely fastened in a box and then sealed in a tamper-evident bag. On occasions the police investigator may advise that the mobile telephone should be left on for monitoring, etc., in which case it should be kept charged. It may also be necessary to transport the telephone while switched on, in which case an anti-static (Faraday) bag may be used to shield it from any signals; however, this will greatly reduce the battery life as the phone searches for an appropriate network for a connection.

12.2 Dendrochronology

Dendrochronology is the study of the growth of tree rings, allowing the dating of events. The width of tree rings varies from year to year and if an assumption is made that similar climatic conditions have occurred for many years, then dates can be established.

If a piece of wood is left by an offender at a crime scene, it should be recovered by the CSI and placed in a solid container such as a box or plastic pot which should then be sealed and labelled. Once recovered, it can be compared against known samples to identify its origin. If wood is stolen from a building and subsequently recovered, it can be compared against a sample of the wood from where it was stolen to demonstrate that both wooden pieces came from the same origin.

The analysis of wood as a means of investigating crime was brought to the attention of the police and public during an investigation, initiated in 1932, into the disappearance of the young son of the famous aviator Charles Lindbergh. A piece of broken wood was left behind at the scene of the kidnapping. Samples of wood were later taken from the house of a suspect, which were matched to the wood recovered from the crime scene. Despite pleading his innocence, the wood and other evidence against him led to the conviction and execution of the suspect.

12.3 Diatoms

Diatoms are minute microscopic organisms that live in fresh water, such as streams and rivers, and marine water, but are not normally found in drinking water. With over 15,000 forms of diatoms (FSS 1998) and different forms found in locations close to each other, their microscopic examination can provide evidence of an individual having been in contact with the water in a particular location. This is particularly useful if an individual is believed to have entered the river in one particular location and been arrested at another – perhaps a suspect for a robbery being chased along a riverbank. In such a case the CSI should take a sample of the water, usually about 2 litres in a large sterile container, from the believed point of entry to the river and a similar sample from where the suspect has been arrested. Another CSI, or police officer, should seize the clothing of the robbery suspect and, after drying the clothing, package the items in separate paper sacks. Comparison by a forensic science specialist of the diatoms within these samples of water recovered by the CSI with diatoms recovered by the forensic scientist from the clothing may provide a match between the diatoms and hence evidence of the suspect having been in a particular location.

Diatoms can also be of use during the examination of samples recovered by a forensic pathologist during the post-mortem examination of a victim of drowning. If diatoms are found in the major organs, then it is likely that the victim was alive when he or she entered the water, whereas if diatoms are found only in the lungs, then it is likely that the victim was dead when he or she entered the water. This is because the live person's heart will still be pumping blood around the circulatory system, causing the movement of diatoms into the bloodstream.

12.4 Drugs

In the UK, drugs are classified under the Misuse of Drugs Act (1971) into the classes A, B and C. The drugs that fall into class 'A' are among the most dangerous; these include cocaine and derivative crack-cocaine, heroin, LSD and ecstasy. Any illegal drug, whatever its original classification, once prepared for injection would also be placed into the 'A' category. Magic mushrooms are now also classified under class 'A'.

Class 'B' drugs include amphetamines and, after a review, cannabis was reclassified from a class 'C' to a class 'B' drug in early 2009. Drugs that are perceived to be the least harmful are classified as 'C'; these include tranquillizers such as temazepam and anabolic steroids. Other substances that may be misused include 'sniffable' solvents, such as aerosols, and alcohol.

Operationally a CSI may come across a believed illegal substance, perhaps during the search of a house by a police team, and be asked to carry out a spot test to identify the presence of a particular drug. There are a number of different spot test kits available, the use of which requires specific training. One of the most widely used spot test kits in the UK is the Marquis test. A small quantity of the drug is added to the Marquis reagent. If heroin, morphine or amphetamines are present, then the reagent will turn an orange-brown or purple colour.

These types of field tests should be followed by toxicological analysis by a forensic scientist in a laboratory. It is also possible for the forensic toxicologist to analyse blood or urine samples for the presence of particular drugs. Although the blood sample should be taken from the suspect by a registered healthcare professional and the urine sample by a police officer, it is useful for the CSI to be aware of the packaging requirements. Both samples should be placed in separate 5ml glass phials containing fluoride oxalate, which is a preservative that will prevent the blood deteriorating but will still allow analysis for drugs. These phials should then be over-packaged with cotton wool and placed in a plastic pot to prevent breakage.

It is more likely that the CSI may come across paraphernalia used to prepare and administer drugs. This paraphernalia may provide intelligence that should be passed on to the investigating officer or may require recovering to provide evidence that a certain substance has been used and/or the container it was in was handled by a particular individual. This may be established by the presence of DNA, perhaps on a mouthpiece or fingerprints, perhaps around the canister. The CSI must therefore be aware of what to look for and how the items should be recovered. Great care must always be taken when handling any drugs or drugs paraphernalia as the drug or its residue can easily be ingested through the eyes, nose and mouth and may enter through the skin directly.

Alcohol

Alcohol should not be forgotten in relation to its effects as a drug. Any glass containers used to commit a crime, such as broken beer glasses, must be packaged in separate solid containers, such as cardboard boxes. These containers should then be over-packaged in polythene bags. It is unlikely that a CSI will become involved in the taking of a sample from a suspect for alcohol analysis, such as for an offence of drinking and driving. However, if advice is sought by an investigating police officer it is useful for the CSI to be aware of the correct packaging for either a urine or blood sample taken from the suspect. As with the examination of blood or urine for any other drug, the samples should be placed in 5ml glass phials containing fluoride oxalate. These phials should then be over-packaged with cotton wool and placed in a plastic pot to prevent breakage.

It is possible, however, that a CSI may be asked to recover glasses or bottles containing alcohol in order to demonstrate that a quantity has been drunk. In such a case the CSI should mark the level of the alcohol present directly onto the glass or bottle before decanting it into a glass container. Both items should then be forwarded to the forensic science provider.

Amphetamines

A synthetic drug used as a stimulant, amphetamines are also known as Billy, speed, uppers or whizz. They are sold in the form of powder, usually white or greyish white, or tablets. Other evidence available may be paper wraps or small plastic bags. Any drugs recovered should be securely packaged and labelled in tamper-evident bags. Paper wraps or plastic bags should all be packaged in separate solid containers, such as plastic pots or cardboard boxes. These containers should then be over-packaged in polythene bags.

Anabolic steroids

Anabolic steroids, also known as gear and roids, consist of many varied compounds that are usually taken orally or injected into muscles in order to improve physique. Tablets may be found or small glass phials from which injectable doses have been drawn. Any drugs recovered should be securely packaged and labelled in tamper-evident bags. The small glass phials should be packaged in separate solid containers, such as cardboard boxes. These containers should then be over-packaged in polythene bags.

Cannabis

Coming from a plant called *Cannabis sativa*, cannabis has numerous street names such as blow, dope, ganja, hash, marijuana, pot or shit. Cannabis is nearly always rolled with tobacco into cigarettes and smoked, although it can also be used in cooking. Evidence of cannabis use includes the butt ends of hand-rolled cigarettes and large cigarette papers. Any drugs recovered should be securely packaged and labelled in tamper-evident bags. Butt ends and cigarette papers should all be packaged in separate solid containers, such as plastic pots or cardboard boxes. These containers should then be over-packaged in polythene bags.

Cocaine and crack cocaine

Also referred to as snow or charlie, cocaine usually comes in the form of a white powder and is often sold in small folded paper wraps. Evidence of its use may be syringes, needles and tourniquet to aid injection, small mirrors on which the drug has been cut and razor blades used to cut the powder into lines before snorting with straws or tightly rolled bank notes. Occasionally users have tiny spoons used for snorting that are on chains to hang around their neck. Crack cocaine comes in rocks, which are heated, and the vapours inhaled. Evidence of crack cocaine use includes small plastic bags in which the rocks have been sold and drinks cans with holes in the side and a burnt underside that have been used to heat the crack and inhale the smoke.

Any drugs recovered should be securely packaged and labelled in tamper-evident bags. Paper wraps, syringes, mirrors, razor blades, straws, spoons, plastic bags and drinks cans should all be packaged in separate solid containers, such as plastic pots or cardboard boxes. These containers should then be over-packaged in polythene bags. Forensic science providers, due to the possibility of needle stick injuries, do not routinely examine needles. If the investigation requires the recovery of the syringe, such as at the scene of a murder, then the end of the needle should be carefully stuck into a cork before being packaged in a solid container and over-packaged in a polythene bag. The packaging must provide a clear warning of the presence of a sharp object.

Ecstasy

Ecstasy, or 'E', usually comes in the form of various coloured tablets or capsules containing a light brown powder. Any drugs recovered should be securely packaged and labelled in tamper-evident bags.

Heroin

Heroin is derived from the poppy. Found as either a white powder or a powder with a brown tinge, it has street names such as 'H', smack, gear or skag. Evidence of its use includes wraps of paper in which it has been supplied, syringes, needles, tourniquets and spoons or silver foil with the base burnt to aid inhalation or injection of the drug. Jif lemon juice, or an alternative form of citric acid, is squirted into the heroin on a spoon to aid injection and it may be drawn through cotton wool to remove impurities. Dealers may also have scales to measure out amounts.

Any drugs and cotton wool recovered should be securely packaged and labelled in tamper-evident bags. Paper wraps, syringes, spoons and silver foil, even the Jiff lemon, should all be packaged in separate solid containers, such as plastic pots or cardboard boxes. These containers should then be over-packaged in polythene bags.

LSD

Lysergic acid diethylamide (LSD) is an artificially created hallucinogenic drug that is usually sold impregnated into pieces of thick paper. The small tab of paper usually has printed on it an attractive motif such as dragons, penguins or the pink panther. Any drugs recovered should be handled with great care, as they can easily be absorbed through the skin. Drugs need to be securely packaged and labelled in tamper-evident bags.

Rohypnol

Rohypnol is more widely referred to as the 'date rape' drug; although its use has not been widely reported in the UK, it can be found in the form of a tablet. A number of other tranquillizers such as temazepam and alcohol can be similarly used. Rohypnol has a powerful hypnotic and sedative effect, reducing anxiety and affecting memory. Rohypnol can only be detected in blood up to 24 hours after the event and in the urine for several days (Pepper and Pepper 2009). Urine samples taken for toxicological examination should be placed in 5ml glass phials containing fluoride oxalate. These phials should then be over-packaged with cotton wool and placed in a plastic pot to prevent breakage. Any tablets discovered should be placed in a plastic pot to prevent crushing, then securely packaged and labelled in a tamper-evident bag.

Solvents

There are numerous solvents that are abused such as aerosols, butane gas, glue, lighter fluid, marker pens and paint thinners. Many of these solvents are sniffed either directly from the container or from a polythene bag. Evidence of abuse may be empty tubes or cans or polythene bags with traces of glue in them. People have died from the abuse of solvents. Any evidence of abuse should be packaged in separate solid containers, such as cardboard boxes. These containers should then be over-packaged in polythene bags.

Tranquillizers such as temazepam

Also known as eggs, jellies and rugby ball, temazepam comes in the form of various coloured tablets or capsules; it may also be injected. Any drugs recovered should be securely packaged and labelled in tamper-evident bags.

Clandestine laboratories and large-scale drug seizures

Lyman (2007) highlights the continued concern among both law enforcement agencies and the general public in relation to the apparent growth in the number of clandestine drugs laboratories. In addition, seizures of drugs have also continued to increase across the UK, for example, in 2008 SOCA (Serious Organised Crime Agency) seized 12.5 tonnes of cannabis resin worth in excess of £35 million aboard a ship docked in a UK port (SOCA 2009).

It is likely that a CSI will become involved in clandestine laboratories and seizures working with a police team to record the scene photographically and assist with the recovery of the drugs and the associated paraphernalia used for its manufacture and/or transportation (such as chemistry equipment). This would usually be in conjunction with a forensic toxicologist. A CSI may also be requested to attend the scene of cannabis cultivation which may have occurred on a relatively small domestic scale (such as in a loft) or an industrial scale (such as a warehouse). At such locations the CSI will once again be involved with recording the scene photographically, which should include the lighting system with close-up photographs of time switches showing when the lights would have been switched on to accelerate growth. These photographs can be particularly challenging due to the many reflective surfaces which are used by the cultivator to increase the light (heat and humidity) applied to the cannabis plants. The CSI will also assist with the recovery (and where possible fingerprinting) of the associated paraphernalia which can include plant pots, growing troughs and lamps. A representative sample of the cannabis plants, including their roots, should also be photographed and seized, then packaged in a brown paper sack to allow them to dry; these plants should then be transported to the forensic science provider as soon as possible.

As when dealing with any crime scene, the health and safety of the CSI and others around them is paramount, but this is particularly important when dealing with drugs when there is the risk of fire and explosion due to the chemicals used and produced as part of the drugs' manufacturing process, as well as the possibility of inhalation, ingestion, accidental injection or absorption of the drugs involved. Specialist forensic advice should always be sought before dealing with large-scale drug-related crime scenes.

12.5 Earprints

The first scientific investigations to identify ears positively can be traced back several hundred years. Alphonse Bertillon is known to have used measurements of the ear in his system of identification introduced in the 1880s (Lugt 2001).

As the CSI conducts an examination of the crime scene, he or she should always consider the location of earprints on surfaces that otherwise would not be examined. An example would be the centre of a painted door or kitchen window where the offender may have listened before breaking in. As the offender pushes his or her ear against the surface, sebaceous sweat may be deposited; the earprint may also be accompanied by impressions of the side of the head or cheek that may help locate it. These crime scene earprints can be recovered photographically if immediately visible or by using fingerprint powders during a sequential examination. There is currently no national database of earprints in the United Kingdom, so crime scene earprints should be retained until a suspect is located.

Once located, the suspect's ears should be copied by placing the head and ear against a rigid surface that can then also be examined with fingerprint powders and lifted. This should be repeated using several pressures to enable the crime scene mark to be compared with a similar earprint from the suspect. Once copied, all of the suspect's earprints and the crime scene earprint should be forwarded to a recognized expert in earprint comparison, who could be located either within a fingerprint bureau or a forensic science organization. The earprints will then be analysed, searching for particular features such as the helix at the top of the ear or lobule at the bottom, before they are compared for similarities and differences. Finally, the earprints are evaluated in an effort to decide on the likelihood that the suspect's earprints can be positively matched with those recovered from the crime scene (Lugt 2001).

In 1996, Dorothy Woods was murdered in her West Yorkshire home. An examination of the crime scene revealed an earprint on a window which was matched to Mark Dallagher who was later convicted of the murder. Dallagher professed his innocence and in 2002 the court of appeal found the conviction was unsafe, and then in 2004, Dallagher was cleared of the murder of Dorothy Woods when it was deemed that the uniqueness of the earprint evidence was in question, as the discipline of earprint comparison was still in its infancy and as such could not be conclusively linked to Dallagher.

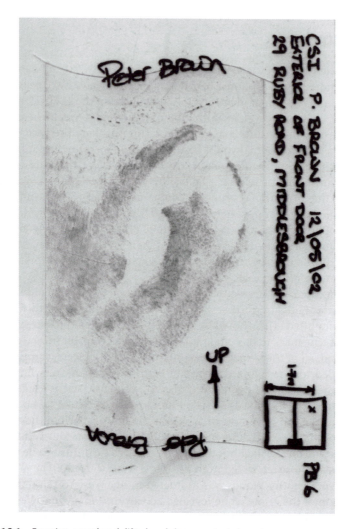

Figure 12.1 Earprint, powdered, lifted and documented at a crime scene

12.6 Entomology

Insects lay their eggs on the rotting flesh of the body of a deceased. The eggs soon mature and turn into larvae before in turn becoming adult insects such as beetles and flies. A study of the stage of growth of the larvae or insect by a forensic entomologist can indicate how long a body has been in a particular location.

In order to maximize the recovery of the entomological evidence, it would be advisable for a forensic entomologist to attend the crime scene to recover suitable samples. The police National Crime and Operations Faculty maintain a database of experts in many fields, including forensic entomology. If the entomologist cannot attend the scene, then the CSI should recover the best evidence possible.

It is better for the entomologist to see the actual larvae, flies, etc. than a photograph. So, after thoroughly photographing the scene, the CSI should use a fine net to capture a selection of flies and/or beetles on and around the body. These should be securely packaged and labelled in a suitable specimen jar. The ambient air temperature should be taken above the body and recorded before taking the temperature of any masses of larvae. A large selection of the larvae should be recovered from across the body and they should be fixed in a preservative, such as Isopropyl alcohol, within a screw-top pot or jar. The preservative is required so that the state of the larvae does not change before it is examined by the forensic expert. Then a second sample of the larvae should be collected and placed alive in a plastic pot that will become a rearing container; the pot should contain a suitable source of food, such as a small quantity of cat or dog food. Finally, after the body has been removed, a number of samples of the soil and flora should be recovered from where the body had been lying; these should then be packaged in solid containers, such as plastic pots or jars, and labelled. These samples will allow the forensic entomologist to recover insects from the fluids shed by the body during decomposition. The samples should be transported to the entomologist as soon as possible after collection.

12.7 Knots

Knots are a source of evidence that can easily be overlooked. The way the knot has been tied, perhaps during a robbery, to hold the hands of an injured party or to strangle a murder victim, may be unique in its construction. Knots tied in a similar way may be located at the suspect's premises.

If knots have been used, they should be comprehensively photographed both without scales and with two scales at right angles to each other placed parallel to the knot. The knot should be removed by cutting through the rope or twine away from the knot; the knot should not be loosened or undone. The knot should then be placed in a polythene bag; this will ensure that any other forms of evidence such as fibres or saliva are not lost. The knot should then be secured in a box, perhaps with sellotape, in order to preserve the knot along with any twists and turns in the rope or twine that are unique to the person who originally tied the knot. The box should then be sealed and labelled.

12.8 National Intelligence Model (NIM)

Not strictly a source of physical evidence but a use for the vast amounts of information collected by the CSI from a crime scene, such as fingerprints identifying an individual, or instrument marks linking crime scenes to the way a crime has been committed. The National Intelligence Model (NIM) is a process of information analysis which aims to share the intelligence generated across police forces and other law enforcement organizations regionally, nationally and internationally.

The NIM model uses what it terms assets focused on knowledge of policing and the law, systems of work, managing information gathering and handling, along with the importance of training and educating personnel as to their roles and responsibilities in relation to the NIM model (National Centre for Policing Excellence 2005). The aim is to compile intelligence products which can impact on policing at three levels. Level one focus on local issues such as crime and anti-social behaviour, level two deals with issues which affect the whole force or another force, level three focuses on serious and organized crime which often impacts nationally and internationally.

12.9 Plant material

Plant material such as flowers or leaves can provide good evidence to link a suspect to a scene. Samples of the whole flower or leaf should be recovered and kept in the state in which it was found at the crime scene. So if it was damp, the CSI should keep it damp in a polythene bag; if it was dry, the CSI should package the sample in a brown paper sack. Such samples will quickly rot so should be transported to the forensic science provider as soon as possible for examination by a botanist.

12.10 Smartwater and forensic property markers

There are a range of commercial products available to mark property forensically to deter an offender from stealing it and to identify the property (and sometimes the offender) if it is stolen and then later recovered by the police. Technology has moved on from using an ultraviolet pen to write a postcode on a product such as a computer or to stamp a postcode on to a bicycle with a punch, although these methods can still be seen. Examples of relatively new technologies are the SelectaDNA products which can be subdivided into an intruder spray which can be used to protect premises such as a petrol station, a grease which can be spread on outdoor surfaces which are at risk of theft (such as lead roof tiles) and a gel which can be spread on to interior surfaces (such as cash tills) that will transfer to an offender when they attempt to steal the product. RedDNA grease and gel can be used in similar circumstances. SelectaMark is a solution containing microdots containing unique codes which can be painted onto a surface of a consumer product (such as bicycle or computer). The microdots can be read using a simple and portable microscope and provide a unique code which is registered to the purchaser. Cypher Mark uniquely stains cash stolen from an ATM or from security staff transporting cash in the street while also staining the thief.

I will detail here the practices and procedures for dealing with Smartwater technology, but such practices are similar for similar products.

Smartwater

In the 1990s, a police officer, who was frustrated with his inability to identify property stolen in burglaries, turned to his brother, a chemist, to help find a solution. Out of this partnership 'Smartwater' was developed. Smartwater is a uniquely coded solution with over 1 billion combinations available. It is manufactured by the Forensic Science Service who maintain a central secure database of users. Smartwater can be deployed by a self-contained sprinkler system, uniquely marking someone who breaks into protected premises. This product has a trade name of Index. One of the first successes with a Smartwater Index installation came in the early 1990s. A local criminal was believed to be responsible for repeatedly burgling a supermarket in Durham City. Covertly a Smartwater unit was installed and two days later the super-market was once again burgled. The unit activated, spraying the offender with the Smartwater. The criminal was arrested several days later and when pre-sented with the evidence, he admitted committing the burglary and several others. An alternative product marketed by Smartwater is Tracer. This works by painting a small amount of the Tracer onto property before it is stolen, which uniquely identifies the item as belonging to an individual if it is later recovered. Tracer has been used by a number of crime reduction initiatives around the UK. A recent development, termed Smartwater Instant, is Tracer with the addition of millions of microdots containing a unique series of letters and numbers. Smartwater products, although centred on the United Kingdom, are also available worldwide.

Smartwater is only visible when viewed under ultraviolet light. Ultraviolet light is part of the electromagnetic spectrum. Red, orange, yellow, green, blue, indigo and violet light come together to provide visible light but this is only a small part of the electromagnetic spectrum. Beyond the visible spectrum at one end is infrared light, microwaves and radio waves; at the other end are ultraviolet light, X-rays and gamma rays. Ultraviolet light can be dangerous and the lights used to search for Smartwater operate on the edge of the visible/

Figure 12.2   Spray pattern of Smartwater Index viewed under ultraviolet light

ultraviolet spectrum under strict guidelines. They should therefore be used with caution and only after suitable training has been given.

If a Smartwater Index installation is activated, perhaps during a robbery or burglary, the person or people standing beneath or close to the unit will be sprayed with a solution that will quickly dry. Once dry, the Smartwater product will only be visible when viewed under ultraviolet light where it will provide either white/blue fluorescence or yellow/green fluorescence.

The CSI should methodically search the crime scene using ultraviolet light to identify any footwear marks or fingerprints, often located between where the unit has been activated and the point of exit. Once found, the location of all the footwear and fingerprints should be marked using chalk, then photographed.

Photographs should be taken with the minimum amount of ambient light, using colour film; the footwear and/or fingerprints should have scales and labels placed beside them before being illuminated with ultraviolet light. If possible, the surface with the footwear or fingerprint on should be recovered, but if this is not possible then the CSI should recover samples of the spray by swabbing a mark on a fixed surface, such as a concrete floor, with a well-diluted solution of Isopropyl alcohol. Alternatively, if the mark is on a moveable surface, such as a carpet, some of the fibres soaked in Smartwater should be cut out. The samples must be securely packaged in brown paper sacks and labelled. The canister which has been activated should also be recovered by the CSI as a control from where the Smartwater has originated.

Spray patterns may be visible on a suspect and should initially be videoed before individual areas are photographed, again using ultraviolet lights. It must be ensured that the ultraviolet lights are used in a safe manner and will not be harmful to the suspect or anyone else present. In order to recover samples of the spray pattern, areas of the skin that appear to have been in contact with Smartwater should be swabbed with a moistened swab of well-diluted Isopropyl alcohol. Clothing from the suspect that fluoresces should also be recovered, packaged, sealed and labelled. However, the CSI should remember that clothing could have been exchanged between individuals and that other substances, such as some washing powders, may also fluoresce.

Swabs and clothing from both the scene and the suspect should be forwarded to the Forensic Science Service or Smartwater's own laboratory for them to prove or disprove that the Smartwater on the swabs matches the unique solution code installed in the burgled premises.

Both Tracer and Smartwater Instant can be painted onto surfaces such as cars, motorbikes, JCBs and computers. The paint can only be seen using ultraviolet light where it will provide green/yellow fluorescence. Once recovered, the stolen property should be checked at the police station with an ultraviolet light, and any fluorescence should be photographed using colour film. The whole item, such as a small engine part or mobile telephone, should be submitted for forensic analysis or alternatively a small amount of the Tracer or Instant should be scraped away with a new scalpel blade into a screw-top pot. These samples should then be forwarded to Smartwater's own laboratory in order for them to demonstrate that the Tracer or Smartwater Instant in the pot matches the unique solution code supplied to a particular individual. Smartwater Instant has the added advantage that a police officer or CSI, correctly equipped with a magnifier, can immediately identify the owner of the property through a unique series of letters and numbers marked onto microdots seeded within the solution on the surface. Once the letter and number sequence has been recovered, then a 24-hour 365-day per year database of owners can be interrogated by the police via the Forensic Science Service.

Please note that the incorrect use of ultraviolet light can cause harm, so ensure that training is received before such light sources are used.

12.11 Sudden Unexpected Death in Infancy (SUDI)

If an infant up to one and a half year of age dies when he or she was previously deemed to be healthy, and any subsequent post-mortem fails to identify a cause of the death, this is categorized as Sudden Unexpected Death in Infancy (SUDI) (also referred to as Sudden Infant Death or Cot Death). A number of theories exist to explain SUDI, such as accidental suffocation, overheating and genetic predisposition, but such theories have yet to be proved.

A police team, including a CSI, will usually examine the scene of the sudden death of an infant. This examination is predominantly conducted in order to recover evidence to help establish how the child died; the joint investigation by the police, medical professionals and children's services is led by the police service on behalf of the coroner. There have, however, been occasions when evidence recovered from such examinations has revealed the malicious killing of a child.

The death of a child is bound to have traumatic effects on the parents and as such the CSI must act with tact, diplomacy and compassion. As soon as it is possible to do so tactfully after arriving at the scene, the CSI should record the room temperature where the child was found unconscious or dead.

Then the CSI should take a comprehensive series of photographs of the scene, although it is suggested that it is explained to the parents that this is routine and the terms such as 'suspicious death' and 'scene of crime' should not be used in order to reduce distress (Foundation for the Study of Infant Death 2005). These photographs should include the following:

- Sectioning (quartering) of the room where the child died. The CSI should consider that the room where the child died may not be where the child was first found unconscious; for example, he or she may have been moved by the parents or paramedics, so other rooms may also have to be photographed.
- The position of the child's body including any visible lines of hypostasis.
- Blood, vomit or staining on the child's face.
- The bed, cot or other surface, such as a sofa, on which the child was found.
- Items that the CSI may later remove such as bedding or nappies.

If the child's body is to be moved, then this should be done with dignity and respect. After removal of the child, it may be necessary for the CSI to recover a number of items for possible future examination. These items may include the following:

- Bedding including pillows. If dry (i.e. not urine-stained), these items should be securely packaged and labelled in separate brown paper bags; if wet, they should be allowed to dry naturally before packaging.

- Nappies and clothing which is soiled and not on the child. These items should be securely packaged and labelled in polythene bags; as soon as possible these items should be frozen. Nappies, etc. which are on the child should be recovered at the subsequent post-mortem examination.
- Samples of food and medication taken by the child. These should be securely packaged and labelled in sterile containers in separate polythene bags.
- Other items that may have contributed to the child's death, such as polythene bags or loose cords or cables around where the child was found. Such items should be securely packaged and labelled in separate polythene bags.

The CSI should also make comprehensive notes at the scene including the following:

- Any fires or air conditioners, which were switched on when he or she first arrived.
- Temperature settings on thermostats.
- The number of layers of bedding where the child was found.
- The widths of gaps where the child may have forced his or her head through, such as uprights on cots or between beds and walls.
- The presence of undesirable insects, such as cockroaches.

The investigation into the death of an infant is bound to be challenging for all involved so the CSI should not be afraid to ask for assistance and guidance.

Self-assessment questions

Answer the following questions without reference to the chapter:

1 In what should the CSI package computer hardware and software?

2 What is dendrochronology the study of?

3 How many forms of diatoms are there?

4 What type of evidence may the CSI find that indicates the use of heroin?

5 Where is the helix of the ear?

6 Can earprints be uniquely matched to prove an individual has committed a crime?

7 What does NIM stand for?

8 What kind of light must be used to see Smartwater?

9 What colours will Smartwater Index fluoresce?

10 What items should a CSI consider removing as evidence from the scene of a sudden unexpected death of an infant?

13 Health and safety at a crime scene

The modern CSI must operate under the Health and Safety at Work Act (1974), which covers both the physical and mental well-being of the CSI. At all times the CSI must take account of issues relating to his/her own health and safety and the health and safety of others who may be affected by his or her acts or omissions (Health and Safety at Work Act 1974). Failure to conform to health and safety legislation may lead to prosecution in a criminal court. There is also a good deal of subsequent legislation, advice and guidance including the Safe Working and the Prevention of Infection in the Mortuary and Post-Mortem Rooms (1991), Personal Protective Equipment at Work Regulations (1992), the Chemical (Hazard Information and Packaging for Supply) Regulations (1994), Carriage of Dangerous Goods (Classification, Packaging and Labelling) Regulations (1996), Management of Health and Safety at Work Regulations (1999), Control of Substances Hazardous to Health (COSHH) Regulations (2002), and Personal Protective Equipment Regulations (2002). Most law enforcement agencies have their own health and safety advisers who can be contacted for specific advice.

I will provide specific examples in relation to the health and safety requirements of recovering particular types of evidence as examples of good practice, but such advice may be superseded by legislation along with policy written by the CSI's employing agency.

13.1 Dealing with bodies and body fluids

Generally CSIs tend to operate in hazardous and demanding situations, often where body fluids, such as blood or semen, have been shed. These body fluids, along with other body materials, such as vomit and faeces, carry varying degrees of risk of infection to the CSI through blood-borne viruses. The main blood-borne viruses the CSI should be aware of are those which may lead to hepatitis or human immunodeficiency syndrome (HIV). The most likely cause of infection for a CSI is coming into direct contact with contaminated blood through splashes into the eyes, nose, mouth or an open cut, or an injury caused by a needle or broken surface such as glass or wood.

When handling small quantities of body fluids or related material, such as taking a swab at a crime scene, a CSI should as a minimum wear latex or nitrile gloves, goggles or safety spectacles and a facemask or respirator that covers both nose and mouth. The facemask or respirator must be of a type that has been specifically designed and approved to prevent ingestion of blood-borne viruses. If larger quantities of blood have been shed, then the CSI would also wear a disposable oversuit (most of which are resistant to splashes) and plastic overshoes in order to prevent the transfer of body fluids to his or her own clothing. If sharp surfaces are to be handled for evidence recovery, then 'slash-resistant' gloves must also be worn.

This type of clothing is termed personal protective equipment (PPE) and includes any items which are to be used or worn by the CSI to prevent injury or illness and should be made available by the employer. Disposable PPE, such as oversuits, may be retained as evidence to show that they were worn in the crime scene by the CSI, thus preventing the contamination of evidence from their own clothing. However, the retention of all disposable articles worn as PPE raises issues in relation to the amount and type of storage available. If there is any likelihood that the clothing has come into contact with body fluids, they should be disposed of through a clinical waste contract arranged by the law enforcement agency. The CSI must make a written note of the disposal of the items and the reason why they have been disposed. All CSIs would be strongly advised to consider inoculations against hepatitis A, B, and tuberculosis and also to receive a tetanus booster.

If dead bodies (or body parts) are to be handled, then full protective clothing including a facemask, goggles or safety spectacles, latex or nitrile gloves, disposable oversuit and overshoes must be worn. By their nature, bodies of deceased are usually heavy and cumbersome to move and when dealt with at a crime scene are often found in locations which themselves create additional hazards such as those present on slippery river banks, in burnt-out buildings or in confined spaces. Once a body is within a mortuary, health and safety risks still continue to be present (such as spilt blood or airborne tuberculosis). Mortuaries are divided into 'clean areas' free from risk of infection and the ideal location to assemble the CSI equipment that may be needed (such as camera and tripod) during the post-mortem examination, and a 'dirty area' within which all appropriate protective clothing must be worn. There is usually a transition zone between the areas where PPE can be donned/removed, equipment can be cleaned and hands thoroughly washed. As well as safe systems of work, safe materials to work with, and a safe working environment, employees should also receive appropriate instruction, training and supervision to enable them to perform their role. This may include, for example, manual handling

Figure 13.1 A CSI in full PPE recovering evidence at the scene of a crime

instruction and training for the moving of dead bodies, first aid training in case of personal injury and ad hoc supervision by the line manager.

Before seeking employment, the potential CSI or other forensic specialist needs to consider carefully that some of the sights he or she may see and probably have to touch can be both gruesome and barbaric, but the CSI still has to conduct his or her work efficiently. I can always remember attending my first 'real murder' post-mortem, that of the common law wife of a football player believed to have been shaken to death. Having been instructed to take a series of photographs of the post-mortem I was reluctant to stick scales on the body and body parts to illustrate the size of injuries. A colleague who was an experienced CSI mentored me, and because I had thought carefully about this part of the job and accepted that as a CSI I had to perform such tasks, I allowed myself to be supported by my colleague and took the necessary photographs. Afterwards I talked about the situation to my colleagues. Such support and subsequent critical incident debriefing can take the form, as in this case, of a discussion with colleagues or through a formalized number of sessions with a counsellor. Health and Safety is not just restricted to what occurs at the scene but also what occurs both before and after the event.

13.2 Dealing with sharps

When recovering samples of glass or other sharp objects for forensic analysis the CSI must wear 'slash-resistant' gloves and goggles to prevent injury to hands or eyes if the glass shatters or breaks.

If syringe needles are to be recovered as evidence, this must be risk assessed; it is then best to pick them up with a remote device such as a mechanical arm. Although little research exists into the occurrences of needlestick injuries to CSIs, research conducted in the late 1990s within a US Metropolitan Police Force found that there were a number of factors which affected the likelihood of police patrol officers receiving a needlestick injury, with one of the main risk factors reported being the lack of experience (Lorentz et al. 2000). Great care should be taken when packaging a needle for forensic analysis and consideration should be given to the necessity of presenting the needle as evidence. It may be that a photograph of the syringe needle *in situ* will suffice and the needle can then be placed in a 'sharps bin' for disposal.

13.3 Dealing with road traffic accidents and vehicles

The scene of a road traffic accident is extremely dangerous; high visibility clothing (PPE) must always be worn and great care needs to be taken when moving around the scene. Moving traffic will have been stopped by the police officers at the scene of a road traffic accident. Always be aware of drivers who pull out of side roads or driveways, or do not even see the police officer stopping traffic. For example, when setting up and looking through the viewfinder of a camera to take a photograph, always have someone watching behind for any hazards and moving traffic.

Other hazards that may be present within a vehicle at the scene of a road traffic accident include body fluids, glass, sharp metal edges, battery acid or spilt fuel that is liable to ignite and explode, as may gas-filled door struts. Airbags can also be a hazard and always ask if these have been disabled prior to entering a vehicle. Advice should always be sought from other emergency service personnel at the scene.

Hydrofluoric acid is a corrosive produced when certain synthetic rubbers are exposed to temperatures in excess of 400° Celsius. This is likely to be found in burnt-out vehicles. If such a vehicle is to be examined, then the CSI must always wear the appropriate PPE, including chemical-resistant goggles, gloves and a disposable oversuit. If skin is splashed with hydrofluoric acid, it needs to be immediately washed and a hydrofluoric acid neutralizing gel applied, then immediate medical attention must be sought.

If a stolen vehicle is to be examined for forensic evidence, the CSI must initially conduct a detailed visual examination of the scene. The CSI will check under door handles and seats for sharp objects, such as syringe needles and razor blades, which may have been left intentionally by the person stealing the car in order to cause injury to the police. Shattered window glass on seats can also cause injury. The CSI must put on the appropriate PPE to protect against sharps and should not sit on the seats.

13.4 Dealing with fire scenes

By its nature the scene of a fire, particularly one that has burnt through a whole building, can be an extremely dangerous place in which a CSI may be asked to search for and recover evidence. The CSI must always seek the advice of the fire service, who will advise if and when the scene is safe to enter. If the CSI is examining premises where the utility supplies, such as electricity and gas, may have been damaged and could cause electrocution or explosion, then he or she must ensure that they have been turned off by the appropriate agencies.

A CSI should never attend a fire scene alone as there are many hidden dangers such as falling debris, damaged asbestos, weakened floors and holes full of water. When entering such a scene the CSI should always wear the appropriate PPE. This must include a hard hat with the chin strap down, in order to provide protection against falling debris and falls into objects, goggles to protect the eyes, 'slash-resistant' gloves for searching through debris and boots with reinforced toe caps and puncture-resistant soles. The CSI must also wear a brightly coloured coverall to allow him or her to be seen by others while in the blackened building; one-piece paper suits should not be worn due to the constant possibility of sparks or warm embers igniting the paper. Reignition of the fire is also a possibility when excavating the seat of the fire as the heat and fuel are still present. As the CSI begins to dig down, such a digging action reintroduces oxygen and the fire triangle can once again form.

It is also important that the CSI has a good source of light, either from those that have been rigged up within the building by the fire service or the police, or brought by the CSI to the scene. It is extremely dangerous to examine the scene of a fire during the hours of darkness, as there are so many hidden dangers.

While within the damaged building the CSI must always be aware of the constant risk of structural collapse. Walls must not be leant against as they may collapse due to the heat damage to the mortar. Upper floors need to be checked underneath by looking at the ceiling of the room below to see whether the fire has damaged the floorboards before they are walked on. Even then it is advisable only to walk where the joists are, as these are the strongest areas of the floors; never rely on the structural stability of stairs. The health and safety considerations outlined above also apply to bodies and sharps found within fire scenes. The key to the safe examination of the scene of a fire is always to check first.

13.5 Dealing with drugs and clandestine drug laboratories

When dealing with drugs of any type, a CSI must be aware that the drug or its residue can easily be ingested through the eyes, nose and mouth and may enter the skin directly through absorption. Care should be taken to wear the appropriate PPE such as latex or nitrile gloves, goggles or safety spectacles, and an appropriate facemask or respirator. Risks may also be present due to the presence of sharps such as needles (see Section 13.2).

I would agree with Cameron (2002) that the investigation of clandestine drug laboratories brings with it a host of dangers while dealing with numerous quantities of chemicals and the associated physical resources to manufacture the illegal drugs. Such dangers not only include the possibility of absorption, inhalation or ingestion of the drugs but also the possibility of fire or explosion. The perceived hazards are so great that Federal Regulations across the USA recommend that those who respond to such laboratories in the USA receive between 24 hours and 40 hours of training in relation to the hazards present (Cameron 2002). Large-scale cannabis cultivation and the associated storage of the cannabis can specifically lead to the growth of a mould called aspergillus as the vegetation decays (particularly in warm and humid conditions). Although most people are immune to this mould, it is possible for those who have compromised immune systems to ingest the mould leading to infection. Advice should always be sought from specialist health and safety advisors and forensic toxicologists before entering clandestine laboratories or large-scale cannabis cultivation.

13.6 Fingerprint powders

There are three main considerations when handling fingerprint powders. First, the incorrect concentration of the dust in the atmosphere plus a source of ignition could lead to an explosion. As such, all powders should be correctly labelled as flammable. Second, the powders can cause irritation to the skin, so it may be prudent to wear cotton gloves when powdering. Finally, in a confined atmosphere, such as a car, the concentration of fingerprint dust is bound to be high so it is advisable to wear an appropriate facemask or respirator.

13.7 Violence at the crime scene

A CSI will often work alone, sometimes at night in all kinds of areas, and may therefore be at risk of becoming a victim of verbal or physical attack. Although no national data are available as to the number of assaults on CSIs, during the financial year 2007/2008 over 11,300 police officers across England and Wales reported assaults against them while on duty and there was one fatality (Home Office 2008a). Whoever controls the CSIs, sending them from crime scene to crime scene, must constantly be aware of the location of each investigator. CSIs will always have a means of contacting their controller in order to ask for assistance, perhaps with a personal airwaves radio or mobile telephone. They should never confront a potentially aggressive situation; instead they must retire from the scene and seek advice and guidance. Effective training, especially using role-play and experience of using the ACPO conflict management model, can help develop reasoning and communication skills that may help a CSI to identify and possibly diffuse potentially violent situations. Some law enforcement agencies have provided personal safety training (self-defence) for their CSIs and even issued protective body armour, but I would suggest that such personal safety training should only to be used as a last line of defence.

13.8 Risk assessment

A risk assessment is a step-by-step consideration of the risk presented by a situation and of how this can be reduced to a reasonable level.

Every crime scene attended by a CSI needs to be risk assessed. This may be in a formal manner such as at the scene of a suspicious fire or sudden death, or in a more informal manner such as at a burglary or theft from motor vehicle. Many police forces have produced generic risk assessments for building types that can easily be reviewed and adapted for specific scenes.

When conducting risk assessments, there are five steps to be followed (HSE 1996). Initially the CSI or other suitably trained person must look for potential hazards that may cause him or her or other people harm (for example, at the scene of a fatal stabbing, body fluids may be leaking from the deceased onto floorboards). Next the CSI needs to consider who might be harmed when entering this murder scene, such as the pathologist, forensic scientist or the CSI him/herself. The CSI must then evaluate the risk of injury or illness arising from the hazard and as a result decide whether further precautions are necessary. The CSI must then decide how he or she can best control the risk sufficiently so that the scene can be examined. In this case the obvious risks are from blood-borne viruses and the knife, so everyone who enters the scene must wear the appropriate PPE. However, the most common causes of injuries at work are slips, trips and falls. When conducting a risk assessment of such a crime scene, it would be prudent for the CSI to consider slips, trips and falls both under normal working conditions and when wearing personal protective equipment such as overshoes. It is likely that blood congealed on the floor may make it slippery, so the CSI may consider using stepping plates, most of which have non-slip surfaces on the top and feet, to enable the examination team to reach the deceased. The CSI acting as the risk assessor must always record their observations and decisions for reference in the future. Finally, the CSI must review any other relevant risk assessments in view of their findings at this particular scene.

Appendix 13.1

Suggested minimum PPE for a CSI

- Hard hat with a chin strap
- Safety spectacles or goggles
- Facemask or respirator designed to protect against blood-borne viruses and dust
- One-piece brightly coloured coverall (preferably flame-resistant)
- Slash-resistant gloves
- Chemical-resistant gloves
- Cotton gloves
- Boots with reinforced toe caps, slip- and puncture-resistant soles
- High visibility tabard
- Waterproof jacket with hood
- Waterproof trousers

Consumable items (i.e. will require replacing after use) constituting PPE

- Disposable oversuits resistant to liquid splashes
- Latex or nitrile gloves
- Plastic overshoes
- Facemasks or parts of respirator may require regular replacing
- Disinfectant wipes (for hands and equipment)
- Hydrofluoric acid gel
- Biological hazard bags
- Sharps bin

Self-assessment questions

Answer the following questions without reference to the chapter:

1   Under the regulations of which Act must a CSI work?

2   What type of material recovered by a CSI may contain blood-borne viruses?

3   What is the most likely cause of infection from blood-borne viruses?

4   What does PPE stand for?

5   What PPE should be worn when handling sharps such as glass?

6   What is produced when synthetic rubber is exposed to high temperatures?

7   What PPE should a CSI wear when examining the scene of a fire?

8   What should a CSI always check before going upstairs in a burnt-out building?

9   What dangers are present for a CSI when attending a clandestine drugs laboratory?

10   What are the three most common causes of injuries at work?

14 The Criminal Law Courts in the United Kingdom

Operational crime scene investigators are very likely to have to give evidence to a court during their career. I have given evidence in Crown, magistrates', and sheriff courts on a number of occasions on the photographic, forensic and fingerprint evidence I had recovered from crime scenes, ranging from murders and assaults to burglaries and theft. Whether newly appointed or with numerous years of experience, a CSI should always come across to the court as a professional and competent witness.

14.1 The role and structure of the Criminal Law Courts in England and Wales

There are numerous sources of law such as those passed by the European Community, legislation passed by Parliament, creation of the law by judicial decisions in certain cases and ancient custom (Slapper and Kelly 1997). The roles of the criminal courts that enforce these laws can broadly be subdivided into three categories. They decide whether an offence has been committed; whether the person that has been brought before the court committed the offence; and decide on a suitable punishment for the offender. In criminal trials the Crown usually brings the prosecution against an individual on behalf of the public, hence the case is often referred to as Regina versus the name of the accused (i.e. *R.* v. *Smith*). The courts across England and Wales use an adversarial system where evidence is gathered, witnesses asked to attend and arguments are presented by legal representatives from the parties involved in the case to the court officials, as opposed to the inquisitorial system (used, for example, in France) where the court officials become actively involved in the gathering of evidence such as calling and questioning witnesses.

The courts themselves are administered by Her Majesty's Court Service (HMCS) and divided into a hierarchical system. The highest court, against whose rulings on Human Rights there is no right of appeal, is the European

Court of Justice which is based in Luxembourg. The highest court in England and Wales is the Supreme Court. The Supreme Court, established in 2009, hears appeals which would previously have been heard by the House of Lords; these are often on points of law or on issues that are deemed by the lower courts to be of importance to the general public. The criminal division of the Court of Appeal hears appeals only on points of law or unsafe decisions by other courts. The Queen's Bench Division can hear appeals from lower courts and hold trials. However, the main courts a CSI is likely to give evidence in are the Crown Courts, magistrates' courts, youth courts or coroners' courts.

14.2 Crown Courts

There are 77 main Crown Courts based in towns and cities throughout England and Wales. During the financial year of 2007/2008 these Crown Courts dealt with 120,000 criminal cases (Her Majesty's Court Service 2008). The Crown Courts deal with 'indictable' offences (generally known as a felony in the USA) and are subdivided into three tiers. The highest or first tier Crown Courts hear both civil and the most serious criminal cases such as murder or rape. The second and third tiers hear only the so-called 'less serious' criminal cases and have no civil jurisdiction. Crown Courts may also be used for sentencing when cases have been referred to them by the magistrates' courts and are also used to try 'either way' offences (such as theft or burglary) which are those cases which can go to trial in either magistrates' or Crown Courts but the defendant has elected to have their case heard in the Crown Court. Perhaps the most famous Crown Court is the Central Criminal Court (the Old Bailey) in London.

When dealing with serious cases, the Crown Court is presided over by a high court judge and a jury. Less serious cases may be dealt with by a circuit judge or Recorder assisted by a jury. The jury consists of 12 men and women aged between 18 and 70 taken at random from the local electoral register. Barristers under instruction usually conduct the prosecution for the case by the Crown Prosecution Service. Other agencies, such as the Health and Safety Executive, may also instruct barristers to conduct a criminal prosecution on their behalf. A barrister acting for the defence defends the accused; he or she may be privately funded or paid for by the government (referred to as criminal legal aid).

The jury decides whether the defendant is guilty on the evidence presented to them within the court; the judge then decides on the sentence. The sentences imposed by the Crown Court can be up to the maximum established by law for a particular offence, such as the mandatory life imprisonment for anyone over the age of 21 who is convicted of murder and a maximum of 14 years' imprisonment for burglary. The court can also decide to suspend a sentence, order service to be performed within the community, impose curfew orders or probation, recommend drug treatment programmes, or fine an individual. Although capital punishment for murder was abolished in 1965, until relatively recently it was still retained for treason; the Crime and Disorder Act (1998) finally removed capital punishment from the list of punishments available to the court.

14.3 Magistrates' courts

Over 700 magistrates' courts in England and Wales deal with the majority of all criminal cases, for example, in the financial year 2007/08 magistrates' courts heard in the region of 2.2 million criminal cases (Her Majesty's Court Service 2008). These are often the less serious 'summary' offences (generally known as misdemeanours in the USA) such as minor assaults or traffic violations, and such offences will not be tried by a jury. Magistrates' courts also deal with committals for more serious offences, deciding whether there is enough evidence to send the accused to Crown Court for trial. In most cases a magistrates' court will consist of three justices of the peace (JPs). They are not professional judges or lawyers, have no experience of working for the criminal justice system and represent the local community. They are expected to be at the court for several days a month but are unpaid, although they can claim expenses, and retire at 70. Although they receive training, if necessary legal advice can be sought from the clerk to the court, who is a legal professional. A district judge (previously known as stipendiary magistrates) can also hold the magistrates' court. District judges are legally qualified solicitors or barristers who are paid to perform the role. They sit alone on the bench but are also aided by the clerk to the court. Lawyers represent both the prosecution and the defence of the case.

Although the magistrates' courts hear the majority of offences, they are limited in the punishments they can give to six months' imprisonment and/or a £5000 fine per offence or up to a maximum of 12 months' imprisonment for consecutive offences. Magistrates can also refer defendants to a Crown Court for sentencing if he or she has opted for a trial at a magistrates' court for an 'either way' offence. The defendant may appeal to the Crown Court on the verdict.

Youth courts are also a type of magistrates' court empowered to hear the cases of children and young persons aged between 10 and 17 years. The court is held in private by specially appointed and trained JPs, with the court consisting of at least one female and one male JP. There are offences that may require the young defendant's case to be heard in magistrates' rather than youth court, such as a serious assault or if they were being tried in conjunction with an adult; however, the defendant must still appear before the specially trained youth court for sentencing.

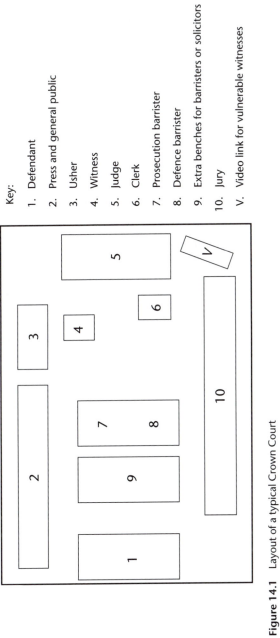

Figure 14.1 Layout of a typical Crown Court

Key:

1. Defendant
2. Press and general public
3. Usher
4. Witness
5. Judge
6. Clerk
7. Prosecution barrister
8. Defence barrister
9. Extra benches for barristers or solicitors
10. Jury
V. Video link for vulnerable witnesses

14.4 Coroners' courts

Coroners are usually barristers, lawyers or doctors who have been in office for at least five years. Although coroners hold a Crown judicial office, they are appointed and paid for by their local authority. The main duties of the approximately 146 coroners in England and Wales (Levine and Pyke 1999), who are spread across approximately 110 districts, are to conduct inquests (inquiries) into deaths that were violent and unnatural, sudden with the cause unknown, or which occurred while the individual was in custody. The inquest is held to establish the identity of an individual, when they died, how they died and where they died, along with establishing a cause of death. This is achieved using a range of evidence types including witness testimony, post-mortem examination results and photographs. The coroner him/herself will view the evidence put before them, and question any witnesses. Other interested parties may also view the evidence and ask pertinent questions of witnesses. There are no legal speeches to the jury and the court is held in public. Verdicts of a coroners' court can include death by natural causes, unlawful or lawful killings or an open verdict (where there is insufficient evidence to come to a conclusion). This may well influence a decision for further criminal investigation. The inquest may be held with a jury of between seven and eleven individuals selected at random from the electoral register, although there are proposals to reduce this number. Coroners are also assisted by coroners' officers who are the link between the coroner, family, police, forensic medical examiner, pathologist and other individuals involved with the death. Coroners' officers are both police and civilian employees who have the aptitude, experience and training to deal with the many issues which exist around dealing with the deceased and their relatives on a daily basis.

If the deceased has already been buried, then a coroner may request an exhumation of the body for the purposes of a police enquiry into the death. This was the case with many of the murder victims of the serial killer Harold Shipman. Shipman had been a general practitioner in Manchester for over 20 years and had been registered with the General Medical Council since 1970, working in Pontefract, Todmorden and Durham (Chief Medical Officer 2001). In 1998, colleagues raised concern over the number of deaths among Shipman's patients and he was arrested by police. The police investigated 192 of the deaths and in January 2000 Shipman was found guilty of murdering 15 of his patients and the police believe that murder may have been possible in a number of the other deaths but evidence was insufficient (Chief Medical Officer 2001). A number of the deceased had been buried; others had been cremated, so the police had to gain the permission of the coroner in order to exhume the buried bodies in an attempt to gather evidence and establish the cause of death.

Like the magistrates' courts, the coroners' courts are sited in major towns and cities. A coroner will usually hold an inquest in the district in which the individual died or in the district where a body, perhaps on an aircraft or ship, entered the country. The coroners' court does not aim to apportion blame.

14.5 The Crown Prosecution Service (CPS)

This is fully discussed in Chapter 15 (Organizations related to crime scene investigation).

14.6 The court systems in Scotland and Northern Ireland

Apart from the European Court of Justice and the House of Lords, Scotland maintains its own supreme courts which are centrally managed by the Scottish Court Service, which as a result of the Judiciary and Courts (Scotland) Act 2008 will be governed by a board which is chaired by the Lord President (Scottish Court Service 2009). The Scottish Court Service is in turn answerable to the Scottish Parliament that has its seat in Edinburgh.

The High Court of Justiciary hears criminal appeals and the most serious of criminal cases such as murder and rape (the type of offences dealt with in first tier Crown Courts across England and Wales). Although based in Edinburgh, the High Court of Justiciary holds trials in towns and cities across Scotland. A judge and a jury, which consists of 15 people selected at random from the electoral register, hear these trials.

The Justice of the Peace (JP) Courts in Scotland deal with offences such as traffic violations (the same type of offences dealt with in magistrates' courts across England and Wales). The sheriff's court deals with some criminal cases, such as theft or assault (again similar types of offences to those dealt with across magistrates' courts in England and Wales).

For administrative purposes Scotland is divided into six regions termed 'Sheriffdoms', containing a total of 49 sheriff's courts (Scottish Court Service 2009). These courts deal with a large proportion of the criminal offences. Presiding over the court is the Sheriff, a full-time judge who sometimes sits alone or in the more serious cases is assisted by a jury of 15 men and women. There are no youth courts in Scotland. As there are also no coroners in Scotland, investigations into suspicious deaths are conducted by the Procurator Fiscal and the sheriff's court.

The Northern Ireland Court Service, established in 1979 by the Judicature (Northern Ireland) Act 1978, manages the court system across Northern Ireland. The court system mirrors that found across England and Wales with the exception that those cases to be heard before the Court of Appeal or High

Courts are initially heard in the Royal Courts of Justice in Belfast where three of the most senior judges in Northern Ireland will hear the appeal. If an issue cannot be resolved in the Northern Ireland Court of Appeal, then this may be taken to the House of Lords for appeal. There are seven Coroners' districts across Northern Ireland (Northern Ireland Court Service 2003)

14.7 Military courts

The Armed Forces Act (2006) has superseded the Army and Air Force Acts (1955) and Naval Discipline Act (1957) making numerous amendments to military law aiming to synchronize process and practices across the Army, the Royal Navy and the Royal Air Force. Summary offences can still be dealt with solely by a military unit's commanding officer, who in effect acts as a magistrate, and can impose punishments such as official reprimands and fines. If the accused wishes to appeal against the finding of a summary judgment by their commanding officer, then he or she may appeal to the tri-service Summary Appeal Court (Crown 2006).

Individuals charged with more serious offences are heard at a court martial which, as a result of the 2006 Act, have been established as standing courts as opposed to being put together as and when required. Court martials are very similar to civilian Crown Courts except that legal representation comes from the military legal branch and the court is presided over by a civilian judge advocate who is assisted by three to five commissioned officers or warrant officers, however, there is no jury. Court martials are subdivided into two categories: a district court martial hears more routine offences (such as disrespectful behaviour) and can impose sentences of up to two years' imprisonment; and a general court martial deals with more serious offences (such as burglary or assisting an enemy) and can impose life imprisonment. Appeals against a sentence can be made to the Court Martial Appeal Court.

In some circumstances, such as the offences committed by members of the reserve forces, an offence may be dealt with by the civilian criminal courts. Service Civilian Courts (with similar jurisdiction to magistrates' courts) also exist within the military to deal with offences committed by civilian staff away from the British Isles, such as those working on military establishments overseas, who commit offences contrary to the military discipline under which they were working at the time.

14.8 Admissibility of forensic evidence in a court of law

In the UK there is currently a general acceptance of forensic evidence in a court of law. This is not the case in the USA. Since 1923, evidence presented by scientific experts, such as forensic scientists, had been accepted in the USA as long as the evidence was based on principles that had been accepted in the scientific community. In the 1993 case of *Daubert* v. *Merrell Dow Pharmaceuticals Incorporated* the trial judge held that all scientific expert evidence must be relevant to the case being heard and highlighted the types of questions that may be used to identify the relevance and scientific reliability of the evidence:

- Has the basic theory or technique used by the scientific expert been tested?
- Has the theory or technique been subject to peer review and publication?
- Are standards in place to control the use of the technique?
- Is there a known error rate for the technique?
- Are the theories and techniques used by the scientific expert generally accepted across the scientific community?

This has thrown into confusion the admissibility of certain types of scientific evidence within a US court. For example, it is unlikely that a forensic scientist would know how many times errors in DNA processing had led to the identification of the wrong person. In the 1999 US case of *Kumho Tire Company Limited* v. *Carmichael* et al., the court suggested that the 'Daubert' tests may also be applied to evidence presented by other experts who are nonscientists; this extensive list could include forensic medical examiners, forensic archaeologists, footwear examiners or crime scene investigators.

With the high profile of forensic evidence and a number of miscarriages of justice such as the mis-identification of fingerprints as belonging to a police officer during the 1997 investigation into the murder of Marion Ross in Scotland, in 2009 the Law Commission in England and Wales reviewed the admissibility of expert evidence in a criminal court in order to supersede the existing test of relevance to the facts of the case being heard and the reliability of the methods used. The Law Commission proposed replacing the existing tests with an appropriate set of new guidelines, this being particularly relevant in cases involving scientific evidence (Law Commission 2009). Such expert evidence could include the examination of forensic and fingerprint evidence from crime scenes.

The proposed new guidelines to assess if the evidence is reliable and therefore admissible in a criminal court include whether the techniques used have been properly tested, margins of error which exist, the existence of a body of peer-reviewed published literature to support the techniques, the qualifications and standing of the expert within the scientific community (Law Commission 2009).

14.9 Appearing in court

A CSI will always receive a warning in order to attend court. When the warning is received the CSI must ensure that he or she knows in which court building in which town the trial is to be held. Familiarity with the evidence that the CSI may be requested to deliver by the court is paramount, and can be achieved by reading through the original crime scene investigation report form and a copy of their statement. The CSI must also have either in his or her possession or know the whereabouts of any evidence that he or she handled. The CSI is representing a professional police and crime scene investigation service and should dress appropriately to reflect this.

Having arrived at the court building with plenty of time to spare, initially the CSI should locate the court in which the trial for which he or she has been warned is proceeding. It is likely that as a witness the CSI will be searched when entering the building so time should be allowed for this procedure. On arrival outside the court the CSI should tell the usher outside the courtroom that he or she has arrived. The CSI will then have to wait until called by the usher to give evidence. Waiting may be in either the public areas or in the police waiting room, but wherever the CSI is waiting, the case should not be discussed as this may lead to the accusation of collusion of evidence.

When called into the court by the usher the CSI must walk calmly to the witness box. Once in the witness box he or she will be led through either the oath or the affirmation. If the oath is to be read, then the Bible should be held and the usher will guide the witness through the words 'I swear by almighty God that the evidence I shall give shall be the truth, the whole truth, and nothing but the truth.' Alternatively, if the witness prefers not to take the oath due to its religious overtones, they may affirm using the words 'I do solemnly, sincerely and truly declare and affirm that the evidence I shall give shall be the truth, the whole truth and nothing but the truth.' Other oaths and affirmations are available for other religions such as Islam or Buddhism. The CSI should then state his or her name, with any relevant qualifications earned, his or her occupation, employer and place of work. For example, a CSI may say 'I am John Smith. I hold a BSc (Hons) in Crime Scene Science, and a Diploma in Crime Scene Examination. I am a crime scene investigator employed by West Yorkshire Police based in Halifax.'

Then the prosecution barrister or solicitor, who is working on behalf of the Crown, will lead the CSI through his or her statement. The statement may have been written for the court many months earlier. The prosecution will ask questions relating to the statement that must be answered truthfully. If unsure of the answer then the witness may refer to the original crime scene investigation report notes that were made at the time, but before reading them the permission of the judge must be sought. Stick to reporting the facts only, as the

CSI cannot say what someone else did, should not provide someone else's account of events (this would be described as hearsay evidence) and should not give an opinion unless asked to do so by the judge. The CSI needs to give answers confidently and in plain English avoiding abbreviations; he or she should not slouch or ask questions back. The defence barristers or solicitors, who are working on behalf of the defendant, will then ask the CSI further questions. Such questions may, for example, explore aspects of the way forensic evidence was recovered, how it was packaged, how the evidence was stored or the experience of the CSI of attending that particular type of crime. However, whatever the questions, the CSI must concentrate on what is being said, remain calm and should not go beyond his or her area of expertise. Once the defence have completed their questioning, then the prosecution will be allowed to ask any further questions in order to clarify points before the CSI will finally be allowed to leave the witness box. During major trials it is not unknown for CSIs to spend many hours giving evidence from the witness box. The most time I have spent in the witness box was half a day, but I have known colleagues spend several days being questioned about their evidence. Once allowed to leave the witness box the CSI should ascertain from the usher that he or she has been released from the court and hence will not be required to give further evidence. If this is the case, the CSI is free to go.

Self-assessment questions

Answer the following questions without reference to the chapter:

1   What is the highest court in England and Wales?

2   In which tier of the Crown Court are murder cases heard?

3   How many men and women sit on a jury in a Crown Court?

4   How many magistrates' courts are there in England and Wales?

5   What are the main duties of a coroner?

6   How many men and women sit on a jury in a sheriff's court?

7   Where are the Royal Courts of Justice in Northern Ireland?

8   Which military court hears the most serious of cases?

9   Who will call a CSI to enter into the courtroom?

10 Can a CSI refer to his or her original notes made on a scene of crime report form?

15 Organizations related to crime scene investigation

There are a number of organizations, such as the Forensic Science Service, LGC Forensics, Interpol and the Serious Organised Crime Agency (SOCA), of which a CSI should have some knowledge. The CSI may work or liaise directly with such organizations or the organizations may influence their practices and procedures during their operational careers.

15.1 Association of Chief Police Officers (ACPO)

ACPO and ACPO (Scotland) were originally established as professional associations for police officers holding senior ranks such as Chief Constables, Deputy Chief Constables and Assistant Chief Constable. Now ACPO and ACPO (Scotland) work to formulate policies and practice which affect every aspect of policing across the police services of the United Kingdom. For example, the *ACPO Murder Manual* provides guidance as to how an investigation into a murder should be conducted.

15.2 Crown Prosecution Service (CPS)

The Crown Prosecution Service (CPS) was established in 1985 to be a fair, independent and objective organization. Led by the Director of Public Prosecutions (DPP), the CPS is organized into 42 regions matching the 43 police forces in England and Wales (the Metropolitan and City of London police areas forming a single CPS region) with a Chief Crown Prosecutor heading each region.

Working in partnership with a number of organizations such as the police, Her Majesty's Courts Service and the Department of Constitutional Affairs, the roles of the CPS within England and Wales are to do the following:

- provide advice to the police prior to their charging a suspect;
- review all police cases before deciding whether they should proceed to the courts of law;
- oversee the progression of such cases;
- provide the prosecution in magistrates' courts and advise prosecution counsel within the Crown Courts.

The CPS works on the premise that it is acting in the interests of the general public. The evidence provided by the police will be checked in every case and the case will only usually be proceeded with if there is a realistic prospect of a conviction by the courts. A specialist CPS division has been established to work in direct partnership with the Serious Organised Crime Agency (SOCA).

15.3 European Police Organization (Europol)

The European Police Organization (Europol) is made up of the member states of the European Union. It was formed in the early 1990s to act as a conduit through which both intelligence and information on serious and organized crime and criminals could be shared between member states. It is based in the Hague.

15.4 Forensic science providers

In 1929, Arthur Dixon, Assistant Secretary at the Home Office, suggested that the police should be trained in forensic investigative techniques (Fido and Skinner 1999). The Metropolitan Police established the first UK forensic laboratory in 1935, located within Hendon Police College. Forensic services today are offered to the criminal justice system by numerous organizations, several of which are detailed below. Each laboratory is separated into specialist sections dealing with evidence types fitting broadly into biological, chemical, toxicological and, in some laboratories, firearms specialisms.

The Forensic Science Service (FSS) was established as an executive agency of the Home Office in 1991. The FSS employs approximately 2500 staff based at seven laboratories around the country in Birmingham, Chepstow, Chorley, Huntingdon, London, Reading and Wetherby, along with a satellite laboratory in Washington, Tyne and Wear. Providing a diverse range of forensic scientific services from drugs analysis and fire debris analysis to the search for semen or firearms comparison, the FSS also operates the national DNA database. During 2001/02, the FSS dealt with 135,000 cases and attended approximately 1700 crime scenes (FSS 2003). The FSS is one of the major suppliers of forensic services to the police in England and Wales.

The other major forensic science provider is LGC Forensics, although alternate providers do exist, such as Scientifics, Key Forensic Services Limited, Forensic Access and Cell Mark Forensic services. Along with the Scottish Police Services Authority (SPSA) Forensic Services and the Forensic Science Service of Northern Ireland, LGC Forensics provides a traditional forensic science service along with specialist services including forensic entomology and archaeology. Scientifics operates from sites across the UK, with its headquarters in Derby. Key Forensic Services Limited operates a range of forensic services from their base in Coventry. Forensic Access provides expert advice and guidance to the legal professions on forensic issues, whereas Cellmark has its main focus on DNA analysis. The Scottish Police Laboratories and the Forensic Science Service of Northern Ireland laboratories specialize in providing a range of traditional forensic services to the criminal justice system within their own geographical area.

15.5 Home Office Scientific Development Branch (HOSDB)

The Home Office Police Scientific Development Branch (HOSDB) is also referred to as the Police Scientific Development Branch (PSDB) and is based at Sandridge, England. HOSDB has a number of scientists, engineers and police officers who work in partnership to develop technologies to assist the police service and other law enforcement agencies across the UK by providing technical and procedural solutions to policing and security issues (Home Office Scientific Development Branch 2009). HOSDB continues to provide innovative solutions to a diverse range of areas within policing, for example, the recovery of fingerprints using powders to the ballistic resistance of body armour.

15.6 Interpol

The first international symposium of police officers and lawyers was held in France during 1914. It had some success, with representatives from 24 countries calling for the establishment of international, centralized criminal records (Bresler 1992). However, the advent of World War I put the ideas on hold and they were not resurrected until 1923 when the International Criminal Police Organization was established in Vienna. In 1956 it became popularly known as Interpol (Bresler 1992).

Interpol is now based in a permanent, purpose-built headquarters in Lyons, France, and focuses on providing assistance to its 187 member states in the investigation of transnational crime including human and drugs trafficking along with counter-terrorism and corruption (Interpol 2009a). To facilitate this assistance, Interpol's activities include the transfer of messages between organizations, analysis and sharing of information and intelligence on crime trends and criminals and the provision of a structure for regional cooperation and collaboration. Interpol also maintains a fingerprint database, advising on compatible systems for member states to share fingerprint data, and facilitates the exchange of information from DNA databases. If a disaster were to occur, then Interpol could assist in the identification of victims by exchanging and collating information between countries.

15.7 National Police Improvement Agency (NPIA)

The National Police Improvement Agency (NPIA) was established in 2007 through the amalgamation of a range of existing police agencies such as Centrex and the Police Information and Technology Organization (PITO). NPIA today consists of a number of specialist departments that provide a range of knowledge and skills including: operational support for policing (such as both uniformed and crime support who can provide specialist skills and deployable resources), departments designed to analyse and disseminate information such as the serious crime analysis section (which aims to identify the existence of serial killers and rapists), and the maintenance of an experts database, called 'Genesis'. Training and examination are conducted at numerous sites ranging from senior leadership training in Hampshire to crime scene investigator training in Durham. Some departments conduct research, development and dissemination while others maintain IT systems (NPIA 2009b). Whatever the product, the NPIA aims to deliver effective, efficient and up-to-date training and educational programmes while developing cutting-edge information and communication technology for use in all aspects of contemporary policing.

15.8 Professional associations

The two main professional associations in the United Kingdom are the Forensic Science Society and the Fingerprint Society.

The Forensic Science Society was established in the UK in 1959. Its aim is to share knowledge of the forensic sciences both nationally and internationally among those within the criminal justice system. Practitioners from all forensic, crime scene investigation and fingerprint disciplines can be members of the society, as can students. The Forensic Science Society formally became a professional body in 2004 providing professional status for its members and fellows. The society also administers a range of educational diplomas for forensic practitioners and in partnership with Skills for Justice can accredit university educational programmes which have the appropriate forensic quantity and quality.

The Fingerprint Society was founded in 1974 as a professional association to advance the use of fingerprints as a means of identification and encourage cooperation (The Fingerprint Society 2009). With over 500 members and fellows around the world, the fingerprint society continues to grow.

In the USA, the main professional associations are the International Association for Identification (IAI), the American Academy of Forensic Sciences (AAFS) and the American Society of Crime Laboratory Directors (ASCLD).

Established in 1915 with the aim of furthering the forensic professions, the International Association for Identification today comprises over 7000 members from 70 countries (IAI 2009); both practitioners and students can be members of the association. Through a blend of operational experience, training opportunities and examination CSIs from across the world can be certified as crime scene investigators or analysts. Other certification programmes are available for footwear examiners, latent print examiners, blood pattern analysts, forensic artists and forensic photographers.

The American Academy of Forensic Sciences was established in the late 1940s as a focus in the USA for the application and requirements of forensic science within the law. The AAFS now has in the region of 6000 members spread across the USA and a number of countries worldwide, representing their needs through a professional society, along with the promotion of education and research in a range of forensic disciplines such as crime scene investigation, dentistry, document examination and engineering (AAFS 2009).

The American Society of Crime Laboratory Directors was formed in the 1970s to provide mutual support and training opportunities for laboratory directors and managers. A spin-off of ASCLD is the American Society of Crime Laboratory Directors – Laboratory Accreditation Boards (ASCLD/LAB). This is a professional organization, established in the 1980s to provide a programme for the evaluation and accreditation of forensic laboratories. The aim of ASCLD/LAB is to raise standards, provide an independent review of the operations of a forensic laboratory, and provide a means of evaluating performance and measure standards across the criminal justice service. This process has been embraced by much of the criminal justice community; by 2004 ASCLD/LAB had successfully accredited 259 laboratories, a number of which are outside the USA (ASCLD/LAB 2009).

15.9 Professional registration of forensic practitioners

The Council for the Registration of Forensic Practitioners (CRFP), a disbanded organization

Launched in 2000, the Council for the Registration of Forensic Practitioners (CRFP) was established as a national independent regulatory body in the United Kingdom with an overarching objective of promoting 'public confidence in forensic practice' (CRFP 2003a). As a result of its introduction a standard minimum level of competence of practitioners was to be ensured within the workplace. A register of these competent forensic practitioners was published and updated by the CRFP.

Professionally managed from its London headquarters, voluntary membership was open to many forensic disciplines, including CSIs, forensic scientists, odontologists, forensic medical practitioners and fingerprint examiners, with the list of disciplines included continually growing. By the middle of 2003 the CRFP had successfully registered 432 CSIs, 266 fingerprint examiners and 195 forensic scientists. The membership was renewable every four years and assessed by appropriate occupationally competent peers, who had been trained to assess fairly against a set of established criteria. The criteria differed between occupational groups such as forensic scientists, CSIs and fingerprint examiners. But each and every member recognized his or her overriding duty was to the administration of justice (CRFP 2003b). At the height of its success in 2008 nearly 1500 crime scene investigators had been registered in a range of disciplines as forensic practitioners with the Council for the Registration of Forensic Practitioners (CRFP 2008). However, in early 2009, funding for the CRFP was withheld and on 31 March 2009 the CRFP ceased to exist as a regulatory body.

The future of the registration of forensic practitioners

Despite the demise of the CRFP, there is still a need for the professional registration of forensic practitioners. Central to such registration is the appointment of the independent forensic science regulator by the Home Office in early 2008 who was appointed to develop, monitor and improve quality across forensic science and its uses within the criminal justice system of England and Wales. At the time of writing a number of questions still exist in relation to registration such as: Against which standards will forensic practitioners be assessed? Who will assess and how will practitioners be assessed for inclusion in a register? Who will maintain the register? How will individuals demonstrate their professional ability to remain on the register? And perhaps above all else, who will pay? The forensic science regulator has stated a preference for accreditation by the United Kingdom Accreditation Service (UKAS), which is well experienced at assessing against national standards, to work with the forensic science regulator to establish an appropriate scheme for the registration of forensic practitioners (Forensic Science Regulator, 2009).

15.10 Serious and Organised Crime Agency (SOCA)

The Serious and Organised Crime Agency (SOCA) was established through the amalgamation of the National Criminal Intelligence Service (NCIS), the

National Crime Squad (NCS), HM Customs and Excise Investigation Branch and the Police National Hi-Tech Crime Unit (NHTCU), which was responsible for the investigation of cyber crime.

SOCA is centrally funded but works independently of the Home Office (SOCA 2009b). SOCA is an independent law enforcement organization with a Director General at its head rather than a Chief Constable. The Director General can designate SOCA employees with powers pertaining to their role (such as those of arrest or investigation) (SOCA 2009b).

Intelligence led, SOCA focuses on organized crime by gathering, storing and analysing information and intelligence on criminal activities, such as human and drugs trafficking. The information is then shared with law enforcement agencies and organizations nationally (such as a police force or the Child Exploitation Online Protection Centre) and internationally (such as Interpol) and is acted upon either by SOCA employees or local police officers. For intelligence to be of use, it needs to be collected, analysed and then disseminated to the right person, in the right place at the right time. To facilitate this process most police forces have at least one Force Intelligence Officer (FIO), Local Intelligence Officer (LIO) and Crime Pattern Analyst (CPA). NCIS originally developed national knowledge products on behalf of the Association of Chief Police Officers, such as the National Intelligence Model. Such National Intelligence Models have been adopted by SOCA and allow users to combine the needs of the task with efficient use of the intelligence, processes, procedures and the systems to collect and collate information. This model of intelligence gathering is used across all police forces in the UK. In the USA, a National Criminal Intelligence Sharing Plan exists for the same reasons as a model to share information across national, state and local law enforcement agencies.

15.11 Skills for Justice

Skills for Justice evolved from the Police Skills and Standards Organization during 2004 to become the National Training Organization for both the police service and elements of the wider criminal justice community. Utilizing specialist expertise from across law enforcement and training/education providers, Skills for Justice (and its predecessor) have designed a suite of national occupational standards for all roles within the police service ranging from driving skills to crime scene investigation. Such standards provide a commonality of competence and professionalism in the workplace and provide a route for qualifications for those across the United Kingdom performing a particular role.

Skills for Justice also administers the 'Skillsmark' quality mark which aims to recognize educational and training providers as delivering programmes which are appropriate for those employed, or hoping to be employed, within the criminal justice community.

15.12 UK Border Agency

In 2008, the Border and Immigration Agency, elements of HM Customs and the Visa Office merged to form the UK Border Agency which has the responsibility for securing the borders of the United Kingdom (UK Border Agency 2009). To aid in the process the Agency collects biometric data (such as facial photographs and fingerprints) from those crossing the UK's borders. The agency has access to a number of police databases such as the Ident1 national fingerprint database.

Self-assessment questions

Answer the following questions without reference to the chapter:

1   When was the first forensic laboratory opened in the UK?

2   Which organization was established in 1959 to share knowledge of the forensic sciences both nationally and internationally among those who work within the criminal justice system?

3   What do the initials NPIA stand for?

4   What is the main function of Europol?

5   Which US professional organization can provide evaluation and accreditation of forensic laboratories?

6   What is the name of the quality mark administered by Skills for Justice?

7   What do the initials IAI stand for?

8   What do the initials SOCA stand for?

9   When was the UK Border Agency formed?

10   Where are the headquarters of Interpol?

Answers to questions

Chapter 1

1 Alphonse Bertillon
2 Evidence is transferred from A to B and vice versa
3 Police Reform Act 2002
4 Police Scientific Development Branch
5 National Police Improvement Agency
6 Serious Organised Crime Agency
7 260,000
6 Scientific Support Manager
9 Volume Crime Scene Investigator
10 Core roles are:
   - photography or video photography at scenes of crime, victims and property;
   - search for and recovery of physical evidence;
   - detection and recovery of fingerprints and palm prints at scenes of crime;
   - package and storage of physical evidence preventing contamination;
   - maintenance of intelligence indices on *modus operandi*, shoe-marks, etc;
   - provision of advice on scientific support matters;
   - preparation of statements and giving evidence in court.

Chapter 2

1 Identify him/herself to the injured party
2 Crime Scene Investigation Report Form
3 Police Reform Act (2002)
4 Victim Support Scheme
5 At the time of the examination
6 CJA label
7 The signature of the CSI
8 What someone else has said has happened
9 Any material that may undermine the case
10 HOLMES II

Chapter 3

1   299,790 kilometres (186,000 miles) a second
2   50mm
3   f22
4   1/500th of a second
5   A type of memory card for a digital camera
6   Taking photographs from all four corners of the room
7   Black and white
8   Information being removed from the image to allow storage
9   40 degrees
10 Immediately an image is recorded

Chapter 4

1   Natural and man-made
2   Tweezers or sellotape
3   Number of contacts, force of contact, nature of surfaces
4   0.5mm
5   Six
6   Glass refractive index measurement
7   Glass in hair combings
8   Top coat colour, layer structure and chemical composition
9   Twenty-five
10 Brown paper sacks

Chapter 5

1   The way the offender entered and exited the premises, where they have been in the scene, the minimum number of people involved, linking scenes
2   Impressed and surface transfer
3   Identification mark and date
4   ESLA
5   Paper
6   Levering, cutting and drilling
7   End wrapped in paper then in a solid container or box
8   Photograph, ESLA, gelatine lift
9   Equivalent to one complete revolution
10 Tyre-specific and accidental marks

Chapter 6

1   Deoxyribonucleic acid
2   Adenine, cytosine, guanine, thymine
3   1986
4   1995
5   One in 1000 million
6   Low copy number
7   Brown paper sacks
8   Frozen
9   Acid phosphatase
10 Blood, buccal swabs, plucked head hairs with roots

Chapter 7

1   Create friction, increase sense of touch, raise up extra sweat pores
2   Invisible
3   Granular, flake
4   Flake
5   Superglue
6   Arch, loop, whorl
7   Two
8   A system which allows the electronic scanning of fingerprints
9   The study of the shape, location and individualization of sweat pores
10 Ident1

Chapter 8

1   Heat, fuel, oxygen
2   Transferred through a solid medium
3   The investigation of any crime
4   Gather information
5   Anything that speeds up the growth of the fire
6   Low and high burning, burn patterns, thermal indicators, smoke patterns
7   The window may have been broken before the fire
8   1 to 2kg
9   Nylon bags
10 Air

Chapter 9

1   As if it is loaded
2   Handguns
3   'A lethal barrelled weapon of any description from which any shot, bullet or other missile can be discharged'
4   Box with a window in the lid
5   Small plastic tube then seal in a polythene bag
6   If possible, cut around the bullet and remove it with a piece of wall still surrounding the bullet, then package in a box
7   Firearms discharge residue
8   Six hours
9   Marks made when the cartridge has been pushed into the chamber of the weapon, marks made by the firing pin, cartridge case extractor and ejector marks
10 National Ballistics Intelligence Service

Chapter 10

1   The saving of life
2   1000 metres
3   Disaster Victim Identification
4   The USA
5   Chemical, biological, radiological and nuclear
6   The explosive charge, means of detonation or ignition, a power supply, a switch, a container
7   Nylon bags
8   DNA, dental records, fingerprints, photography, personal viewings, X-rays, personal effects, tattoos and by other means
9   255
10 Over 226,000 people

Chapter 11

1   Inner and outer
2   Senior Investigating Officer
3   70–90 per cent
4   Forensic medical examiner, forensic pathologist, forensic biologist, forensic chemist, toxicologist, firearms expert
5   Hyoid
6   Forensic odontologist

7   Scientific Support Coordinator
8   Scientific Support Manager
9   National Crime and Operations Faculty
10   Take a strategic view of the forensic examination and coordinate forensic submissions

Chapter 12

1   Anti-static (Faraday) bags
2   The study of the growth of tree rings
3   Over 15,000
4   Evidence of its use include wraps of paper, syringes, needles, tourniquets and spoons or silver foil with the base burnt, Jif lemon juice, cotton wool, measuring scales
5   The top of the ear
6   No
7   National Intelligence Model
8   Ultraviolet
9   White/blue fluorescence or yellow/green fluorescence
10   Bedding including pillows, soiled nappies and clothes, food and medication, other items such as plastic bags, cables or cords

Chapter 13

1   Health and Safety at Work Act (1974)
2   Blood, semen, vomit, faeces
3   Contact with contaminated blood through splashes into eyes, nose, mouth or open cut
4   Personal protective equipment
5   'Slash-resistant' gloves and goggles
6   Hydrofluoric acid
7   Hard hat with chin strap, goggles, 'slash-resistant' gloves, boots with reinforced toe caps and puncture-resistant soles, brightly coloured coverall
8   The ceiling of the room below to see if the floorboards are still intact
9   The possibility of absorption, inhalation or ingestion of the drugs and the possibility of fire or explosion
10   Slips, trips and falls

Chapter 14

1   The Supreme Court
2   First tier
3   Twelve
4   Over 700
5   The main duties of the coroner are to conduct inquests (inquiries) into deaths that were violent and unnatural, sudden with the cause unknown or occurred in prison
6   15
7   Belfast
8   General Court Martial
9   The usher
10 Yes, if permission is granted by the judge

Chapter 15

1   1935
2   The Forensic Science Society
3   National Police Improvement Agency
4   To share intelligence and information on serious and organized crime and criminals between member states of the EU
5   ASCLD/LAB
6   Skillsmark
7   International Association for Identification
8   Serious and Organised Crime Agency
9   2008
10 Lyons, France

References

AAFS (2009) *American Academy of Forensic Sciences (AAFS): About Us*. Available from: http://www.aafs.org/ (accessed 30 June 2009).

ACPO (Association of Chief Police Officers) (2000) *The Manual of Standard Operating Procedures for Scientific Support Personnel at Major Incident Scenes*. London: ACPO Crime Committee.

ACPO: 7Safe (2007) *Good Practice Guide for Computer Based Electronic Evidence*, 4th edn. London: ACPO.

ACPO/FSS (Association of Chief Police Officers/Forensic Science Service) (1996) *Using Forensic Science Effectively*. Birmingham: ACPO/FSS.

ACPO/NPIA (2009) *Guidance on Emergency Procedures*. Wyboston: National Police Improvement Agency.

Adair, J. (1984) *The Skills of Leadership*. London: Gower Publishing.

Adderley, R. and Bond, J. (2008) The effects of deprivation on the time spent examining crime scenes and the recovery of DNA and fingerprints, *Journal of Forensic Science*, 53(1): 178–82.

Adderley, R. and Musgrove, P. (2001) Police crime recording and investigation systems: a user's view, *Policing: An International Journal of Police Strategies and Management*, 24(1): 100–14.

Anon. (2009) Personal Communication, email, 25 November.

ASCLD/LAB (2009) *American Society of Crime Laboratory Director – Laboratory Accreditation Boards*. Available from: http://www.ascld-lab.org (accessed 19 March 2009).

Bandey, H. (2007) *Fingerprint Powders Guidelines*, Publication 09/07. Sandridge: Home Office Scientific Development Branch

Bandey, H. (2008) *Fingerprint and Footwear Forensic Newsletter*, Publication 24/08. Sandridge: Home Office Scientific Development Branch.

Becker, R. (2006) *Underwater Forensic Investigation*. New Jersey: Pearson Education.

Bellefeuille, J., Bowen, K., Dixon, P., Hanniman, J., Hillier, E., Lama, D. et al. (2003) Crime scene DNA collection: research and practical considerations, *Journal of Forensic Identification*, 53(6): 729–34.

Bevel, T. and Gardner, R.M. (2002) *Bloodstain Pattern Analysis*. Boca Raton, FL: CRC Press.

Blakey, D. (2000) *Under the Microscope: Thematic Inspection Report on Scientific and Technical Support*. London: Her Majesty's Inspectorate of Constabulary.

Bodziak, W.J. (2000) *Footwear Impression Evidence*, 2nd edn. Boca Raton, FL: CRC Press.

Brady, N.C. (1990) *The Nature and Properties of Soils*, 10th edn. Englewood Cliffs, NJ: Prentice-Hall.

Bresler, F. (1992) *Interpol*. London: Sinclair-Stevenson.

Bridges, B.C. (1942) *Practical Fingerprinting*. New York: Funk & Wagnalls.

Bryant, R. (ed.) (2008) *Investigating Digital Crime*. Chichester: John Wiley & Sons, Ltd.

Cabinet Office UK Resilience (2009) *Case Study, Mass Fatalities, Incident: Indian Ocean Tsunami, 26 December 2004*. Available from: www.cabinetoffice.gov.uk/ukresilience/ (accessed 11 August 2009).

Caddy, B. (2001) *Forensic Examination of Glass and Paint: Analysis and Interpretation*. London: Taylor and Francis.

Cameron, M. (2002) Health and safety concerns for law enforcement personnel investigating clandestine drug labs, *Chemical Health and Safety*, 9(1): 6–9.

Charlton, D. (2003) Obituary, *Fingerprint Whorld*, 29(111): 27.

Chief Medical Examiner (2009) Update on the results of DNA testing of remains recovered at the World Trade Center site and surrounding area. Available from: http://www.nyc.gov/html/ocme/html/home/ (accessed 13 August 2009).

Chief Medical Officer (2001) *Harold Shipman's Clinical Practice 1974–1998*. Norwich: Her Majesty's Stationery Office.

Communities and Local Government (2009) *Fire Statistics Monitor: Covering Period up to 31st March 2008*. Available from: http://www.communities.gov.uk/news/corporate/firestatsmonitor31march2008 (accessed 30 March 2009).

Cooke, R.A. and Ide, R.H. (1985) *Principles of Fire Investigation*. Leicester: Institution of Fire Engineers.

Corbett, C. (2003) *Car Crime*. Cullompton, Devon: Willan Publishing.

CRFP (2003a) *Promoting Confidence in Forensic Practice*. London: Council for the Registration of Forensic Practitioners.

CRFP (2003b) *Good Practice for Forensic Practitioners*. London: Council for the Registration of Forensic Practitioners.

CRFP (2008) *The Registered Post: The Newsletter of CRFP*. London: Council for the Registration of Forensic Practitioners.

Critchley, T.A. (1967) *A History of Police in England and Wales 1900–1966*. London: Constable and Company.

Crown (2006) *Explanatory Notes to the Armed Forces Act 2006 c.52*. London: The Stationery Office.

DeHaan, J.D. (2007) *Kirk's Fire Investigation*, 6th edn. Englewood Cliffs, NJ: Prentice-Hall.

De Kinder, J., Lory, S., Van Laere, W. and Demuynck, E. (2002) The deviation of bullets passing through window panes, *Forensic Science International*, 125(1): 8–11.

DeLisi, M. (2002) The Columbine High School massacre and criminal justice system response: an exploratory case study, *The Social Sciences Journal*, 39: 19–29.

Eller, R. (2000) *Secrets of Successful Aerial Photography*. Buffalo, NY: Amherst Media Inc.

Emsley, C. (1991) *The English Police: A Political and Social History*. London: Longman.

English, B. and English, J. (2003) *Police Training Manual*, 10th edn. London: McGraw-Hill.

English, J. and Card, R. (1996) *Butterworths Police Law*, 5th edn. London: Butterworths.

English, J. and Card, R. (2003) *Butterworths Police Law*, 8th edn. London: Butterworths LexisNexis.

Faulds, H. (1880) On the skin furrows of the hand, *Nature*, 22 (605): 28 October.

FBI (2009a) *Next Generation Identification*. Washington, DC: FBI. Available from: http://www.fbi.gov (accessed 1 July 2009).

FBI (2009b) *CODIS-NDIS Statistics*. Washington, DC: FBI. Available from: http://www.fbi.gov (accessed 5 March 2009).

Fennell, D. (1988) *Investigation into the King's Cross Underground Fire*. London: HMSO.

Fido, M. and Skinner, K. (1999) *The Official Encyclopedia of Scotland Yard*. London: Virgin Books.

Fire and Rescue Service Circular (2006) *The Investigation of Fires Where the Supposed Cause is Not Accidental*. Circular 1–2006. London: Office of the Deputy Prime Minister.

Flood-Page, C. and Taylor, J. (2003) *Crime in England and Wales 2001/2002: Supplementary Volume*. London: Research, Development and Statistics Directorate.

Forensic Science Regulator (2009) *Consultation Paper: A Review of the Options for Accreditation of Forensic Practitioners*. London: Forensic Science Regulation Unit.

Foundation for the Study of Infant Death (2005) *'Responding when a baby dies' Campaign. Sudden Unexpected Deaths in Infancy: A Suggested Approach for Police and Coroner's Officers*. The Foundation for the Study of Infant Deaths. Available from: http://www.sids.org.uk/ (accessed 30 June 2009).

Fridell, R. (2001) *DNA Fingerprinting: The Ultimate Identity*. New York: Franklin Watts.

FSS (Forensic Science Service) (1998) It's all in the water, *Contact*, April (26): 40–1.

FSS (1999) *The Scenes of Crime Handbook*. Chorley: Forensic Science Service.

FSS (2003a) *The Scenes of Crime Handbook*. Version 4. Chorley: Forensic Science Service.

FSS (2003b) *The Forensic Science Service*. Available from: http://www.forensic.gov.uk (accessed 1 July 2003).

Galton, F. (1888) Personal identification and description, *Scientific American Supplement*, 26(659): 10532–3.

Galton, F. (1892) *Finger Prints*. London: Macmillan and Co.

Goodchild. S. and Lashmar. P. (2005) Up to 4m guns in the UK and police are losing the battle, *The Independent*, 4 September 2005. Available from: http://www.independent.co.uk/news/ (accessed 27 April 2009).

Goodwin, W., Linacre, A. and Hadi, S. (2007) *An Introduction to Forensic Genetics*. Chichester: John Wiley & Sons, Ltd.

Greaves, P.H. (1995) *Microscopy of Textile Fibres*. Oxford: BIOS Scientific Publishers.

Green, R. (2007) Forensic investigation in the UK, in T. Newburn, T. Williamson, and A. Wright (eds) *Handbook of Criminal Investigation*. Cullompton: Willan Publishing.

Griffin, T.J. (2009) Personal Communication, email, 16 and 30 October.

Griffin, T.J. and Andrist, C. (2000) *Mass Crime Scene Handbook*. Denver, CO: Colorado Bureau of Investigation.

Haberfeld, M.R. (2002) *Critical Issues in Police Training*. Englewood Cliffs, NJ: Pearson Education.

Hale, G., Lewis, C. and Silverstone, D. (2006) *Gun Crime: The Market in and the Use of Illegal Firearms*. Research Study 298. London: Home Office.

Hartink, A.E. (1996) *Encyclopaedia of Pistols and Revolvers*. Lisse, Netherlands: Rebo Productions.

Henry, E.R. (1934) *Classification and Uses of Finger Prints*, 7th edn. London: HMSO.

Her Majesty's Court Service (2008) *Annual Report and Accounts, 2007/08*. Norwich: TSO.

Herzog, A. and Ezickson, A. (1940) *Camera Take the Stand!* New York: Prentice-Hall.

Holborn, P.G., Nolan, P.F. and Golt, J. (2003) An analysis of fatal, unintentional dwelling fires investigated by London Fire Brigade between 1996 and 2000, *Fire Safety Journal*, 38(1): 1–42.

Home Office (1988) *Civilian Staff in the Police Service*, Circular 105. London: Home Office.

Home Office (2002) *Guidance on Powers for Designated Civilian Investigating, Detention and Escort Officers*, Circular 67/2002. London: Home Office.

Home Office (2008a) Statistics on the number of police officers assaulted on duty from 2005/06 to 2007/08 in England and Wales, 26 August. Available from: www.homeoffice.gov.uk/rds (accessed 17 July 2009).

Home Office (2008b) Supplementary note on (a) recorded crimes involving firearms and (b) violent and sexual offences involving the use of knives or sharp instruments, in *Crime in England and Wales: Quarterly Update to June 2008*. London: Home Office.

Home Office (2008c) *Crime in England and Wales 2007/2008: A Summary of the Main Findings*. London: Home Office.

Home Office Science Policy Unit (2003) *Police Science and Technology Strategy 2003 to 2008*. London: Home Office.

Home Office Scientific Development Branch (2009) *About Us: About Our Work*. Available from: http://scienceandresearch.homeoffice.gov.uk/hosdb/ (accessed 1 July 2009).

Horswell, J. (2000) Major incident scene management, in J. Siegel, P. Saukko, and G. Knupfer (eds) *Encyclopedia of Forensic Sciences*. London: Academic Press.

HSE (Health and Safety Executive) (1996) *Five Steps to Risk Assessment*, 7/96. Sudbury: Health and Safety Executive Books.

Hughes, M. (2009) Police lost evidence at Barrymore's house, *The Independent*, 25 February 2009. Available from: http://www.independent.co.uk/news/uk/crime (accessed 18th June 2009).

IAI (1999) *Crime Scene Investigation Guidelines*. Mendota Heights: International Association of Identification.

IAI (2009) *International Association for Identification*. Available from: http://www.theiai.org/ (accessed 18 March 2009).

Interpol (2009a) *About Interpol*. Available from: http://www.interpol.int/public/icpo/default.asp (accessed 20 March 2009).

Interpol (2009b) *PM Evidence Collection*. Available from: http://www.interpol.int/Public/DisasterVictim/Guide (accessed 13 August 2009).

Jeffreys, A.J., Wilson, V. and Thein, S.L. (1985) Individual-specific 'fingerprints' of human DNA, *Nature*, 316: 76–9.

Johnson, A. (2009) *Written Ministerial Statement: DNA and Fingerprint Retention*. London: Home Office.

Jones, R. and White, A. (2008) *Jane's: Guns Recognition Guide*, 5th edn. London: HarperCollins Publishers.

Joyce, J. (2007) *Bullet Proof! The Evidence that Guns Leave Behind*. New York: Scholastic Inc.

Kershaw, C., Nicholas, S. and Walker, A. (2008) *Crime in England and Wales 2007/2008: Findings from the British Crime Survey and Police Recorded Crime*. London: Home Office.

Kidd, C. and Robertson, J. (1982) The transfer of textile fibres during simulated contacts, *Journal of the Forensic Science Society*, 22: 301–8.

Kimber, C. (2000) Interpretation of mitochondrial DNA sequencing, *Science and Justice*, 40(3): 217–18.

Knowles, R. (2000) The new (non-numeric) fingerprint evidence standard – is it pointless?, *Science and Justice*, 40(2): 120–1.

Lambert, J., Satterthwaite, M. and Harrison, P. (1995) A survey of glass fragments recovered from clothing of persons suspected of involvement in crime, *Science and Justice*, 35(4): 273–81.

Lambourne, G. (1975) Glove print identification: a new technique, *Police Journal*, 4(3): 219–46.

Lander, P. (2009) Forensic evidence sees murder conviction quashed, *Police Professional*, March 26: 8.

Langer, M. and Dunaski, M. (2007) Aerial photography: an elevated perspective, *Evidence Technology Magazine*, 5(4): 28–33.

Langford, M. and Andrews, P. (2007) *Langford's Starting Photography: The Guide to Great Images with Digital or Film*, 5th edn. Oxford: Focal Press.

Law Commission (2009) *The Admissibility of Expert Evidence in Criminal Proceedings in England and Wales: A New Approach to the Determination of Evidence Reliability*, Consultation Paper No. 190. London: Law Commission.

Levine, M. and Pyke, J. (1999) *Levine on Coroners' Courts*. London: Sweet and Maxwell.

LGC (2003) Behind the scene, *LGC Forensic News*, 1: 2.

Lorentz, J., Hill, L. and Samimi, B. (2000) Occupational needlestick injuries in a metropolitan police force, *American Journal of Preventive Medicine*, 18(2): 146–50.

Lugt, C. (2001) *Earprint Identification*. Gravennage: Elsevier Bedrijfsinformatie.

Lyman, M. (2007) *Practical Drug Enforcement*, 3rd edn. Boca Raton, FL: Taylor and Francis.

Malcolm, J.L. (2002) *Guns and Violence: The English Experience*. Cambridge, MA: Harvard University Press.

Marshall, L. and Armstrong, J. (2002) Double murder at Poynzpass: a case study involving secondary transfer, *Proc-European Fibres Group*, 10 (June): 117–19.

Martin, P.D., Schmitter, H. and Schneider, P.M. (2000) A brief history of the formation of DNA databases in forensic science within Europe, *Forensic Science International*, 119(2): 225–31.

Martini, F.H. (2001) *Fundamentals of Anatomy and Physiology*, 5th edn. Englewood Cliffs NJ: Prentice-Hall.

Martis, R. (2005) Service cannot track down firearms used on UK streets. *Police Review*, 113 (5820): 6.

McLay, W.D.S. (1990) *Clinical Forensic Medicine*. London: Pinter Publishers.

Metropolitan Police (2002) *History*. Available from: www.met.police.uk/history (accessed 8 July 2004).

Midkiff, C.R. (1993) Lifetime of a latent print. How long? Can you tell?, *Journal of Forensic Identification*, 43(4): 386–92.

Miller. L. (2006) *Police Photography*, 5th edn. New York: Anderson Publishing.

Morgan, O., Sribanditmongkol, P., Perera, C., Sulasmi, Y., Alphen, D. and Sondorp, E. (2006) Mass fatality management following the South Asian tsunami disaster: case studies in Thailand, Indonesia and Sri Lanka, *PLoS Medicine*, 3(6): e195.

National Centre for Policing Excellence (2005) *Guidance on the National Intelligence Model*. Wyboston: Centrex.

Newburn, T., Williamson, T., and Wright, A. (eds) (2007) *Handbook of Criminal Investigation*. Cullompton: Willan Publishing.

Nickell, J. and Fischer, J.F. (1999) *Crime Science: Methods of Forensic Detection*. Lexington, KY: Kentucky University Press.

Northern Ireland Court Service (2003) Northern Ireland Court Service [online]. Available from: http://www.courtsni.gov.uk/en-GB/AboutUs/ (accessed 4 August 2009).

NPIA (2009a) *The National Police Improvement Agency: Fingerprint Database*. Available from: http://www.npia.police.uk (accessed 5 March 2009).

NPIA (2009b) *The National Police Improvement Agency: Welcome to the NPIA Website*. Available from: http://www.npia.police.uk (accessed 20 March 2009).

Pepper, I. and Pepper, H. (2009) *Keywords in Policing*. Maidenhead: Open University Press.

Portugal, F.H. and Cohen, J.S. (1977) *A Century of DNA: A History of the Discovery of the Structure and Function of the Genetic Substance*. Cambridge, MA: Massachusetts Institute of Technology.

Pounds, C. and Smalldon, K. (1975) The transfer of fibres between clothing materials during simulated contacts and their persistence during wear – Part 1: fibre transference, *Journal of the Forensic Science Society*, 15: 17–27.

Pressly, J. (1999) Ninhydrin on latex gloves: an alternative use for an old technique, *Journal of Forensic Identification*, 49(3): 257–60.

PSDB (Police Scientific Development Branch) (1998) *Manual of Fingerprint Development Techniques: A Guide to the Selection and Use of Processes for the Development of Latent Fingerprints*, 2nd edn. Sandridge: Home Office.

PSDB (2002) *Digital Imaging Procedure*, Version 1. London: Home Office.

Quirk, A., Bellerby, J., Carter, J., Thomas, F., and Hill, J. (2009) An initial evaluation of stable isotopic characterization of post-blast plastic debris from improvised explosive devices, *Science and Justice*, 49(2): 87–93.

Radzinowicz, L. (1956a) *A History of English Criminal Law and its Administration from 1750*, vol. 2. London: Stevens and Sons.

Radzinowicz, L. (1956b) *A History of English Criminal Law and its Administration from 1750*, vol. 3. London: Stevens and Sons.

Rhodes, H.T.F. (1956) *Alphonse Bertillon: Father of Scientific Detection*. London: Harrap and Co. Ltd.

Rinehart, D.J. (2000) Developing and identifying a latent print recovered from a piece of latex glove using ninhydrin-heptane carrier (Case 1), *Journal of Forensic Identification*, 50(5): 443–6.

Robertson, J. (1999) *Forensic Examination of Hair*. London: Taylor and Francis.

Rohde, R. (2000) Crime photography, *Photographic Society of America*, 66(3): 15–17.

Rutty, G.N., Watson, S. and Davison, J. (2000) DNA contamination of mortuary instruments and work surfaces: a significant problem in forensic practice?, *International Journal of Legal Medicine*, 114: 56–60.

Schwoeble, A.J. and Exline, D.L. (2000) *Current Methods in Forensic Gunshot Residue Analysis*. Boca Raton, FL: CRC Press.

Scottish Court Service (2009) *Welcome to the Scottish Courts Website*. Available from: http://www.scotcourts.gov.uk/ (accessed 4 August 2009).

Sheriff, Jefferson County (2000) Statement, April 20 1999. Available from: http://www.cnn.com/SPECIALS/2000/columbine.cd/Pages/INTRO_TEXT.htm (accessed 20 August 2009).

Siegel, J.A., Saukko, P.J. and Knupfer, G.C. (2000) *Encyclopaedia of Forensic Science*. San Diego, CA: Academic Press.

Skills for Justice (2009) *National Occupational Standards*. Available from: http://www.skillsforjustice.com/ (accessed 2 March 2009).

Slapper, G. and Kelly, D. (1997) *Principles of the English Legal System*, 3rd edn. London: Cavendish Publishing.

SOCA (2009a) *SOCA, Press Release, 36 million spliffs incinerated as international crime gang is convicted*, 2 June. Available at: http://www.soca.gov.uk/ (accessed 29 June 2009).

SOCA (2009b) *SOCA, About Us*. Available from: http://www.soca.gov.uk/ (accessed 20 March 2009).

Steck-Flynn, K. (2005) Getting down and dirty: the soil at a crime scene, *Law Enforcement Technology*, 32(2): 32–40.

Steers, R.M., Porter, L.W. and Bigley, G.A. (1996) *Motivation and Leadership at Work*, 6th edn. New York: McGraw-Hill.

Stroebel, L. and Zakia, R. (1993) *Encyclopedia of Photography*, 3rd edn. Boston, MA: Focal Press.

Szibor, R., Michael, M., Plate, I. and Krause, D. (2000) Efficiency of forensic mtDNA analysis: case examples demonstrating the identification of traces, *Forensic Science International*, 113(1–3): 71–8.

The Fingerprint Society (2009) *History of the Society*. Available from: http://www.fpsociety.org.uk/ (accessed 18 March 2009).

Thorwald, J. (1965) *The Marks of Cain*. London: Thames and Hudson.

Tilley, N. and Ford, A. (1996) *Forensic Science and Crime Investigation*, Crime Detection and Prevention Series Paper 73. London: Home Office.

Touche Ross (1987) *Review of Scientific Support for the Police*, vol. III. London: Home Office.

Travis, A. (2008) 17 Judges, one ruling – and 857,000 records must now be wiped clear, *Guardian*, 5 December.

Tucker, J.B. (2000) *Toxic Terror: Assessing Terrorist Use of Chemical and Biological Weapons*. Cambridge, MA: MIT Press.

Tullett, T. (1981) *Famous Cases of Scotland Yard's Murder Squad: From Crippen to the Black Panther*. London: Triad Grafton.

UK Border Agency (2009) *UK Border Agency*. Available from: http://www.bia.homeoffice.gov.uk (accessed 19 March 2009).

Walls, H.J. (1968) *Forensic Science*. London: Sweet and Maxwell.

Warlen, S.C. (1995) Crime scene photography: the silent witness, *Journal of Forensic Identification*, 45(3): 261–5.

Warlow, T.A. (1996) *Firearms, the Law and Forensic Ballistics*. London: Taylor and Francis.

Warlow, T.A. (2005) *Firearms, the Law and Forensic Ballistics*, 2nd edn. London: Taylor and Francis.

Williams, R. (2004) *The Management of Crime Scene Examination in Relation to the Investigation of Burglary and Vehicle Crime*. Home Office Online Report 24/04. London: Home Office.

Williams, R. and Johnson, P. (2008) *Genetic Policing: The Use of DNA in Criminal Investigation*. Cullompton: Willan.

Index

absorption
drugs residue, 170
accelerants
use in arson, 107–8
ACE-V analysis
fingerprints, 92–3
acid phosphatase
for recovering semen, 74
ACPO conflict management model, 171
Adair, John, 136
adhesive tape
lifting fibres with, 46
lifting fingerprints with, 82
recovering hairs with, 51
admissibility
forensic evidence, 180–1
aerial photography, 35–6, 41–2
earliest, 41
equipment for, 41
road traffic accidents, 37
affirmation
alternative to oath, 182
Air Accident Investigation Branch, 127
Air Force Act (1955), 180
air support units, 41
airbags
hazard at road traffic accidents, 168
airguns, 112
alcohol
use in crime, 151
aluminium flake powder, 83
ambulance service
role in major incidents, 123
American Academy of Forensic Sciences
(AAFS), 188
American Society of Crime Laboratory
Directors (ASCLD), 188
American Standards Association (ASA), 34
amido black, 85–6
ammunition
composition of, 113–5
amphetamines, 151
anabolic steroids, 151
Anglo-Saxons

ancient customs of, 3
Animal Liberation Front
incendiary devices used by, 126
anthrax
used in US terror campaigns, 125
anthropometry, 6, 79
anti-static bags (Faraday bags), 148
aperture settings
camera, 31
arch pattern group
fingerprints, 93
Armed Forces Act (2006), 180
Army Act (1955), 180
arson
incidence of, 104
photography, 36
suspicion of, 106–7
task forces set up to investigate, 106
to cover other crimes, 107
use of accelerants in, 107–8
artist's impression
for identifying criminals, 6
asbestos
dangers of at fire scenes, 169
aspergillus, 170
Asquith, Lord Herbert Henry [1852–1928], 79
assault rifles, 112
assault victims
photographing, 39–40
Association of Chief Police Officers (ACPO),
11, 184, 190
guidance on major incidents, 123
audit trail
digital images, 43
Australia
police force, 5

backward fragmentation
breaking window, 49
bacteria
biological weapons, 125
ballistics, 118–9
battery acid
present at road traffic accidents, 168

bedding
  from scene of SUDI, 162
Belper, Lord Henry Strutt [1840–1914], 80
Bertillon, Alphonse [1853–1914], 6, 79
  earprints used by, 155
bifurcation
  fingerprints, 100
biological weapons
  terrorist incidents involving, 124–5
  types of, 125
blood
  contact with contaminated, 166
  evidence of in O.J. Simpson trial, 139–41
  from bodies, 138
  information elicited from examination of,
    70–1
  recovering from crime scene, 70–4
  smears, 73
  splashes, 70–2
  spots dropped from different heights, 71
  sterile swabs for recovering, 73–4
blood groups, 65
blood samples, 66
  alcohol, 151
  for drug testing, 150
blood-borne viruses
  risk from, 165–6
bodies
  contamination of, 138
  decomposition, 157
  difficulties of recovery from Indian Ocean
    tsunami (2004), 131
  escorting to mortuary, 137
  fingerprinting, 144
  forensic evidence from, 144
  health and safety when dealing with,
    165–8
  insects providing evidence about, 156–7
  obtaining evidence from, 137–9
  packaging, 144–5
  photographing, 144
  processes for recovering evidence from,
    144–5
  recovery of, 137
  removal of child's from scene of SUDI, 162
  samples from, 138, 145–6
  temperature, 138
  training for handling, 166–7
  tyre marks on, 62
  visual examination, 137
body fluids

health and safety when dealing with, 166
  present at road traffic accidents, 168
body parts
  recovery from major incidents, 124
bomb fragments
  recovering, 129
bones
  mitochondrial DNA profiling of, 69
Border and Immigration Agency, 191
Bose, Hem Chandra, 79
botanists
  examination of plant material by, 158
Bow Street Runners, 4
boxes
  as packaging for evidence, 20
Bradford football stadium fire (1985), 105
brand
  tyres, 63
branding
  recidivists, 6
brass flake powder, 83
breaking window
  backward fragmentation, 49
British Transport Police, 8
brown paper sacks
  as packaging for evidence, 20
Buddhism
  oaths and affirmations for adherents of,
    182
Buffalo Medical Journal, 111
bullet holes
  examining, 129
bullets
  examination of, 111
  laboratory analysis of, 118–9
  packaging, 117
  reconstructing path of, 116
  recovery of, 115–7
  retrieving impacted, 117
burglary, 52
  questions to be asked at scene of, 18
burn patterns, 108
Byford, Sir Lawrence, 141

calibre
  definition of, 113
  identification by, 119
cameras
  aperture settings, 31–2
  digital, 34–5
  flash synchronization, 33

shutter speed, 32
tripods, 35, 37–8
types of, 31
Canada
  police force, 5
cannabis, 151–2
  cultivation, 154, 170
  samples, 154
career progression
  CSI, 13
Carriage of Dangerous Goods (Classification,
    Packaging and Labelling) Regulations
    (1996), 165
cartridge cases
  examination of, 111
case law, 174
casting
  footwear marks, 53, 56
  tyre tracks, 62
Cell Mark Forensic Services, 186
cells
  structure of, 66
Central Criminal Court (Old Bailey), 175
Central Police Training and Development
    Authority (Centrex), 8
Charlies *see* watchmen
charring
  depth of, 108
chemical content
  soil, 53
chemical weapons
  terrorist incidents involving, 124–5
chemical-resistant goggles, 168
Chemicals (Hazard Information and
    Packaging for Supply) Regulations
    (1994), 165
Chief Constable
  role of, 7
Chief Constable of Avon and Somerset v Jest
    (1986), 80
Chief Crown Prosecutor, 184
child
  removal of body from scene of SUDI,
    162
  unexpected death of, 161–3
Child Exploitation Online Protection Centre,
    190
Cho, Seung-Hui
  identified as mass murderer at Virginia
    Polytechnic Institute, 120
chromatography, 47

cigarette ends
  source of saliva evidence, 75
cigarettes
  cannabis in, 152
  careless disposal of causing fires, 104
'Cinderella analysis', 59
circuit judges, 175
circular plastic tubes
  as packaging for evidence, 20
Civil Nuclear Constabulary, 8
CJA labels, 21, 23–5
clandestine laboratories
  drugs manufacture, 154
classification
  drugs, 150
  fingerprints, 92–101
clean-ups
  following investigations, 19
clinical waste disposal, 166
clothing
  firearms discharge residue on, 118
  from scene of SUDI, 163
  spray patterns, 161
  vacuuming, 50
cocaine, 152
Colquhoun, Patrick [1745–1820], 4
Columbine High School
  mass murder at, 128–30,
    137
Combined DNA Index System (CODIS), 69
commercial high explosives, 126
committals, 176
common approach paths (CAPs), 134
compact flash cards, 34
comparison
  DNA samples, 76–7
  fibres, 46–7
  footwear, 58–9
  glass, 48–50
  glove marks, 61
  hairs, 50–1
  instrument marks, 60
  paint, 52
  soil, 53
  tools, 60
  tyre marks, 63
comparison microscopes, 60
composites
  fingerprints, 96, 98
computer screens
  photographing, 40

computers
　ghosting contents, 148
　packaging, 148
　use in committing crime, 147–8
concentric cracks
　glass, 49
　windows, 48
conservation
　evidence, 18–9
constables
　establishment of role of, 3–4
contact trace DNA, 68
contaminants
　soil, 53
contamination
　bodies, 138
　DNA samples, 68
　evidence, 139–41
　prevention of, 12–3, 20, 133
control cartridges, 119
Control of Substances Hazardous to Health
　(COSHH) Regulations (2002), 165
control samples
　fibres, 46
　footwear marks, 56
　glass, 48–9
　hair, 51
　paint, 52
　particulates, 56
controlled area
　major incidents, 123
converging loops
　fingerprints, 85, 98
coordination
　forensic examination of major crime
　　scenes, 141–2
'coppers'
　origin of nickname, 5
cordons
　crime scenes, 134
　major incidents, 123
coroners
　Northern Ireland, 180
　reporting fire deaths to, 105
　role of, 178
coroners' courts, 178–9
　verdicts in, 178
coroners' officers, 178
corruption, 186
cot death *see* sudden unexpected death in
　infancy (SUDI)

Council for the Registration of Forensic
　Practitioners (CRFP), 188–9
　demise of, 14
counter-terrorism, 8, 186
county sheriffs
　early recorded appointment of in Virginia, 5
Court Martial Appeal Court, 180
Court of Appeal, 175, 179
court system
　Northern Ireland, 179–80
　Scotland, 179
Court Witness Service, 19
courts
　CSIs appearing in, 182–3
crack cocaine, 152
cracks
　windows, 48
Crick, Francis Harry Compton [1916–2004],
　65
crime
　alcohol and, 151
　glass containers involved in, 151
　use of firearms in, 111
Crime and Disorder Act (1998), 176
crime laboratories
　early, 6
Crime Pattern Analyst (CPA), 190
crime prevention advice, 19
Crime Scene Investigator NOS units, 11
crime scene investigators (CSIs), 9
　appearing in court, 182–3
　career progression, 13
　civilian, 19
　clean-up after investigations, 19
　common standards for, 14
　consumable items of PPE for, 172
　educational qualifications for, 14
　equipment available to, 27–9
　fire scenes, 169–70
　fires, 105–10
　first to visit scene of suspicious death, 133
　giving evidence in court, 174–83
　health and safety in dealing with drugs,
　　170
　identifying themselves, 25
　inoculations for, 166
　job description for
　　UK, 14–5
　　US, 15–6
　photographic equipment available to,
　　43–4

providing crime prevention advice, 19
psychological considerations for, 167–8
relationship with injured party, 17–8
report form, 21–3
requirement for tact when dealing with
    SUDI, 162
role of, 11–4
statement writing, 25–6
status of, 14
suggested minimum PPE for, 172
training of, 10–1
crime scene manager (CSM)
    appointment of, 133
    example for role of, 139–41
    qualifications for, 134
    role of, 135–6
crime scenes
    approaching, 17–29
    bodies at, 137–9
    coordinating forensic examination of,
        141–2
    cordons, 134
    difficulty in securing extended, 133
    examination, 18–9
    first arrival at, 17–8
    health and safety at, 165–72
    leading forensic examination of, 135–7
    management in US compared to UK,
        139–41
    management of forensic examination at,
        132–46
    matrix of, 142
    organisations relating to investigations,
        184–91
    photography, 30–44
procedure for, 35–6
    police assessment of incident, 132
    recording, 134
    rendezvous point (RVP), 18
    risk assessment, 171–2
    risk of violence at, 171
    scene log, 133
    security, 133
    zoning, 18–9, 134
crimes
    number recorded, 132
criminal court system, 174–83
criminal courts
    operation of, 174–5
Criminal Justice Act (1967), 23, 25
Criminal Justice Act (2003), 67

Criminal Justice and Police Act (2001), 67
Criminal Justice and Public Order Act (1995),
    75
criminal legal aid, 175
Criminal Procedures and Investigation Act
    (1996), 21, 25
criminals
    identification of before use of fingerprints,
        6–7
crossover
    fingerprints, 100
Crown Courts, 175–6
    typical layout of, 177
Crown Prosecution Service (CPS), 25, 175,
    179, 184–5
Crownstone, 56, 62
CS canisters, 112
cyber crime, 147–8
Cypher Mark, 159

Dallagher, Mark
    conviction of murder through earprint
        evidence, 155
Dando, Jill [1961–99]
    murder of, 120
Darwin, Charles Robert [1809–82], 79
date rape drug (rohypnol), 153
Daubert tests, 181
Daubert v Merrell Dow Pharmaceuticals Inc, 181
De Simone, Teresa
    murder of, 70
death
    determining cause of, 138
    timing of, 138
debris
    dangers of falling at fire scenes, 169
deceased persons
    fingerprinting, 89, 92
    photographing, 124
    recovery from major incidents, 123–4
    samples of hair from, 51
decomposition
    bodies, 157
decontamination
    terrorist incidents, 125
dendrochronology, 148–9
density
    glass, 50
Denstone KD, 56, 62
deoxyribonucleic acid (DNA), 65–77
    advances in, 69–70

as means of identification, 65–6
background to use of, 65–9
comparing samples, 76–7
description of, 65
identification and recovery of, 70–5
preserving samples of, 75
recovering from firearms, 116
samples from bodies, 138
samples from suspects, 75–6
detection
  fingerprints, 81–6
detective department
  first, 5
detention officers
  fingerprinting by, 87
detonation
  IEDs, 127
Devaney, June Anne
  early mass fingerprint screen to identify
    murderer of, 80
diagrams
  recording fire scene, 108
diatoms, 149
diazafluoren-9-one (DFO), 85
digital cameras, 34–5
  advantages of, 31
  formats used by, 42
  settings, 38
digital imaging
  police investment in, 42
  security of, 43
digital photography, 1
  pixels, 35
  problems with, 42–3
digital recording
  major incidents, 124
digital technology
  developments in, 31
diopter lenses, 37–8
Diploma in Crime Scene Examination, 13
Director of Public Prosecutions (DPP), 184
disaster
  definition of, 122
Disaster Victim Identification (DVI) team,
    123
disasters, 14, 130–1
  international response to, 131
discharge residue
  recovery of firearms, 118
disclosure
  rules of, 25

disposable oversuits, 166
district judges, 176
Dixon, Arthur, 185
DNA database, 185
  establishment of, 67
  growth of, 68
  inclusion on, 76
DNA profiling, 66–7
  hair, 51
DNA samples, 19, 26
  contamination, 68
  drugs, 150
  ECHR challenge to taking of, 67
  retention on national database, 67
  tracking, 27
documentation
  evidence, 17–29
drowning
  use of diatoms in cases of, 149
drug testing, 150
drugs, 150–4
  absorption of residue of, 170
  care when handling, 153
  classification of, 150
  DNA samples, 150
  examination of hair for presence of, 51
  health and safety when dealing with, 170
  identification of, 150
  illicit manufacture, 154, 170
  ingestion of residue of, 170
  large scale seizures, 154
  paraphernalia for preparation and
    administration, 150
  spot tests for, 150
  toxicological analysis, 150
drugs trafficking, 186
Dumfries and Galloway Constabulary, 8
Dunblane school massacre (1996), 112
dyes
  abstraction from fibres, 47

earprints, 155–6
ecstacy, 152
EDTA, 75
educational programmes
  police, 8
electrocution
  dangers of at fire scenes, 169
electronic evidence
  recovering, 147–8
electrostatic detection apparatus (ESDA), 57

electrostatic lifting apparatus (ESLA), 57, 61–2
elongated whorls
fingerprints, 95, 98
equipment
CSI, 27–9
etymology *see* forensic etymology
European Court of Human Rights (ECHR)
challenge to taking DNA samples in, 67
European Court of Justice (ECJ), 174–5, 179
European Police Organization (Europol), 185
European Union (EU)
as source of law, 174
establishment of Europol by, 185
Evaluating the Crime Scene Investigation
NOS unit, 11
evidence
automated examination and recovery of, 14
cocaine and crack cocaine, 152
conservation, 18–9
contamination of, 139–41
CSIs giving in court, 174–83, 182–3
documentation, 17–29
earprint, 155
firearms, 111
from scene of SUDI, 162–3
giving in court, 12
heroin, 152–3
knots, 157
packaging, 17–29
processes for recovering from bodies, 144–5
receipts for, 19
recovery from fire scenes, 104–10
retrieval from major incidents, 123–4
search and recovery of, 11
solvent abuse, 153
evidence management systems, 26–7
exhumation, 178
expert evidence, 181
experts
database for, 187
National Crime and Operations Faculty
database of, 157
explosions
dangers of at fire scenes, 169
examination of seat of, 127–8
trace evidence from, 128
zoning seat of, 127
explosives, 126–8

residue, 128
Explosives Ordnance Disposal (EOD) teams, 126
exposure
camera, 32
external ballistics, 118–9
extra digits
noting, 89

fablon lifts, 61–2
fabric gloves, 61
facemasks, 166, 170–1
familial searching, 69
family liaison officer (FLO), 134
Faraday bags, 148
Faulds, Henry [1843–1930], 78–9, 81
Federal Bureau of Investigation (FBI), 69, 102
Federal Disaster Mortuary Operational
Response Team (DMORT), 124
Federal Fingerprint Bureau, 102
fibre taping, 46
fibres, 45–8
abstraction of dyes from, 47
categorisation, 45
control samples, 46
evidence in investigation of murder of
Sarah Payne, 47–8
microscopic examination, 47
recovery and comparison, 46–7
Fielding, Henry [1707–54], 4
Fielding, John [1721–80], 4
film
choice of, 33–4
speeds, 34
types of, 31
Finger Prints
publication of, 79
fingernails
samples from bodies, 138
Fingerprint Bureau, 1
Fingerprint Development Laboratory (FDL), 84
fingerprint powders, 82
glove marks, 61
health and safety, 170–1
to enhance footwear marks, 58
to lift tyre marks, 62
Fingerprint Society
establishment of, 188
fingerprinting
bodies, 144

deceased persons, 89
fingerprints, 11, 19, 78–102
  background to use of, 78–80
  classification, 97–100
  computerized identification, 101–2
  dangers of reliance on as sole form of
    evidence, 80
  detection and recovery of, 81–6
  development of classification system for,
    79
  early mass screen to identify murderer, 80
  early use in Indian prison, 79
  electronic taking of, 87
  first use of in crime detection, 80
  fluorescence examination, 85
  identification and classification, 92–101
  introduction of use of for identification, 6
  latent on gloves, 61
  lifting, 82
  methods of taking, 87
  online transfer of latent, 14
  pattern groups, 93–6
  photographing, 37–8, 82, 85
  primary classification, 97
  reasons for taking, 87
  ridge count, 98–9
  secondary classification, 97
  taking of, 87–92
  tertiary classification, 98
  types of, 81
fire and rescue services
  role in major incidents, 123
Fire and Rescue Services Act (2004), 105
fire appliances
  tampering with, 107
Fire Investigation Teams (FIT), 106
fire officers, 105
firearms, 111–20
  amnesties, 112
  definition of, 112
  discharge residue recovery, 118
  DNA recovery from, 116
  illegal, 112
  laboratory analysis of, 118–9
  microscopic examination, 119
  most common used in crimes, 112
  packaging, 116
  recovery of, 115–7
  safety, 119
  structure of, 111–2
  types of, 112–3

used in crime, 111
Firearms Act (1968), 112
firearms discharge residue (FDR), 118
  evidence used in conviction of Barry
    George, 120
  laboratory analysis of, 118–9
firearms intelligence service, 119
firearms-related injuries, 111
fires
  agencies involved in investigating, 105–6
  classification of, 105
  CSIs at scene of, 169–70
  deaths caused by, 104
  deliberate ignition, 106–8
  diagrams recording scene of, 108
  environment for, 104–5
  examination of evidence from scene of,
    109–10
  flashovers, 108
  glass at scene of, 108
  health and safety at scene of, 169–70
  ignition of, 104–5
  investigation at scenes of, 104–10
  involvement of forensic pathologist, 106
  locating seat of, 107–9
  London Fire Brigade research into cause of,
    104
  multiple ignition points, 107
  photographing scene of, 108
  protective clothing and scene of, 169
  recovery of samples from, 108–9
  thermal indicators, 108
  video recording scene of, 108
flake powders
  introduction of, 83
  selection of type to use, 83–4
flammability
  fingerprint powders, 170
FLARE system, 27
flash synchronization
  camera, 33
flashguns
  photography, 33
flashovers
  fires, 108
flowers
  samples, 158
fluorescence examination
  fingerprints, 85
footwear
  changing soles of over time, 58

comparison, 58–9
impressions of, 55–9
overt copying for purpose of intelligence, 58
samples from suspect, 58
footwear marks, 19
casting, 53, 56
control samples, 56
fingerprint powders to enhance, 58
indented impressions, 56–7
photographing, 37–8, 56
Force Intelligence Officer (FIO), 190
Force Linked Intelligence System (FLINTS), 26–7
Foreign and Commonwealth Office (FCO), 14
Forensic Access, 186
forensic after incident review (FAIR), 136
forensic anthropologists, 139
forensic biologists, 51
forensic chemists, 52
forensic entomology, 139, 156–7
forensic evidence
admissibility, 180–1
from bodies, 144
forensic examination, 19
background to at crime scene, 132–4
computer equipment, 147–8
coordinating major crime scenes, 141–2
leading examination at crime scene, 135–7
management at crime scene, 132–46
mobile telephones, 148
water, 149
forensic medical examiners (FME), 51, 134
role in major incidents, 124
forensic nurses, 51
forensic odontologists, 138
forensic pathologist
involvement with fire, 106
forensic practitioners
professional registration of, 188–9
forensic samples
taken at post-mortems, 138
forensic science
early use of, 6–7
Forensic Science Advisory Group (FSAG), 138
Forensic Science Regulator, 1
Forensic Science Service of Northern Ireland, 186
Forensic Science Service (FSS), 11, 27, 58, 66–9, 142, 185

establishment of, 187
manufacture of Smartwater by, 159
forensic scientists, 134
forensic services
providers, 185–6
forensic submissions, 26
forensic toxicologists, 51
forensic vehicle examiner, 10
friction ridges, 81–2
structure of, 82
sweat, 81
fuel
spilt at road traffic accidents, 168
furniture
arrangement of at scene of fire, 107

Galton, Sir Francis [1822–1911], 79, 81, 100
Galton's system of fingerprinting, 79, 100
gelatine lifts, 57–8, 61–2
gelatine-coated photographic paper, 82
Genesis database, 187
genetic code, 65
GENIE, 27
George, Barry
FDR evidence leading to conviction of, 120
GF111 form, 26
ghosting
computer contents, 148
glass, 48–50
at scene of fires, 108
control samples, 48–9
cracks, 49
density, 50
effects of fire on, 108
location of, 50
present at road traffic accidents, 168
recovery and comparison, 48–50
varieties of, 48
glass containers
involvement in crime, 151
glass refractive index measurement
equipment (GRIM), 50
glove marks, 60–1
categories of, 61
comparison, 61
fingerprint powders to enhance, 61
photographing, 61
gloves
latent fingerprints on, 61
goggles, 166, 168
Goldman, Ronald

murder of, 139–41
Gordon Riots (1780), 4
Gregson, Mary
   murder of, 69–70
Grew, Nehemiah [1641–1712], 78
Griffiths, Peter
   fingerprint evidence used to convict, 80
ground granular graphite powder, 82
group needs, 136
gunshot residue (GSR), 118

hair, 50–1
   combings, 49–50
   control samples, 51
   evidence in investigation of murder of
      Sarah Payne, 47–8
   firearms discharge residue in, 118
   recovery and comparison, 50–1
   samples from bodies, 51, 138
   samples from rape victims, 51
hand-held fingerprint scanners
   trialling, 87
handguns
   types of, 113
handling
   bodies, 166–7
Haque, Azizul, 79
Harker, David
   convicted of murder of Julie Paterson,
      141
Harris, Eric
   commits mass murder at Columbine High
      School, 128–30
hazards
   present in vehicles at road traffic accidents,
      168–9
Head of Crime Scene Investigation, 9
health and safety
   at crime scene, 165–72
   dealing with bodies, 165–8
   dealing with drugs, 170
   dealing with major incidents, 124
   fingerprint powders, 170–1
   fire scenes, 169–70
   firearms, 111, 115, 119
   needles, 168
   road traffic accidents, 168–9
   sharp objects, 168
   vehicles, 168–9
Health and Safety at Work Act (1974), 165
Health and Safety Executive (HSE), 175

helicopters
   aerial photography, 41
Hendon Police College, 185
Henry, Sir Edward Richard [1850–1931], 6,
   79, 97
Henry system
   worldwide acceptance of, 80
hepatitis
   risk of, 165
Her Majesty's Court Service (HMCS), 174,
   176
heroin, 152–3
Herschel, Sir William James [1833–1917], 79,
   81
hierarchy of needs, 136–7
High Court, 175
high court judges, 175
High Court of Justiciary, 179
high explosives (HEs)
   categories of, 126
high intensity light, 62
high visibility clothing, 168
hit and run collisions
   paint samples from, 52
HIV
   risk of, 165
HM Customs and Excise Investigation
   Branch, 190
HM Revenue and Customs, 8, 191
Hodgson, Sean
   overturning of conviction of using DNA
      evidence, 70
Home Office, 84, 185
   appointments, 1
Home Office forensic pathologists, 137
Home Office Large Major Enquiry System
   (HOLMES), 26
Home Office Scientific Development Branch
   (HOSDB), 186
Home Secretary
   responsibility for police, 7
home-made high explosives, 126
horseborne patrols, 4
House of Lords, 179
hue and cry, 3
human rights, 174
   DNA sampling and, 67
Hungerford shootings (1987), 122
hydrocarbon detector dogs, 108
hydrofluoric acid
   hazard at road traffic accidents, 168–9

hypostasis
lines of, 138
photographing, 39

Ident1 national fingerprint database, 101–2
identification
criminals before use of fingerprints, 6–7
DNA, 70–5
drugs, 150
fingerprints, 92–101
victims of Indian Ocean tsunami (2004),
131
identity parades
photographing, 40
ignition points
multiple, 107
immigrants
traditions of sheriffs brought to US by, 5
implied consent, 19
impressed marks
footwear, 55–7
impressions, 55–63
footwear, 55–9
improvised explosive devices (IED), 126
characteristics of, 127
incendiary devices, 126
indented impressions
footwear marks, 56–7
independent ridge
fingerprints, 100
Index
trade name of Smartwater, 159
India
introduction of anthropometric system of
identification in, 6
Indian Ocean tsunami (2004), 122, 130–1
indictable offences, 175
Indonesia
effects of Indian Ocean tsunami (2004),
130
infants
unexpected death of, 161–3
infection
risk from bodies, 166
information analysis, 158
information collation, 18
information technology (IT), 8
evidence management, 26
use in committing crime, 147–8
ingestion
drugs residue, 170

inhalation
heroin, 153
injection
cocaine and crack cocaine, 152
heroin, 153
injured parties
relationship with CSI, 17–8
injuries
photographing, 39
inquests, 178
insects
providing evidence about bodies, 156–7
samples, 157
instrument marks, 59–60
comparison, 60
photographing, 37–8, 60
Integrated automatic Fingerprint
Identification System (IAFIS), 102
Integrated Ballistic Identification System
(IBIS), 119
intelligence, 8, 158
overt copying of footwear for purpose of, 58
recognition of importance of, 4
intelligence indices
maintenance of, 12
internal ballistics, 118–9
International Association for Identification
(IAI), 188
International Standards Organization (ISO),
34
Interpol, 69, 186–7
background to, 186
Islam
oaths and affirmations for adherents of,
182

Jackson, Harry
fingerprint evidence used to convict, 80
Jeffreys, Sir Alec John, 65–6
job description
CSI, 14–6
JPEG files, 42
Judicature (Northern Ireland) Act (1978), 179
Judiciary and Courts (Scotland) Act (2008),
179
juries, 175
inquests, 178
Justice of the Peace Act (1361), 3
Justice of the Peace (JP) Courts, 179
Justices of the Peace (JPs), 176
establishment of role of, 3

juveniles
deletion of DNA profiles, 67–8

kastle mayer (KM), 72
Key Forensic Services Ltd, 186
King's Cross underground station fire (1987),
110
Klebold, Dylan
commits mass murder at Columbine High
School, 128–30
knife tubes, 20
knots
as evidence, 157
Kosovo
bones recovered from mass grave in (1999),
139
Kumho Tire Co Ltd v Carmichael, 181

labelling
packaging, 209
laboratories
illicit drugs manufacture, 154, 170
lake
fingerprints, 100
Landsteiner, Karl [1868–1943], 65
Lantern project, 87
latent fingerprints, 81–3
vacuum metal deposition to detect, 86
latent marks
gloves, 61
lateral pockets
fingerprints, 96, 98
latex gloves, 61, 166, 170
law
sources of, 174
Law Commission
report on expert evidence, 181
law enforcement
police role in, 8
leather gloves, 61
leaves
samples, 158
legislation
as source of law, 174
lenses
camera, 31
leucomalachite green (LMG), 72
LGC Forensics, 142, 186
lifting apparatus
photography from, 41
light meters, 32

lighting
photography, 36
Lindbergh kidnapping
use of dendrochronology in investigation
of, 149
Livescan
electronic fingerprint taking, 87
Local Intelligence Officer (LIO), 190
Locard, Edmond [1877–1966], 6–7
Locard system, 26–7
Locard's principle, 7
location
glass, 50
Lockerbie
bombing of Pan Am 103 over (1988), 127
London
growth of, 3–4
mob rule in, 4
transport bombings (2005), 122
London Fire Brigade
research into cause of fires, 104
loop pattern group
fingerprints, 93
low copy number (LCN) DNA process, 68
low oblique photographs, 41
Lowther, Ian
conviction of using DNA evidence, 69–70
Lubbock, Stuart
murder of, 133
lysergic acid diethylamide (LSD), 153

MAC 10 submachine pistol, 112
magistrates' courts, 176
magnetic powders, 83
Major Disaster Advisory Team (MDAT), 141
major incidents, 122–31
appointment of Scene Evidence Recovery
Manager (SERM), 123
appointment of Senior Investigating
Officer (SIO), 123
categorisation, 122
controlled area, 123
cordons, 123
digital recording, 124
establishment of mortuaries in, 124
photographing, 124
recovery of body parts, 124
recovery of deceased victims from, 123–4
rescue phase, 123
response to, 123–4
retrieval of evidence from, 123–4

role of emergency services in, 123
role of forensic medical examiner in, 124
safety in dealing with, 124
video recording, 124
zoning for search purposes, 123
Malaysia
effects of Indian Ocean tsunami (2004), 131
man-made fibres, 45
Management of Health and Safety at Work Regulations (1999), 165
mapping
scene of shooting, 116
marking
property, 158–61
Markov, Georgi
assassination of by ricin in tip of umbrella, 125–6
Marquis test, 150
Maslow, Elijah Abraham [1908–70], 136–7
mass graves
investigations into, 14
mass murder, 128–30
definition of, 122
investigation at scene of, 129
Mayne, Sir Richard [1796–1868], 5
memory cards
digital cameras, 34
Metropolitan Police
divisions of, 5
establishment of, 4–5
fingerprint bureau established by, 80
first detective department established by, 5
forensic laboratory established by, 185
largest force, 8
Metropolitan Police Act (1829), 5
MG/FSP forms, 26
MG11 statement from witness form, 25
microscopic examination
fibres, 47
firearms, 119
paint, 52
Miescher, Friedrich [1844–95], 65
military courts, 180
military high explosives, 126
Ministry of Defence Police, 8–9
mis-identification of fingerprints, 181
miscarriages of justice, 181
missing fingers
noting, 89
Misuse of Drugs Act (1971), 150

mitochondrial DNA profiling, 69
hair, 51
mixed DNA, 68
mobile fingerprint scanners, 1
Mobile Identification at Scene (MIDaS), 88
mobile telephones
forensic examination, 148
packaging, 148
modus operandi
report form, 22
mortars, 112
mortuaries
escorting bodies to, 137
establishment of in major incidents, 124
mould characteristics
tyres, 63
mouth swabs
DNA smpling by, 75–6
multilocus probe (MLP), 65–7
Municipal Corporation Act (1835), 5
murder
DNA profiling to detect, 66
using advances in DNA technology to review cases, 69–70

nappies
from scene of SUDI, 163
National Automated Fingerprint Identification System (NAFIS), 101
National Ballistics Intelligence Service (NaBIS), 1, 119
National Crime and Operations Faculty (NCOF), 141
database of experts held by, 157
National Crime Squad (NCS), 8, 190
National Criminal Intelligence Service (NCIS), 8, 189
National Criminal Intelligence Sharing Plan, 190
National DNA Database (NDNAD), 26
National Intelligence Model (NIM), 158, 190
National Occupational Standards (NOS), 11, 14
National Police Improvement Agency (NPIA), 8, 187
guidance on major incidents, 123
National Training Centre for Scientific Support to Crime Investigation (NTCSSCI), 2
establishment of, 10
National Training Organization, 190

natural fibres, 45
Navy Discipline Act (1957), 180
needle stick injuries
  avoidance of, 152
needles, 152
  health and safety, 168, 170
neighbourhood policing, 8
New South Wales
  police force, 5
New York City Police, 5
ninhydrin, 85
nitrile gloves, 116, 166, 170
Norman Conquest, 3
Northern Ireland
  coroners, 180
  court system, 179–80
Northern Ireland Court of Appeal, 180
nutant loops
  fingerprints, 95, 98
nylon bags
  as packaging for evidence, 20

oath
  taking in court, 182
oblique lighting
  photography, 38
Old Bailey, 175
Omagh bombings, 68
organized crime, 14
overshoes, 166

packaging
  bodies, 144–5
  bullets, 117
  computers, 148
  evidence, 17–29
  firearms, 116
  materials for, 19–20
  mobile telephones, 148
paint, 51–2
  control samples, 52
  microscopic examination, 52
  recovery and comparison, 52
  samples from hit and run collisions, 52
  samples from road traffic accidents, 52
  samples from suspects, 52
  samples from victims, 52
palm prints, 11
  electronic taking of, 87
  methods of taking, 87
  reasons for taking, 87

taking of, 87–92
Pan Am, 103
  bombing of (1988), 127
parenthood
  DNA testing for, 65
partial DNA, 68
particle size
  soil, 53
particulates
  control samples, 56
paternity testing, 69
Paterson, Julie
  murder of, 141
path
  bullets, 116
pathfinder, 57
pathologists, 134
pattern groups
  fingerprints, 93–6
pay and conditions
  police, 7
Payne, Sarah
  hair and fibre evidence in investigating
    murder of, 47–8
Peel, Sir Robert [1788–1850], 5
people trafficking, 186
personal equipment
  CSI, 27–8
Personal Protective Equipment at Work
    Regulations (1992), 165
personal protective equipment (PPE), 166
  consumable items for, 172
  suggested minimum for CSI, 172
Personal Protective Equipment Regulations
    (2002), 165
photographic equipment
  care of, 44
photography, 11
  arson, 36
  assault victims, 39–40
  basics of, 30–1
  bodies, 144
  computer screens, 40
  crime scene, 30–44, 134
procedure for, 35–6
  cyber crime, 147–8
  deceased victims of major incidents, 124
  fingerprints, 37–8, 82, 85
  footwear marks, 37–8, 56
  for identifying criminals, 6
  glove marks, 61

hypostasis, 39
identity parades, 40
injuries, 39
instrument marks, 37–8, 60
lighting, 36
major incidents, 124
oblique lighting, 38
post-mortem examinations, 39, 138
road traffic accidents, 36
procedure for, 37
scene of fires, 108
scene of SUDI, 162
suspects, 39–40
tyre tracks, 37–8, 62
underwater crime scenes, 36
victims, 39–40
weapons, 116
physical developer, 85
Pitchfork, Colin, 66
pixels
digital photography, 35
plain arches
fingerprints, 94, 97
plain loops
fingerprints, 94, 98
plain whorls
fingerprints, 95, 98
plan drawers, 134
plant material
samples, 158
plastic overshoes, 166
plastics
effects of fire on, 108
police
educational programmes, 8
initial assessment of crime scene, 132
regionalization, 8–9
reporting fires to, 105
training, 8
Police Act (1919), 7
Police Act (1964), 7
Police and Criminal Evidence Act (1984),
75
police authority, 7
police collision accident investigators, 37
police community support officer (PCSO), 8
police custody suite
DNA samples taken in, 75
police duties
civilianization of, 7–8
Police Elimination Database, 68

police employees
DNA samples taken by, 75
police firearms officers, 116
police forces
Australia, 5
autonomy of, 7
Canada, 5
Texas, 5
Police Information and Technology
Organization (PITO), 8, 187
Police National Hi-Tech Crime Unit
(NHTCU), 190
police officers
fingerprinting by, 87
police photography, 9
Police Reform Act (2002), 8, 19
Police Scientific Development Branch
(PSDB), 8, 43, 84–5, 186
police search advisers (POLSAs), 134
police service
structure of, 7–9
Police Skills and Standards Organization, 190
police system
background to, 3–5
polydactylism
noting, 89
polymerase chain reaction (PCR), 67
polythene bags
as packaging for evidence, 19–20
poor quality DNA, 68
Port of London
theft from, 4
post-event deposits of DNA, 68
post-mortem examinations, 137–9
photographing, 39, 138
pre-event deposits of DNA, 68
preservatives
insect samples, 157
presumptive blood testing kits, 72
primary classification
fingerprints, 97
primary fires, 105
Printscan, 58
PRISM, 27
Procurator Fiscal, 179
professional associations, 187–8
professional registration
forensic practitioners, 188–9
prohibited weapons, 112
projectile holes
examining, 129

property
    forensic marking of, 158–61
protective clothing
    dealing with bodies, 166
    fire scenes, 169
    road traffic accidents, 168
Purkinje, Johannes Evangelista [1787–1869],
    78

Queen's Bench Division
    High Court, 175

radial cracks
    glass, 49
radial loops
    fingerprints, 98
rape
    DNA profiling, 66
    recovering semen from scene of, 74–5
    samples of hair from victims of, 51
RAW files, 42–3
receipts
    for evidence, 19
recidivists
    branding, 6
    committee to examine identification of, 79
recorders, 175
recovery
    blood, 70–4
    bodies, 137
    body parts from major incidents, 124
    bomb fragments, 129
    bullets, 115–7
    cartridges, 115–7
    deceased victims of major incidents, 123–4
    DNA, 70–5
    electronic evidence, 147–8
    fibres, 46–7
    fingerprints, 81–6
    firearms, 115–7
    firearms discharge residue, 118
    glass, 48–50
    hairs, 50–1
    paint, 52
    process for evidence from bodies, 144–5
    samples from fire scene, 108–9
    samples from terrorist incidents, 125
    soil, 53
RedDNA, 159
regionalization
    police, 8–9

reignition
    dangers of at fire scenes, 169
rendezvous point (RVP)
    crime scene, 18
replica firearms, 112
report form
    CSI, 21–3
rescue phase
    major incidents, 123
respirators, 166, 170–1
revolvers, 112
    types of, 113
rickettsia
    biological weapons, 125
ridge characteristics
    fingerprints, 100–1
ridge count
    fingerprints, 98–9
ridge ending
    fingerprints, 100
ridge tracing
    fingerprints, 99
rifles, 112
rifling, 119
rigor mortis, 138
risk assessment
    crime scenes, 171–2
River Police
    establishment of, 4
road traffic accidents
    aerial photography, 37
    health and safety, 168–9
    paint samples from, 52
    photography, 36
    procedure for, 37
    protective clothing, 168
rocket launchers, 112
rohypnol (date rape drug), 153
Ross, Marion
    investigation of murder of, 181
Rowan, Sir Charles [1782–1852], 4–5
Royal Air Force Police, 9
Royal Courts of Justice (Belfast), 180
Royal Military Police, 9
Royal Photographic Society, 31
Royal Society
    lecture on fingerprinting given at, 78
rubber gloves, 61
Russian royal family
    mitochondrial DNA profiling of skeletons
      to identify, 69

Ryan, Michael
  perpetrator of Hungerford shootings, 122

Safe Working and the Prevention of Infection in the Mortuary and Post-Mortem Rooms, 165
safety *see* health and safety
safety spectacles, 166
St Valentine's Day Massacre, 111
saliva
  recovering from crime scene, 75
  sampling, 66
samples
  cannabis, 154
  flowers, 158
  from bodies, 138, 145–6
  from scene of SUDI, 163
  insects, 157
  leaves, 158
  plant material, 158
  unique identifying mark, 25
sarin
  toxicity of, 125
saving life
  priority in major incidents, 123
scaling, 39–40
Scene Evidence Recovery Manager (SERM)
  appointed for major incidents, 123
scene log
  crime scene, 133
scientific advice, 12
*Scientific America*i
  features of fingerprints published in, 79
Scientific Support College, 10
Scientific Support Coordinator (SSC), 141–3
Scientific Support Department
  operation of, 143
scientific support managers (SSM), 9, 143
scientific support units
  development of, 9–10
Scientifics, 186
Scotland
  court system, 179
Scotland Yard, 5
Scottish Court Service, 179
Scottish Parliament, 179
Scottish Police Laboratories, 186
Scottish Police Services Authority (SPSA)
  Forensic Services, 186
searching
  zoning, 123
second generation multiplex (SGM), 67

secondary classification
  fingerprints, 97
secondary fires, 105
secure digital cards, 34
security
  crime scene, 133
  digital images, 43
SelectaDNA, 158
SelectaMark, 159
self-loading pistols, 112
  types of, 113
semen
  acid phosphatase for recovering, 74
  DNA profiling, 66
  recovering from crime scene, 74–5
Semtex, 126
Senior Investigating Officer (SIO)
  appointed for major incidents, 123
sentences, 175–6
  limit to in magistrates' courts, 176
  youth courts, 176
Serious and Organised Crime and Police Act (2005), 8, 58
Serious Organised Crime Agency (SOCA), 8, 14, 185, 189–90
  seizure of drugs by, 154
Service Civilian Courts, 180
sexual assault
  recovering semen from scene of, 74–5
Sexual Assault Referral Centre (SARC), 74
shared equipment
  CSI, 28
sharp metal edges
  present at road traffic accidents, 168
sharp objects
  health and safety in handling, 168, 170
sheriffs
  introduction of in US, 5
sheriff's courts, 179
Shipman, Harold
  mass murder by, 178
Shoeprint Image Capture and Retrieval version 6 (SICAR6), 58
shooting
  suicide, 111
  surveying and mapping scene of, 116
short tandem repeat (STR) techniques, 67–8
shotgun cartridges
  composition of, 113, 115
  laboratory analysis of, 118–9
  recovery of, 115–7

shotguns, 112
shutter speed
    camera, 32
SIM cards, 148
Simpson, Nicole
    murder of, 139–41
Simpson, Orenthal James (O.J.)
    murder trial of, 139–41
single shot pistols, 113
Skills for Justice, 11, 190–1
Skillsmark, 190
skin
    firearms discharge residue on, 118
    make-up of, 81
skin irritation
    fingerprint powders causing, 170
slash-resistant gloves, 166, 168
SLR digital cameras, 31, 42
smart media memory cards, 34
Smartwater, 159–61
    operation of, 159–60
Smartwater Instant, 159, 161
smears
    blood, 73
smoke damage, 108
smoking materials
    careless disposal of causing fires, 104
snow
    recovering footwear marks from, 56
    tyre tracks, 62
snow print wax, 56
SOCIMS, 27
SOCKET, 27
SOCRATES, 26–7
sodium cyanide gas
    terrorist incidents, 125
soil, 52–3
    chemical content, 53
    contaminants, 53
    particle size, 53
    recovery and comparison, 53
    samples from vehicles, 53
SoleMate database, 58
soles
    footwear changing over time, 58
solvent abuse, 153
Somalia
    effects of Indian Ocean tsunami (2004), 131
Special Constables Act (1831), 5
specialist advisors (previously known as
    Byford scientists), 141

Spjut, Scott Russell
    killed while examining rifle, 111
splashes
    blood, 70–2
spontaneous combustion, 108
spot tests
    drugs, 150
spray patterns, 161
sprinklers
    tampering with, 107
spur
    fingerprints, 100
Sri Lanka
    effects of Indian Ocean tsunami (2004),
        131
stains, 26
standards
    CSI, 14
Starting the Crime Scene Investigation
        Process
    NOS unit, 11
statement from witness form, 25
statements, 25–6
    preparation of, 12
States of Jersey Police, 9
Statute of Winchester (1285), 3
sterile swabs
    for recovering blood, 73–4
stolen vehicles, 169
strike
    police forbidden to, 7
structural collapse
    dangers of at fire scenes, 169
submachine guns, 112
sudden unexpected death in infancy (SUDI),
        161–3
    evidence from scene of, 162–3
    photographing scene of, 162
suicide
    by shooting, 111
Summary Appeal Court, 180
summary offences, 176
superglue
    in recovering fingerprints, 86
Supreme Court, 175
surface transfer marks
    footwear, 55–7
surveying
    scene of shooting, 116
suspects
    footwear samples from, 58

paint samples from, 52
photographing, 39–40
taking DNA samples from, 75–6
suspicious death
assessment of scene, 132
CSI first to visit scene of, 133
swabs
sterile for recovering blood, 73–4
sweat
friction ridges, 81
sweat pores
examination of, 93
syringes, 152

tamper-evident bags, 20
team work
crime scene, 136
Technical Support Units (TSU), 9, 134
teeth
examination of at post-mortems, 138
mitochondrial DNA profiling of, 69
telephoto lenses, 31
tenprint forms
classified, 99–100
example of, 90–1
fingerprint taking on, 87
tented arches
fingerprints, 94, 98
terminal ballistics, 118–9
terrorism
definition of, 122
Terrorism Act (2000), 122
terrorist incidents, 124–8
bombing of Pan Am 103 (1988), 127
chemical, biological, radiological and
nuclear (CBRN) explosions, 124
decontamination, 125
London transport bombings (2005), 122
recovering samples from, 125
World Trade Centre bombing (1993), 125
World Trade Centre attacks (2001), 128
tertiary classification
fingerprints, 98
Texas
police force, 5
thermal indicators
fires, 108
'thief takers', 4
third generation multiplex (TGM), 69
TIFF files, 42–3
Tokyo subway attacks (1995), 125

tools
comparison, 60
used to gain entry, 59–60
Toronto
full-time constable appointed in, 5
Touche Ross Report (Review of Scientific
Support for the Police) (1987),
10–1
tourniquets, 152
toxicological analysis
drugs, 150
toxins
biological weapons, 125
trace evidence, 45–53
explosions, 128
Tracer, 159, 161
traffic
stopping at road traffic accidents, 168
training
handling bodies, 166–7
police, 8
tranquillizers, 154
transnational crime, 186
tread wear
tyres, 63
Treadmate database, 63
tripods
camera, 35, 37–8
Troup, Charles [1857–1941], 79
TTL metering system, 32
twinned loops
fingerprints, 96, 98
tyre tracks/marks, 61–2
casing, 62
comparison, 63
fingerprint powders to lift, 62
identification, 63–4
impressions of, 61
photographing, 37–8, 62
snow, 62
tyres
determining brand, 63
tythingman, 3

UK Border Agency, 14, 101, 191
UK Immigration Service, 8
ulnar loops
fingerprints, 98
ultraviolet light, 160–1
underwater crime scenes
photography, 36

unique identifying mark
  samples, 25
United Kingdom
  crime scene management compared with
    US, 139–41
United Kingdom Accreditation Service
  (UKAS), 189
United States
  admissibility of forensic evidence in,
    181
  crime scene management compared with
    UK, 139–41
  DNA databases in, 69
  Federal Disaster Mortuary Operational
    Response Team (DMORT), 124
  fingerprint records in, 102
  job description for CSI, 15–6
  professional associations, 188
  sheriffs, 5
urine samples
  alcohol, 151
  for drug testing, 150
  rohypnol (date rape drug), 153
US Marshalls, 5

vacuum metal deposition, 86
vacuuming
  clothing, 50
vehicle identification
  tyre marks assisting, 63
vehicle-borne explosive device, 126–7
vehicles
  hazards present at road traffic accidents,
    168–9
  health and safety, 168–9
  soil samples from, 53
  stolen, 169
  test marks from suspect, 63
verdicts
  coroners' courts, 178
vertical images, 42
Victim Support Scheme, 19
victims
  identification of following World Trade
    Centre attacks (2001), 128
  paint samples from, 52
  photographing, 39–40
  wide spread of from Indian Ocean tsunami
    (2004), 130–1
video
  recording fire scene, 108

Video Identification Parade Electronic
  Recording (VIPER), 40
video photography, 11
video recording
  crime scene, 134
  major incidents, 124
vinyl gloves, 61
violence
  risk of at crime scene, 171
Violent Crime Reduction Act (2006), 112
Virginia
  earliest recorded appointment of county
    sheriff in, 5
Virginia Polytechnic Institute
  mass murder at, 120
viruses
  biological weapons, 125
Visa Office, 191
visible fingerprints, 81,
  84
volume crime scene investigator (VCSI), 10–1

Waco siege (1993), 138
Washington, George [1732–99], 5
watchmen
  establishment of role of, 3
water
  forensic examination of, 149
  recovering footwear marks from, 56
Watson, James Dewey, 65
weapons
  photographing, 116
West Midlands Police, 27
Whiting, Roy
  hair and fibre trace evidence used to
    convict, 47–8
whorl pattern group
  fingerprints, 93
wide-angle lenses, 31
window glass
  composition of, 48
Women Police Service
  establishment of, 5
wood
  dendrochronological examination of,
    148–9
Woods, Dorothy
  murder of, 155
World Trade Centre
  attacks on (2001), 128
  bombing (1993), 125

World War I, 5
Write Once, Read Many (WORM) format,
43

xD picture cards, 34

youth courts, 176
Yugoslavia

investigations into mass graves in former,
14

Zephyr type brush, 83, 85
zoning
crime scene, 18–9, 134
for search purposes in major incidents, 123
seat of explosions, 127